*The French nobility
in the eighteenth century*

The French nobility in the eighteenth century

From feudalism to enlightenment

GUY CHAUSSINAND-NOGARET

translated by

WILLIAM DOYLE

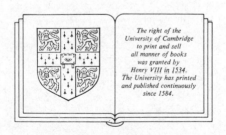

The right of the
University of Cambridge
to print and sell
all manner of books
was granted by
Henry VIII in 1534.
The University has printed
and published continuously
since 1584.

CAMBRIDGE UNIVERSITY PRESS

Cambridge

London   New York   New Rochelle

Melbourne   Sydney

Published by the Press Syndicate of the University of Cambridge
The Pitt Building, Trumpington Street, Cambridge CB2 1RP
32 East 57th Street, New York, NY 10022, USA
10 Stamford Road, Oakleigh, Melbourne 3166, Australia

Originally published in 1976 as *La
Noblesse au XVIIIe siècle: de la
féodalité aux lumières* by
Librairie Hachette

English translation © Cambridge University Press 1985

First published 1985

Printed in Great Britain by the University Press, Cambridge

Library of Congress catalog card number: 84–19898

British Library Cataloguing in Publication Data

Chaussinand-Nogaret, Guy
The French nobility in the eighteenth century:
from feudalism to enlightenment.
1. France—Nobility—History
I. Title II. La noblesse au XVIIIe siècle: de
la féodalité aux lumières. *English*
305.5′224′0944   HT653.F7

ISBN 0 521 25623 2   hard covers
ISBN 0 521 27590 3   paperback

Contents

Introduction: the gilded ghetto of royal nobility

May 1789. The Estates-General met at Versailles. The three orders processed ceremonially. The second order, the nobility, shone with all the brilliance of gold-embroidered coats and capes, white-plumed hats, and engraved ceremonial swords. Alongside the nobility the third estate was dark and sombre, a sorry sight. Yet: brilliant as it still appeared, still today at the head of the procession, the nobility could already feel the cold wind of defeat.

It had become, by imperceptible stages which had mostly escaped its notice, a marginal minority in French society, under sentence. In 1789 nobles were the kingdom's Jews.

To be sure, the nobility still exercised an irresistible attraction, and for broad areas of opinion it was the only model. Its code of honour, its ritual refined from the politeness born of court ceremonies, its style, behaviour and way of life, were still dominant. Nobility remained the supreme ambition of the unrepentantly elitist middle classes, who saw in ennoblement a way of escaping the confusions which ranked them with the most despised elements of a third estate with which fundamentally they felt so little in common. But, at the same time as it engendered social imitation, the nobility aroused envy and indeed hostility, mingled with feelings of frustration and anxiety in the face of a group ill-understood, perceived as alien, and easily enough as antagonistic. This sharp awareness of *difference*, no doubt stronger among non-nobles than nobles themselves, could and indeed soon did give rise to delusions which the 'aristocratic plots' of the Revolution would bring to the surface. Even before that, however, turning the nobility's own arguments against itself, the third estate had adopted a racist attitude towards it. Sieyès denounced this 'people apart, a counterfeit people which, unable to exist by itself for lack of useful organs, latches on to a real nation like those vegetable growths which can only live on the sap of the plants they exhaust and suck dry'. And, using the argument inopportunely provided by Boulainvilliers, he suggested sending the second order back to its mythic origins: 'Why does not [the third estate] send all these families who still make the crazy claim that they are descended from a race of conquerors back to the forests of Franconia?' And it was true enough that the nobility, from La Roque to Boulainvilliers via Saint-Simon, had fashioned this rod for its own back. Justifying its own privileges on grounds of race and history, it ceased to be identified with the Nation and made inevitable the rejection it was to suffer.

Efforts made in the second half of the eighteenth century to remodel its image were inefficient and came too late to make much impact. The damage was done. All it had taken was half a century, roughly the reign of Louis XIV, with its development of the phenomenon of the Court, centralisation and the uprooting of the nobility that followed it, the vanity of the ducal caste and its official theorists, for the nobility to shatter the cohesion of the kingdom and cut itself off from the rest of the Nation. After that, right down to the Constituent Assembly, nobles' attempts to escape from the gilded ghetto in which they had allowed themselves to be shut up were mostly fruitless; as Sieyès' words show, there was a determination to keep them out.

This was the paradox of the nobility, to be at one and the same time the official elite of the kingdom, and a body of rejects, seen as alien, useless and harmful. Any elite produced by a given political and social system is bound to appear a parasitic excrescence once the system which has spawned it is called into question. Today, wherever socialist models are the rule or the aspiration, elites spawned by capitalist states have fallen into disrepute and are denounced as impediments to national cohesion. The French nobility was no exception to the general rule and, despite worthy efforts in 1789 to blend itself into the Nation and identify with it, it was unable to turn back the tide that was sweeping it away.

Yet the French nobility never turned itself into a caste, or cut itself off from the nearest levels of the third estate. The absence of a general register of nobility, which was never drawn up, the ease of ennoblement, the encroachment on privileges by the office- and fief-holding middle class: all this proved how open the group remained. In France it was never entirely clear who was and who was not in the nobility.

First and foremost it was a national nobility. To be sure, it took in foreign nobles, but only immediately to naturalise them. In Alsace, it overlapped with the Imperial nobility; it recognised that of newly acquired provinces like Corsica and Lorraine and assimilated foreign elements, whether Swedish, German, Polish or Swiss, and above all the imposing mass of Jacobite refugees. Even so the percentage of assimilations must have remained less than 2%. But what in fact were the numbers of the French nobility? 80,000 persons or 400,000? Since the old regime figures have varied between these two extremes. It is difficult to work out, but not impossible. Nor is this a purely academic issue. First of all the satisfaction or failure to satisfy the needs of the nobility depended on its numbers. Opportunities for service were not unlimited, especially since the nobility seldom had a monopoly of any career, even in the army. And without figures, how can we estimate the renewal rate of the order? As the linchpin of social morality, the nobility's capacity to absorb newcomers or to allow progress from one end of the noble hierarchy to the other was important both for the renewal of the second order, and for the satisfaction of the third estate's desire for promotion. For complex reasons, the chances of rising for the petty nobility of the provinces and the countryside were almost non-existent. The way was beset with filters so fine that practically nobody could get through.

For the third estate to get into the second order was a very different matter. The middle classes had opportunities as various as they were most often costly, for attaining the privilege of nobility. They could even gain an instant promotion which lifted them at one leap to the highest level. The Bourgeois de Boynes family, ennobled by the office of King's Secretary in 1719, received the honours of the court[1] with dispensation from proofs of ancestry, less than 50 years later. The Peyrenc de Moras, or the Laurent de Villedeuil families, and many others had the same meteoric rise. This penetration into the nobility, and above all into its higher reaches, by the cream of the third estate, had consequences of great importance for the perpetuation of the order, and indeed determined its evolution. The order was maintained at an adequate demographic level for its existence, even though it was plainly on the wane from the mid seventeenth century. In addition, the nobility drew on the wealth and the abilities of the third estate. Even more important were the transformations affecting noble psychology and the order's view of itself. Its invasion since the sixteenth century by new elements, at a time when the identity of the middle class was emerging, led to the warping of noble ideology and a conversion of the second order to values foreign to its traditional ethic.

Sometimes not without reluctance or regret; noble racism was deeply ingrained. But it was not all-embracing, and both acknowledgement of middle-class ideology and the ideas of Boulainvilliers could be found together in the same person. Boulainvilliers, however, perhaps for lack of opportunity, made little appearance in that last will and testament of the nobility, its *cahiers* of 1789. Birth is never mentioned in them, but references to individual merit appear with the regularity of a *leitmotiv*. The collective value of the group had been abandoned. Traditionally, a noble was defined by his lineage. His merit was inseparable from that of his ancestry, and the worth of his forebears underlay his own virtue. In one extreme sense he had no individual existence, no separate self. He was merely a link in an ancestral chain. This was the tradition that the nobility, or at least a large segment of the order, abandoned in 1789. Just like commoners, nobles demanded recognition of their personal merit, put off the protective veil of ancestry and, not without pride, offered themselves to the judgment and the competition of the third estate. Uncertainly, and running up sometimes against insuperable obstacles, little by little the middle class model supplanted the noble one. Transformations in behaviour followed. The nobility joined in the development of productive forces, absorbed capitalism into its outlook, and took on the ways of the middle class.

The nobility was not sealed off by impenetrable social barriers, or by some ideological frontier. It was not forbidden territory. Various nobilities could be defined by profession within the order; but only secondarily. For profession itself was determined by a decisive factor, a far more fundamental reason for profound gradations than length of lineage: money. Money mingled ranks and spread confusion, for it opened the way to the acquisition of land, including noble land – fiefs – which had not conferred nobility since the sixteenth century but were available to anybody at a time when to be well endowed was becoming more important than, or at least confused with, being well born. But at the same time it deepened differences and shattered noble unity. The hierarchy of wealth, which can be established from fiscal documents and personal accounts, shows precisely not only the limitations from lack of means which paralysed part of the nobility, and the particular outlook which this often bitterly resented situation gave rise to; but also the discrepancy between the model of society longed for by these frustrated nobles and the model favoured by a noble elite less professionally specialised, less exclusive in its inclinations and ambitions, and more easily contaminated by the intellectual currents it encountered.

Throughout the eighteenth century the petty military nobility, kept from Court through principle, from office through penury, from distinctions through obscurity, looked to professionalism for a definition and an identity.

They tried to establish the model of a nobility entirely dedicated to the profession of arms, finding justification in an ascetic ideal. The disappointed hopes of the petty nobility thus led them to dream of a class of heroes and an antidote to a society devoted to luxury and the rising power of money. It was the equivalent, on a chivalric level, of the religious mysticism of the Jansenistic middle class of the previous century. The frustration of this petty nobility, kept out of senior posts and sometimes the army itself by venality and the privilege of courtiers, bred a mystique of heroism and selflessness. The chevalier d'Arc, who gave his book the characteristic title of the *French Patriot*, gave vigorous expression to this yearning for sacrifice, and his frenzied debate with the abbé Coyer elevated this ideal of austerity, purity and service to the fatherland to paradoxical heights.

None of this was calculated to fire the gilded nobility with much enthusiasm. They had evolved differently. They did not escape their own crisis of identity. The transformation of the noble outlook had not been spontaneous. The monarchy had pushed it along, and public opinion had forced it to consider its position. First, with respect to itself, what it was and what it ought to become. Then with respect to the Nation, a Nation which, breaking into self-awareness, threatened to condemn the nobility to exclusion. Of course, attempts to define the nobility were nothing new. Jurists had long identified nobility with virtue, usually in order to provide a better justification for a hereditary nobility. Moralists had warned against accepting this too readily. The thought of the Enlightenment had thrown doubt on its certainty. And the nobility joined in the game of self-examination; a fashionable game perhaps, but a disturbing one. Bossuet was their defender, but it was Bossuet himself who opened the crisis with the charge that 'Nobility is often but empty, ignorant, coarse and idle poverty, vain in despising what it lacks; are these grounds for such swollen pride?'[2] It was a terrible condemnation left for the eighteenth century to ponder. If nobility was supposed to be virtue above all, why was virtue not a principle of the nobility? Nobles supposed to be falling so short were bound to be concerned! Was there no escape from such worries? Some refuge from agonising, perhaps, in well-worn certainties? Many petty gentlemen thought so, threatened and alarmed by equality, clinging haughtily to the fickle illusion of superiority. Comte de Ségur, thrust onto the side of change more by fashion than conviction, was a clear-eyed observer while in the army of this hardening attitude among petty nobles under threat:

The great lords and courtiers were less to blame than the poor and unenlightened nobility of the provinces; and this should come as no surprise, for all these people had were their titles, which they endlessly invoked against the real superiority of the middle class by whose wealth and education they were crossed and humiliated.[3]

Well-born and something of a rebel, he could overlook such things. Yet there were limits to the Enlightenment's appeal to high society. For many it was little more than a game. One could throw oneself energetically and elegantly into English fashions, liberal ideas, republicanism and equality. But how many of these triflers merely feigned Enlightenment? Many a frivolous dabbler was playing the innocent sorcerer's apprentice who would wake up the next day horrified by the forces he had so rashly let loose.

Ségur, one himself, clearly picked out the inconsistency of these socialites, foppishly playing the aristocratic rebel, unaware of the importance of the stakes, spoilt children who thought that turning on their nurses was revolutionary:

We deeply respected the remnants of an ancient order whose habits, ignorance and prejudices we gaily defied . . . We lent enthusiastic support to the philosophic doctrines professed by bold and witty scribblers. Voltaire won us over, Rousseau touched our hearts, and we felt a secret pleasure when we saw them attack an old structure that appeared to us gothic and ridiculous. So whatever our rank, our privileges, the remains of our former power eaten away beneath our feet, we enjoyed this little war. Untouched by it, we were mere onlookers. These battles were mere pen- or word-play which did not seem to us likely to affect the worldly superiority we enjoyed and which centuries-old possession made us believe indestructible . . . Liberty, whatever its tones, appealed to us through its courage, and equality through its convenience. It can be pleasurable to sink so long as one believes one can rise again at will, and, heedless of the future, we tasted in one draught patrician advantages and the delights of plebeian philosophy.

How many, indeed, of these laughable young democrats saw equality as more than an appealing game, and resisting the absolutist State as a more than a pastime? They turned tail at the first warning. But not all were so empty. Many appreciated how important these changes were, accepted them with thoughtful enthusiasm, and kept to their course with the generous conviction of disinterested believers. A young aristocrat like de Pont, the correspondent of Burke, remained faithful to his ideals even after his 'mentor' became the 'defender of despotism' in denouncing the Revolution. He was no dilettante: for him liberty, equality, a constitution were not simply fashionable trimmings, but necessary innovations replacing (at the cost of some excesses, as he frankly but unsentimentally admitted) all that he deplored in the name of national dignity and honour.[4]

Official historiography has often interpreted the crisis of the old order as the embryo of a class struggle, a conflict between the nobility and a middle class destined by century-long evolution to challenge them in a life or death struggle for power. There was indeed such a conflict; but it antedated Louis XVI's reign, and indeed the eighteenth century itself, and those involved were not quite the parties they are thought to be. It began when absolutism began, and it was a quarrel between different nobles. It was not middle class against noble, but noble against noble. It took place within the nobility, a civil war that lasted as long as the old order, from the sixteenth to the eighteenth century, and was only resolved in the crisis of absolutism, after 1787, when the opposed nobilities came together on the defeat of the monarchy. Only after this reconciliation did the ground shift, and third estate begin to oppose nobility and attack privilege under the banner of equality.

But we need to go even further back. Absolutism was established on the ruins of feudalism when it overthrew the liege nobility, an aristocracy enjoying sovereign powers. To secure its authority and meet its growing fiscal needs, the monarchy surrounded itself with a class of retainers owing direct allegiance to its authority, closely supervised but granted noble privileges in return for services rendered, and completely subservient. In this way it brought about a transfer of power from the feudal nobility to a royal nobility, to which it delegated, under its immediate control, segments of public authority in the form of offices and commissions. Thus was created a new nobility which gradually replaced feudal remnants as they shrank to a purely decorative role. The representatives of this former feudal power, real or presumed, and helpless victims of this revolution which was the final ruin of their power, regarded it as a collapse. 'I confess I can scarce restrain myself when I think on the cruel state to which the late government reduced the order from whence I take my life and honour.' Saint-Simon, the outraged witness of noble debasement, saw clearly how this transfer of power worked. The second order – meaning the old nobility – fell into dependence on the 'Third', lawyers, clerks and bankers, all servants of the absolutist state which distributed power among them. He depicted this third estate, this middle class ennobled by crown and office, and holding the reality of power under Louis XIV, as a new nobility. Provincial government, once in the hands of governors who were true nobles, was now exercised by commissioners, royal nobles. The latter held the second order (for in Saint-Simon's eyes they were not part of it) in complete economic and political dependence. They were rich, and had cornered all the powers that the warrior nobility had lost. Nobody was more sensitive than Saint-Simon to whatever demeaned old stock, and he deplored:

The way rich men command poor, regardless of their birth, by means of places in authority attained through venal offices whose price far outstrips their yield. These ways of matching the nobility will not be easily given up, especially when they lead to yet greater things through the continual want that nobles have, from the most renowned to the least, of the goods and protection, to speak plainly, of rich office holders of the third order, which is almost entirely made up of them . . . As to offices, notwithstanding that the number of judicial, clerical and financial ones is wellnigh infinite, there is not one among them without direct or indirect authority or power, whose measure is in no way comparable with that of any military office whatsoever . . .[5]

With wealth and power engrossed by the royal nobility and the feudal nobility obliged to accept its protection and authority, the latter order sank to being 'the most oppressed of all, with least resources, although the only one to have existed in most distant times'.[6]

The ground of this conflict between two nobilities shifted in the eighteenth century. The cause of the royal nobility was won once absolutism triumphed. But now battle was rejoined over another issue, no longer political power, but the army. Here the clash between money and privilege was resolved at the point of absurdity in the Ségur law under Louis XVI, that last episode of the war between the two nobilities which, in giving official recognition to two classes within the royal nobility, shattered the painfully constructed compromise made by absolutism between the rival segments of the order.[7] Ultimately absolutism paid the price for this political mistake. The two nobilities, their cohesion under threat, came together in opposition and even sought, in alliance with the third estate, to bring the monarchy down. And this alliance lasted. Revolutionary rhetoric might subsequently denounce nobility, as later it would denounce the Girondins and their supporters, but these episodes did not prevent the middle classes and the nobility from triumphing in a post-revolutionary society conforming in general to the wishes expressed by both in 1789.

Scarcely a century separated the peak of absolutism from its end. During that century it passed through a sort of blessed state, a state of grace following from the governmental momentum built up by Louis XIV. Early successes allowed the crown to impose its authority benignly, without recourse to force. It seemed to have reached that perfect position where obedience came automatically and there was no need to threaten violence or coercion. But was this an illusion? When the Constituent Assembly met it found a kingdom that the government no longer governed or even administered. Ruled by women, the monarchy put up no resistance. For all its sporadic revivals, it had given up.

This was the logical result of a long slide, from the time of absolutism at its height down to the meeting of the Constituent Assembly, which had reduced the crown to a marginal sham. But the illusion of authority was so complete that when it was revealed for what it was, the Nation could not at first believe its eyes.

This running out of power, this long downward drift into oblivion, happened in two phases. The first occurred under Louis XIV, when government became self-absorbed and set up for its subjects a cult of its own omnipresence, worshipped at the altar of the hero-sovereign, hiding behind the protective screen of ritual and man-made institutions which performed a double function designed at one and the same time to hide both strengths and weaknesses and to neutralise all threats, all criticism and all opposition. This protective layer was the Court. Court was the catalyst of all ambitions, the sole focus of all thinking beings, a world cut off from natural life where compromises were secretly elaborated. It was a frontier sealing off the crown from all contact with diversity, sheltering it from contamination, yet at the same time operating in a vacuum. It made the birth and development of opposition outside its own ambit ridiculous if not impossible. Opposition could only become effective at Court, and there everything was smothered, controlled, smoothed over. The Court of Louis XIV was a political edifice designed to neutralise any attempt to organise external criticism or opposition. It operated by centralising threats. Nothing must overflow. It was a system for neutralising dangerous forces which turned opposition into intrigue, a formula which turned bombs into squibs, political conflict into courtiers' games or harem conspiracies. The Court channelled, naturalised and neutralised opposition. The Crown watched over it, and was all the stronger in consequence.

In the course of the eighteenth century this mechanism changed, became debased and fell apart. The first cracks appeared under the Regency and in the early years of Louis XV's reign. Authority was on the slide, and the threat of being by-passed took shape, once resistance or even political reflexion escaped from the closed world in which Louis XIV had shut them. Fleury understood this, and that was why he closed down the Entresol club, a centre of political discussion that could have posed a real danger. But the breach had been made. After the death of Louis XIV and the liberalisation or 'de-Stalinisation' of the Regency, the function and the effectiveness of the Court were under threat. It was no longer the sealed world of power, veiling it from unwelcome scrutiny. This was so well appreciated that government shrank away into Versailles' 'little apartments' whose private and secret architecture made ever more obvious the fact that the whole structure had become top-heavy for a government that had ceased to believe in itself. After me, the deluge, said a king who could see the defences raised for his protection crumbling all around him. The Court ceased to function properly at the very moment when it was codifying its practices. Its political function, to draw a circle of fire around the crown, was becoming blurred. The clouds which hid it from the masses were blowing away. Salons, academies, dining-clubs, all the circles of the Palais Royal and soon enough secret or semi-secret societies too seized upon it; it became a subject for talk, argument, and envy. Suddenly shorn of its secrecy, and thus of its magic too, and now an everyday subject thrown open for the Nation's discussion, it shrivelled, paled and half-consciously abandoned itself while everybody, led by the nobility, transferred their interest elsewhere. But to what? Perhaps this essay will explain.

1

The Enlightenment and noble ideology

The eighteenth century can be characterised in a number of different ways. Whether it was a great bourgeois century or a great noble one, it was certainly the century of Enlightenment. But what divergent trends had produced this Enlightenment? Viewed as a bourgeois frame of mind, produced by an expansive social class coming up against the resistance of a society too rigid to accommodate its appetite for power, the Enlightenment looks very like the ideology of a frustration complex. Doubtless this is a one sided and socially unbalanced definition, but it does convey the sense of seemingly inbuilt dissatisfaction which scarred the consciousness and fertilised the thought of a century which ended in permanent revolution, and which spoke, felt, reasoned, and fantasised about revolution, in the written word and even in music, before it committed the act which made revolution a reality.

But who were the authors of this overture to both the exultation and the fury of the revolution? Who were the frustrated ones, the leaders, the prophets of the great shining tomorrow that would bring forth a new world? Were they bourgeois? They could not fail to be. In a society which seemed to be gaily burying the old aristotelian categories which stood in its way, how could the bourgeoisie, an elite already competing for power, not play a leading role in planning the changes? We need only mention Voltaire, Diderot, Rousseau, Raynal, Sieyès. But surely it would be quite misleading to claim that they monopolised the Enlightenment, that they alone felt frustrated or wished to overturn the world! For the frustration which afflicted this century was not primarily social; it was above all political. First and foremost the Enlightenment was about redefining power, or rather realising that power now lay somewhere new. Until then, government was something not seen and therefore not controlled by the citizen. Power emanated from Heaven, and dwelt in one charismatic person, the object of religious veneration and the instrument of a force not his own which could perform miracles.

The first consequence of Enlightenment thought was to secularise government, to cut the umbilical cord linking it to Heaven, to give it back to men. The most important effect was to fragment it, make it divisible, and at the same time to redefine its purpose, diversify what it could do, and set out its limits. So long as it was sanctioned by religion, government touched men's souls as well as their bodies. Without that sanction, their souls no longer concerned it, but their bodies came more obviously under its sway. Once government lost its role as divine legislator, it became subject to the judgement of the citizen, and found itself assigned a specific function: to protect and benefit him materially. It should guarantee men's wordly happiness. Its ability to do this was closely dependent on how the relationship between those who exercised power and those subject to it was organised; any model, from despotism through to socialism, could be equally desirable provided that it brought about human happiness.

The nobility, always conscious that it was an aristocracy, could not stand apart from government, or its forms and manifestations, and indeed felt obliged to treat it as a prime concern. The more so as its heritage and the particular situation into which it had been thrust, largely under Louis XIV, left it bitterly resentful and frustrated at a power which had set itself apart, beyond noble influence or reach, free of all check, out of control and out of sight. So naturally the nobility was the particular opponent of government, and it was to be expected that nobles should want a say in redefining it, bringing it down from the heights it had reached, forcing it to take account of mankind, giving it full rein under the control of those who, by taking it over, would give it legitimacy.

Such a redefinition of power sprang from the thought of those whom power had most affected, those most wounded by a scandalous authority answerable to none, without limits, justified only in metaphysical terms. It had robbed them of one justification for their existence and at the same time destroyed their fundamental rights: the right to advise, the right to check, the right to govern. It was hardly surprising after that that criticism of government should be led by nobles who profoundly resented its pharaoh-like personalisation. In their eyes, government should merely be the expression, individualised and magnified in the person of the sovereign, of the noble order's collective capacity to rule or to delegate its authority without surrendering its original rights.

In divorcing government from its social foundations, in setting it ideologically apart, Louis XIV had excluded the official elites from the essential pact between power and its object, between government and governed. He had broken the tacit contract made at the beginning of the monarchy: the noble contract, a sort of aristocratic social contract. This made men think, it made them bold, it made them rebel. For henceforth the very legitimacy of government was at issue. Even in the most respectful eyes, Louis XIV's power could appear intolerably despotic, contrary indeed to the contract which alone gave it legitimacy. Shorn of his natural advisers, the monarch no longer embodied sovereign and unalterable power; a power guaranteed only by force, fear, and despair was a mere caricature. The right to resist then became a duty.

The duc d'Orleans, sitting in 1715 amid the peers and magistrates of the parlement, symbolised the re-emergence of true legal and hallowed authority, and together they were able to annul the last wishes of a misguided monarch in the full awareness that law was being restored and power returned to the plenitude of joint sovereignty.[1] The memorable session of the parlement at which Louis XIV's last wishes were overriden was in fact the official manifestation of the ideological revolution from which the whole of Enlightenment thinking about government stemmed. From then on government was no longer a thing of religious mystery, but rather a rational activity and a focus of society.

An authority rooted in reason, for a century which thought history all-pervasive, must also be rooted in history. And history in its turn gave rise to ideologies. Some were cyclical, and so they looked back to better times. Some were progressive, and they spawned ideas of progress and visions of future happiness. Insofar as the partnership between the nobility and history remained more attractive than the idea of a self-governing nation, an ideology first developed among those who felt the partnership most clearly, because they were most concerned with it and because it was they who resented the scandalous warping of history most deeply. Inversely, history provided them with arguments to underpin the legitimacy of their outlook and to condemn a government which usurped the rights of those it existed to support. A dialectic of the present and the future constructed a future of progress and happiness in a golden age some time before power was usurped. For those who rejected that golden age, history was the other way round. The usurpation of power for them was a stage in a forward movement, a step in the ascent to happiness. At the two extremes of these opposed currents, coming together with a golden age either restored or seen as possibly to come, stood feudalism or socialism, Boulainvilliers or d'Argenson. In both cases, whether government was seen as the destroyer of liberties or the founder of the State, there was an awareness of a right to happiness, to be achieved either through government founded on old rights recovered or on reasonable rights justified by the advance of history. Whether seen as the instrument for the achievement of happiness, or the obstacle to its spread, government could be improved. And this is the capital point: Enlightenment meant reform.

The situation of the French nobility was the result of an evolution that had locked it into a contradiction from which the whole intellectual effort of the eighteenth century sought to free it. Subjected, 'debased' some writers said, by authority, devalued by a usurping power, it still retained great pretensions which could now only be satisfied by shams and substitutes for power in the form of precedence and dignities. The defeat of the Fronde had consolidated absolutism, a regime in which the State and its incarnation, the king, recognised only subjects and thralls, not power sharers; slaves of the law, not its guarantors. The victory of the monarchy marked the end of a dialogue between government and nobility which whether peaceful or violent had been between equals. Henceforth the nobility was to be a mere associate. It had ceased to be the state, or at least one of its essential components, and become an estate.

In exchange for submission it found itself assigned a role. In the great show put on by the monarchy to celebrate its own grandeur and cult, the nobility played a symbolic part: it personified luxury, highlighting the leading character and hiding his usurpation. In the lavish jewel-box of Versailles, the petted and powerless nobility, the deified king, and religious and profane pomp became confused with everyday life. Nobles took part in the display but, constantly on stage, they had no entry to the recesses where government shut itself away. Transformed into sumptuous celebrants of the great liturgy presented by the monarchy to its people and to Europe, nobles lost on all fronts; their power was reduced to mere trappings, their local influence given up for gorgeous slavery. Their leaders had become royal retainers. And from then on nobles began to realise how far they had slipped. Throughout the eighteenth century – from the duc de Bourgogne's circle down to the Estates-General – all their efforts were bent towards reversing the relationship that Louis XIV had established between the crown and the nobility: they sought to replace their domestication with control of the monarchy.

Or at least that was one of their aims; for the whole second order was not involved in it, nor even the whole of the elite among the nobility. There were in fact many nobilities. A whole segment of the second order, the petty and middling nobles of the provinces, had no designs on high offices that were closed to them, or on political power which they only saw in charismatic terms. For them, absolutism meant the divinely ordained state, which in everyday terms meant the employer state; they submitted willingly, even religiously, to its authority; and in return it provided them with employment. The state must retain an army to satisfy their professional needs. They could live with absolutism so long as the king guaranteed their privileges and plenty of noble employments. It was the monarchy's failure to satisfy this demand from the majority of the nobility that turned them belatedly into advocates of limited monarchy. Having tamed it too well without managing to satisfy it, the monarchy alienated the nobility. But at the same time it failed to win onto its side a third estate that had been sacrificed to the nobility, and whose political ambitions followed the pattern of noble one.

The beginning of noble resistance coincided with the greatest extent of royal power, under Louis XIV. In questioning the established order, the nobility opened the way to the politics of the Enlightenment whose criticism was progressively to undermine the foundations of absolutism. Fénelon, Chevreuse and Beauvilliers developed the idea of an aristocratic monarchy, a regime that would put responsible government in place of the despotic power of a monarch answerable to none but himself; in place of unitary and therefore arbitrary government, a shared authority divided between men of power and men of position – a meritocracy in fact. A decentralised monarchy would be controlled by the elite of the nobility and the third estate, established in the administration, the army and the judiciary according to their ability and their worth, and independent of ministerial despotism.[2] Throughout, nobles would enjoy preference when they combined worthiness with dignity. Councils would appoint the best, or in Saint-Simon's words, people of 'a certain attainment': people who by their birth and their 'establishment' were most interested in the State's wellbeing, and above all people who were independently-spirited, and most likely to resist arbitrary tendencies. Fénelon and Chevreuse adopted the *parlementaire* doctrine that founded the principle of government on law. It was this that placed limits on the sovereign's authority, and curbed popular excesses.

'The tyrannical despotism of sovereigns is an affront to the rights of human brotherhood; it upsets the great law of nature, that kings are but the custodians of. The despotism of the multitude is a mad, blind force that rages 'gainst itself; a people spoiled by excess of liberty is the most insupportable of all tyrants. *The wisdom of all government consists in finding the mean betwixt these two dread extremes, in a liberty tempered by the sole authority of the laws.*'[3]

It matters little that Fénelon had difficulty in shaking off his nostalgia for an idyllic past. What matters is his criticism of government. It established Enlightened political thought on two principles that the whole century was to exploit – that tyranny infringed natural law, and that law was a necessary limitation on power.

This theorising had only been made possible by the crisis of conscience that had shattered, fragmented, and warped relations between the king and his subjects, driving them apart, disrupting the links between government and governed – in a word confronted authority with a new concept that soon became defined as the Nation. Before emerging fully this idea had to go through an intermediate stage made necessary by the pyramid structure of society and the dictates of history. The national idea was built up over a number of phases, each marking a wider definition of what Nation meant. First it could be, and had to be, thought of in its noble phase. The awakening of the nobility's awareness that it was a national body, often misinterpreted as a 'feudal reaction', was both the leaven and the embryo of the Nation. It was from the aristocracy that the Enlightenment received and transformed the idea of something with inalienable rights that was opposed to established authority yet antedated it. Confronted by absolutism, power of limitless pretensions which recognised nothing existing outside its own ambit, the nobility turned to history for proof of its prior existence and the principle of its being: 'The nobility derives neither its establishment nor its rights from the monarchy.'[4] Here was a Nation, for the moment confined to a nobility whose superiority was neither natural nor biological, but historical, defining itself against a power bent on reducing it to absolute submission, and demanding rights, liberties and autonomy. Boulainvilliers, with his noble liberties and powers, became authority's most dangerous critic.[5] It was he who opened the way to the emergence of the Nation, henceforward embracing all citizens. To deal with government, the idea of the rights of the Nation (initially on the reduced scale of the nobility), having served monarchical usurpation, turned to history for a challenge to despotism. It also lent legitimacy to 'revolution' in the sense of a return to first principles. And this could easily be turned, if historical underpinnings were removed, in a reforming direction, towards forward-looking revolution.

For Montesquieu, who produced a synthesis of noble claims, absorbed the thought of great magistrates like d'Aguesseau, denied the distinction between noble Germans and common Gauls, and recognised that the nobility had never been closed to outsiders, the Frankish monarchy became a time when 'liberties' and limited monarchy had coexisted. Shorn of Boulainvilliers' historical racism, the attack on absolutism was now pressed home through a judicial doctrine of limited powers. Magistrates had already asserted that there were brakes and buffers: that law was above kings, that the Parlement exercised controls, that the nobility had hallowed privileges: 'A monarchical State is characterised, and distinguished from a despotical State, by the diversity within it of classes and orders of subjects, and those prerogatives and exemptions that are attached to them.'

This was a jurists' interpretation, which with Montesquieu led to the famous dictum: 'in order that power be not abused, matters must so be arranged that power checks power'. This blocking, tempering, power had three foundations: in history (Frankish liberties), in law (judicial control), but also in dignity. For who had more capacity to resist the abuse of power than the great, who else had so much power without imposing servitude? And so Montesquieu was at one with Saint-Simon:

> The moment Louis XIV was dead, envy of rank appeared. The people added to what royal authority had already accomplished. They would willingly abase themselves before the king's ministers; but would in no wise defer to an officer of the Crown, and looked with indignation on all subordination that was not servitude.[6]

For Montesquieu nobility and the noble hierarchy were joint guarantors of the Nation's liberties against levelling authority; they guaranteed that authority was just.

Mably, too, turned to history for his national claims. But he widened the Nation by postulating two alternate sets of usurpations. The Nation's liberation, which would establish it, would be accomplished by throwing off both monarchical usurpation and feudal usurpation. Here the liberty of the Nation was no longer confused with that of the nobility. It derived on the contrary from the destruction of the two forms of tyranny which had brought fatal consequences to the course of history. For if kings had separated 'their interests from those of the Nation' and seen themselves 'more as masters of a fief than magistrates of a great society, destroying the Estates-General to put arbitrary administration in their place', the nobility too had misconstrued the natural rights of the Nation by aspiring to become a class of 'tyrants' by the use of force and the weight of heredity.[7] With Mably the Nation (and its substitute the Estates-General) went beyond the definition given it by both Fénelon and Boulainvilliers, ranked the nobility among the obstacles in the way of its own fulfilment, and assumed the form that would be acknowledged in 1789.

Boldly, noble thinking had made absolutism its particular target. For the crisis which afflicted it was primarily political. But nobles could not challenge authority without thinking about themselves, defining their own nature, and justifying, in the face of government and society, their ambitions and their very existence. This meant they needed to establish terms of reference. History provided an arsenal full of arguments: the superiority of victors had been established by conquest. This argument, though historical, could be variously interpreted by historians. Based[8] theoretically in biology, the racial argument was weakened by evidence of contamination and the way governments had created nobles. The spirit of the Enlightenment was unreceptive to arbitrary values which looked more like acts of faith than natural truths. It was becoming more and more obvious that social selection could depend on criteria other than heredity.

Once this principle was established, nobility was bound to appear an obstacle to progress, indeed a superstition incompatible with the philosophy of an enlightened age, an age which wished to be guided by the evidence of reason alone. The first enlightened generation had undermined absolutism. Would the second reject nobility, on the same principles, as a usurpation? In fact, it was not until the revolutionary generation of d'Antraigues and Sieyès that nobles became victims of their own line of thought, and found the argument of conquest and the Gaulish Nation turned back against them with Sieyès advising them to get back to . . . their Franconian forests. But even before this was thrown back at them, the nobility's self-examination and self-doubt had called their whole legitimacy into question.

René Louis de Voyer, marquis d'Argenson, minister of Louis XV, was dubbed 'the beast' by a frivolous Court, but was a cultivated man, a friend of Voltaire, and a great scribbler who left behind him after his death 56 manuscript volumes, a treatise on *Royal Democracy*, and *Essays* in the manner of Montaigne. He also elaborated a vigorous model of a nobility based on merit. For d'Argenson, the triumph of merit over heredity was the essential stage in the transition from a society of violence to a society of happiness. Breaking with his predecessors and above all with Boulainvilliers, he turned historical reasoning round. Imagine looking in an idealised past for a model of the desirable society! On the contrary, the seeds of progress lay in the present and the future. For throughout history things have got better: the golden age is in front of us, not behind. Absolutism had taken a progressive step by struggling against anarchy and feudal despotism. But in turn it became despotic itself, for it wished 'to rule all by direct royal agents'. 'Royal democracy' should restore it to its proper limits and bring the historic evolution of France to its logical conclusions. The crown had put an end to 'feudal usurpation'. But in its turn it was both author and victim of a new usurpation: venality, which essentially benefited the nobility. Even so, the crown had begun the struggle against this new form of subjection: people of no birth were being admitted as royal officers, and 'today commoners are said to be preferred to nobles for all matters of government. Thus little by little heredity and the venality of offices are being eliminated.' All that was now needed was to transform royal officers into municipal ones so as to limit arbitrary power, and while preserving governmental rights, to interest the Nation in the management of its interests. But to achieve these results, certain prerequisites were essential: first destroy seigneurial property, for 'separation between the owner of the land and he who works it is the greatest of ills'; then abolish nobility: this was a direct consequence of democracy and the way to guarantee monarchical authority.

Should we not count the strength of the nobility among the safeguards that monarchical authority has no need of? It is said it supports the Crown; but many reasons say it is more likely to overturn it if remedies are not applied. All we need know is whether an order cut off from the rest of the citizens, nearer the throne than the people, whether high birth, independent of the prince's grace, is more subservient to royal authority than subjects equal between themselves.

These then are the two desires formulated as early as 1739 by an enlightened representative of the second order: to establish civil equality, and organise a meritocratic society. 'Let all citizens be equal to each other, so that each works according to his talents and not by the whims of others. Let each be the child of his works and his merits; all the demands of justice will be met, and the State will be better served.'⁹ Hereditary nobility is denounced as an 'evil'; contrary to morality and to virtue, and besides it offends all those who are not noble: 'What could be more cruel than to be surpassed by people whose only talent is to be born noble and rich?' D'Argenson favours the aristocracy of merit: 'We must in fact move towards a goal of equality where the only distinction between men is that of personal merit.' Nobody before 1789 would go further than d'Argenson, whether in his criticism of nobility, 'That rust . . . that inborn greatness which is not only without merit, but actually excludes it for lack of education', or in the call for equality (even of goods) which makes him the first socialist.

D'Argenson and Boulainvilliers, however far apart their thought may seem, are found mingled in a thinker who was less original, but who had a greater influence on his contemporaries, the comte d'Antraigues.

From one he took the condemnation of nobility, from the other hostility to absolutism in the name of Frankish liberties. Born in 1753, a great traveller, disciple of Rousseau and friend of Voltaire, he had links with the young liberal nobility, the Encyclopedists and Mirabeau. D'Antraigues was a violent opponent of all tyranny, political or religious, a free thinker and free liver (marrying an opera singer), one of the last generation of the Enlightenment. Beginning as a soldier, he soon embraced civil life and became a frequenter of salons and a paid ministerial publicist, living partly by his pen. But it was the imminence of the meeting of the Estates-General which showed him to be a political writer and thinker. In 1788 he published his *Memorandum on the Estates-General* which went through 14 successive editions and shared public favour with Sieyès' pamphlet *What is the Third Estate?* He was as famous in his time as Sieyès himself, and the third estate electors of Paris wished to nominate him for their list. As early as 1785 he had set out the two principles of his popularity: the calling of the Estates-General, and the abolition of nobility. 'There are for us', he wrote in that year, 'two ways of recovering liberty without recourse to the extreme but legitimate way of insurrection. More fortunate than the Turks, formerly we had general assemblies in which the Nation met together through its representatives and set up formidable barriers against the crown. Let the Nation realise the absolute necessity of assembling the States-General, and know that this is the only way to avoid tyranny.' And he added, opening the second line of his argument, 'Hereditary nobility is a scourge which is devouring the land of my birth.'[10]

Like his predecessors, d'Antraigues sought and found hope of national resurrection in the past of France. Royal power – since d'Antraigues regretfully recognised there was a king, preferring a republic himself – royal power held executive authority, since the Nation could not exercise it directly in a state as big as France. But it could alienate the power of making laws without renouncing its liberty.

If any man is disqualified by his position from exercising legislative power, that man is a king and above all a hereditary king. Born amid corruption, his first sight is of the natural enemies of public order. Their poisoned maxims are the first things his inexperience hears. He grows up in the midst of courtiers; so all he sees around him is a debased crowd of slaves.[11]

It was also for the Nation to set up courts to remove despotism from the judicial arm: 'Its existence and its liberty reside in this imprescriptible power.' And consent to taxation. All these rights had once been enjoyed by the Nation in the assemblies of March and May. But the Franks had failed in their duty, and had not known how to safeguard public liberty. They had committed two serious faults which had opened the way for the nation's enserfment. Firstly they had enserfed the Gauls: this political mistake had bred 'corrupters of the throne and satellites of tyrants'. Then they had made fiefs hereditary: 'From this fatal change hereditary nobility was to blossom, the most appalling scourge with which heaven in its wrath can afflict a free nation.'[12] The nobility was no longer the best part of the Nation, constituting thereby the Nation itself, the guarantor of liberties: on the contrary, it was an excrescence, a foreign body, 'a new Nation hostile to peoples'. 'Since the hereditary nobility formed a numerous body in the midst of the Nation, the result was that there existed a sort of particular Nation within the Nation'. Not even Sièyes went further in rejecting this foreign parasitic nation, which opposed its own interests to greater ones.

Like d'Argenson, d'Antraigues condemned a society based on orders, and in a unified Nation wanted henceforth only individuals. This quest for an individualistic society, cemented by the equality of citizens, went together with an instinctive mistrust with regard to the quasi-religious power of the monarch. D'Antraigues proclaimed the necessity of shaking off the sentimentalism surrounding the devotion of subjects to their king. The latter was simply a master, whom it was well to watch closely. A man in power could manage to be an object of veneration of love; but also of fear, and vigilance was the first duty of a free people. 'It is known (in the depths of the poorest province) that kings are chiefs and not fathers of their peoples.' D'Antraigues was attempting to rid France of the poisoned maxims which had established absolutism and the omnipotence of kings. 'The king's will is law' was a doctrine as perverse as the claim of kings that they held their crown from God alone. Citizens owed government no sacrifices, but owed their all to the Nation.

Thus, noble thinking followed two complementary tracks. In the search for its identity, it had begun by trying to justify its own 'difference', to set up a principle of apartness. The aim was to distance itself from a subject Nation, to combat absolutism in the name of primitive liberties. Later, playing down the idea of singularity, it tried to integrate nobility into the emerging Nation. To do this it went to great lengths, denying the values on which it was established, together with a society of orders that had become the main obstacle to its integration into the national community. From then on the nobility took up the values of individualistic society: merit and equality of opportunity. And so it merged with bourgeois thinking. The noble identity crisis, having provoked a stress on difference, ended up with the annihilation of the order in a model of egalitarian meritocracy.

It is impossible to discern two opposed social currents in Enlightenment thought, one bourgeois and the other noble. In cultural development, and in the political and social thought of the Enlightenment nobles played a role as important as the representatives of the third estate. In fact they defined together a single and selfsame culture: one which culminated in the self-realisation of a Nation individualistic, egalitarian, free to choose, and keen to take control of its destiny. The grievance lists (*cahiers de doléances*) of the nobility and the third estate show the cultural identity which the two orders had reached by 1789.

2
The nobility between myth and history

It matters little in itself whether there were 100,000 nobles or 500,000. Like every elite, the old regime nobility defined itself not so much by volume as by weight, by structure rather than by numerical strength. What mattered was its social density. If its influence, its role in the state and its weight in public life had been reduced to the exact level and proportion of its numbers, it would have been nothing in a Nation of 26 millions. But an elite is measured by its dynamism; its existence is linked to the image made of it by the society which secretes and encapsulates it. It is rooted in the magic of social symbolism, as something worth competing for, and/or imitating. Part of its survival depends on the aspiration or the capacity of outsiders to copy and/or challenge it, to admire and/or oppose it, to join and/or supplant it; and part depends on the credibility of its chosen image. This needs to be all the more sound when, as in the case of the old regime nobility, the elite is better defined, its frontiers more rigorous, and the barrier separating it from outsiders institutionalised and juridically defined. In this case it must match a more-or-less imaginary model based on myth.

Thus the nobility's existence was rooted in two concepts both objective and mythic: race and history, twin mirrors in which all nobility was reflected, two poles in which the distinctive worthiness of the elite was invested. Frankish conquest, superior seed. That was how the nobility set itself apart and assessed itself. Conquest gave it a fabulous image which Boulainvilliers turned into history by setting it down. Inherited virtue, theoretically given a biological basis by La Roque, perpetuated the heroic worth of the founders. It hardly mattered that reality could not be bent to the demands of this legendary account. So far from rendering it fanciful, the contamination of the myth by everyday evidence reinforced it and integrated it into history. The ennobled bourgeois instinctively bent to the rules of the aristocratic game. Nor was this perversity or fantasy on his part; it was coherent acceptance

23

of a system of symbols that must be taken as a whole if the entire edifice was not to collapse. Proof of that was the profound upset brought about in the second half of the 18th century by the emergence of the new idea – not universally accepted, but never mind – of merit, and its substitution for *worthiness* in the definition of what a noble was.

So the first task is to get the measure of the myth. History is the yardstick that will falsify or confirm it. Ennoblement first. It is true that immemorial nobility, which fits the myth most closely, was quantitatively negligible. Most nobles owed their existence to one or other form of ennoblement. But myth hid or at least considerably obscured this reality. All that mattered in practice was what was seen as a negation of the myth and by that very fact, theoretically at least, improper: recent ennoblement. The historian's viewpoint here blends with that of contemporaries. Within the limits of the eighteenth century, every entry into the nobility appears to us as promotion of the middle class. Yet it was only in the eighteenth century that membership of the nobility of race began to be defined (although its juridicial definition was older) by exclusion of those with less than four generations or a century. Here the myth shows itself in the accord between the attempt to redefine identity, and the reaction intended to exclude from the group those marked out by merit and no longer by worthiness. Yet the latter were more and more numerous and blended perfectly into the noble group because that group allowed its values to be increasingly infringed and, recognising the normality of this, allowed itself to be contaminated, apart from certain special areas where barriers remained insurmountable. But the group as a whole, insofar as it retained its social cohesion, was profoundly affected. And divided.

The ways to ennoblement, which were very various, had the same virtues in common. They brought promotion first of all, entry into the official elite; but above all regeneration. The new noble, cleansed of the commonness which stained him by his 'soap for scum' (*savonette à vilain*),[1] henceforth shared in the noble ethic and the myth which underpinned it. It was only quite late, after 1750, that commoners brought in turn to the nobility absorbing them a regenerative virtue of their own: merit. Until then a new noble had come from nothing; he brought nothing to the group he was joining. So he had no option but to accept completely the new universe that was opening up to him. Henceforth, on the contrary, he brought with him something to add to the noble heritage, something that would enhance and transform it increasingly. Thus it is essential to measure the importance of the group's renewal in the course of the century in order to understand the importance of the transformation it had undergone, quantitatively in terms of recruitment, and qualitatively in terms of the operational symbols which dictated its values and its behaviour.

A major path to ennoblement was through offices. Thanks to them the gateway to nobility was wide open: the barrier was crossed in one step by the newcomer and his descendants. This was called first degree ennoblement. Less rapid was ennoblement by degrees, called gradual nobility; two or three generations sloughed off the old man by a slowly maturing process of purification. Assimilation worked more obscurely. Here possession was nine points of the law. Three or four generations lent the authority of time to an ascent. Usurpation encountered the same resistance from the passage of time.

From this viewpoint the only certain indicator is the number of ennobling offices, and that is the first obstacle. They were open to nobles, and indeed in certain cases – the highest levels of the judiciary and certain offices at Court – they were in practice a noble monopoly. For some, nobility only came at the end of a slow ascent. Necker estimated that 4,000 people in the course of the eighteenth century owed their ennoblement to the exercise of office. Jean Meyer has recently preferred the lower estimate of 2,000. Only monographs giving a complete list of the personnel of all the parlements, courts of accounts and other sovereign courts would allow us to distinguish between offices conveying ennoblement and those which actually brought ennoblement to those who held them. There were 3,020 ennobling offices in the sovereign courts. But Necker, who gives this figure (its rough exactitude is confirmed by detailed checks), does not itemise the nuances, and here they are essential.

Some offices ennobled in the first degree: their holders enjoyed full and transmissible nobility after 20 years in office or passed on their nobility to descendants if they died in office before completing the required period. This privilege was enjoyed by the court of requests (*Requêtes de l'Hôtel*), the parlements of Besançon, Dombes, Flanders, Grenoble, Paris, the chambers of accounts of Dôle and Paris, the court of aids of Paris, the court of moneys of Paris, the superior councils of Artois and Dombes, the bureau of finances of Paris, and the Châtelet. But there are numerous complications. The Châtelet only began to ennoble in the first degree very late: this provision only took effect in 1768 and was accompanied by a restriction which, as a result of the Revolution, nullified its effect: exceptionally, nobility was only acquired after 40 years in office. The council of Dombes was abolished in 1762, the parlement of Dombes in 1771, and the court of moneys of Paris had only ennobled in the first degree since 1719.

In the other courts offices conferred only gradual nobility. Father and son had each to spend 20 years in the same office in order to bequeath perfect nobility to the third generation. This accordingly reduced the rate of ennoblement over the century. Affected were the parlements of Aix, Bordeaux, Dijon, Metz, Nancy (from 1766), Navarre, Rennes, Rouen and Toulouse, the chambers of accounts of Bar-le-Duc (from 1766), Blois (until 1778), Aix, Dijon, Lorraine (from 1766), Metz, Montpellier, Nantes and Rouen, the courts of aids of Caen, Clermont-Ferrand, Guyenne, Montauban and Rouen, the court of moneys of Lyons (until 1771), the superior councils of Alsace, Artois, Corsica (from 1768), Roussillon, Guadeloupe (from 1768), Martinique (1768 also), Cap Français (from 1766), Saint Domingue (1766 also), and bureaux of finances other than that of Paris.

To these difficulties must be added the hardening which is supposed to have occurred in the second half of the eighteenth century in the recruitment of the parlements. According to Bluche, the parlement of Paris made itself throughout the century the instrument of an aristocratic reaction.[2] It only took in an average of 10 % non-nobles. The term 'aristocratic reaction', here as in the army, is ill-chosen. If the parlement of Paris recruited relatively few commoners, this was because under the old regime there was a recognised hierarchy of promotion. It was rare to go straight from the counting-house to the bench. Among the 'new men' entering the parlement of Paris, there were many who had previously held, or whose fathers had held, offices in less illustrious bodies like the bureaux of finances or courts of aids, or (a third) who had been King's Secretaries. These offices brought them nobility, but the parlement added the distinction they lacked, and constituted a sort of second degree of ennoblement. The parlement of Paris found the company of King's Secretaries a nursery of magistrates naturally selected by recent nobility and wealth. There was no trace of noble reaction here, but for the present purpose the consequence of this type of recruitment was considerable: ennoblements through office-holding in the parlement of Paris were greatly reduced. The same type of recruitment was found at Nancy, Grenoble, Aix, Toulouse. At Rennes, by tradition, only nobles were allowed in.

Elsewhere matters were different. Jean Egret has been able to show, using A. de Roton's collection of *Arrêts du Grand Conseil portant dispense du marc d'or de noblesse*, that the recruitment of non-nobles in the last 15 years of the old regime was sometimes considerable: at Colmar all newcomers were non-nobles, at Metz and Perpignan two thirds, more than half at Pau, Douai and Bordeaux, a third at Rouen and Dijon and a quarter at Besançon, where Maurice Gresset confirms it holds good for the whole century.[3] Doubtless the proportion was somewhat higher in companies with less prestige than the parlements, and less able to be lofty about the origins of their members. Out of 25 counsellors replaced between 1780 and 1789 at the court of accounts of Aix-en-Provence, 11 were commoners,[4] as were 10 of the 21 members of the bureau of finances of Besançon.[5]

It is rash to generalise from these rare samples. However, taking into account the reservations made earlier, such as the gradualness of ennoblement in certain cases, it does not seem excessive to suggest that one fifth of ennobling offices actually ennobled their holders over the century. That makes over 3,000 which, counting 20 years for a generation and in certain cases two, as a normal time for acquiring complete nobility[6] (it could be less when death came prematurely), makes a minimum of 1,200 ennoblements for the whole century.

To this figure can be added the 900 King's Secretaries in the grand chancery and provincial chanceries. In the course of the eighteenth century the Parisian chancery took in 1,500 secretaries;[7] over the same period the provincial chanceries admitted about twice that number. This makes 4,000 commoners enjoying this type of ennoblement, the most complete in that it absorbed the newcomer into the nobility of race by allowing him 4 quarterings of nobility. Even so, the last to get in did not have time to reach the end of their 20 years in office, so they must be deducted. Let us say a round figure of 4,000. But some of these, 20%, already held ennobling offices; that leaves 3,200.

Other ennoblements through office occurred in the course of the century, but in the present state of research it is impossible to draw up a complete list. Military nobility, resulting from an edict of 1750, which granted transmissible nobility to all generals and gradual nobility for three successive generations of knights of St Louis, only provided 110 new nobles: 92 through promotions to general and just 18 through the long road of the cross of St Louis. The lowness of the latter figure is attributable to the revolutionary break, since only two generations had time to benefit from this provision.[8]

This leaves ennoblement by municipal office. Nobles 'of the bell',

mocked and yet envied, must have been numerous, for although municipal offices which ennobled their holders were not common – about
30 in all – the period in office was often as short as a year, so that in a
century they had time to benefit a fair number. Even allowing that
certain of them might have been held by nobles, a thousand would
doubtless be a minimal figure, since there were, at Toulouse alone, 700
capitouls in the course of the eighteenth century.[9]

So a total of 5,510 were ennobled by office in the space of a very
short century. However, ennoblement by office did not constitute the
only way of getting into the second order. What figure could we
suggest for numbers joining the nobility through patient waiting or
through usurpation?[10] Less problematic is ennoblement by letters.
From 1712 to 1787, the court of aids of Paris registered 500 letters,
and the court of accounts of Brittany 57 between 1715 and 1787; for
its part the parlement of Dijon offered a score from 1720 to 1782, not
counting confirmations, upholdings and recognitions of nobility which
were often in reality ennoblements.[11] In total, 1,000 letters for the
kingdom as a whole is surely not an excessive figure.

Office, bell, and merit add up then to a total of 6,500 ennoblements:
a very low figure in relation to the total of families which at the end of
the eighteenth century owed their nobility to one or other of these
forms of recruitment to the second order since 1700. For actually it
represents not 6,500 newcomers but that number of living families,
some of whom had had time by 1789 to give birth to several branches.
So it is a far more considerable number of nuclear families that we
should compare with the total of noble families in 1789 in order to
measure exactly the renewal of the order in the course of the century.

A further difficulty. The estimates which have been made offer a
spread of figures whose very disparity shows how arbitrary they are.
They vary between 80,000 and 400,000. But not all are talking about
the same thing. Some speak of individuals (Coyer, Lavoisier, Sieyès,
Gouy d'Arsy), others take families (Chérin, Bouillé, Expilly): but are
these families of kinship or nuclear families? In any case most of these
figures were for propaganda purposes. Coyer, to defend his call for a
trading nobility, had an obvious interest in exaggerating the differences
between the number of nobles and the range of available places in the
royal armies. Sieyès was perhaps tempted to play it down in order to
make noble privileges appear more scandalous. We find the same diver-
gencies among modern historians, but there is a tendency to raise the
figure. Henri Carré settled on a figure of 230,000 nobles, but he

included in that everybody who enjoyed noble privileges. Recently R. Dauvergne felt impelled towards the high figure of 400,000. The wisest course is to recalculate on a different basis and using other sources. Taine gave an estimate by using La Roque and Barthélémy's lists of electors at the *bailliage* assemblies of 1789, and reached a total of 130,000 nobles or 26,000 families. None of the weaknesses attributed to this source appear to me to survive serious examination.[12]

It is said to exclude nobles without fiefs, and also those recently ennobled. But this is to confuse or misread the regulation. Those without fiefs were not excluded, they were simply summoned in a different way, collectively, whilst those with fiefs received an individual summons. As to the recently ennobled, they were only passed over if their nobility was incomplete: this meant people like King's Secretaries who had not yet been in their offices for the required 20 years. They indeed had no right to take part in the noble assemblies.

In Paris there is said to have been a large number of abstentions. This argument too appears groundless to me. A great number of Parisian nobles voted in assemblies in the provinces, where their lands were held, and had no right to be represented by proxy in Paris where they owned no fiefs, since there were very few in the capital.

The only argument worth consideration works against the position of those who reject La Roque's lists: the fact that by the use of proxies the same person could appear simultaneously in several assemblies. This means we should reduce rather than raise Taine's figure by taking only the number of members who were actually present in the *bailliage* assemblies. The result is that even if we take into account possible abstentions, the figure of 26,000 families is a maximum one. And there is a way of checking this result: the separate noble lists for the capitation tax. Only a part of them have survived, representing over ⅓ of the kingdom (38%). They include 13 generalities: Amiens, Châlons, Grenoble, Limoges, Bourges, Bordeaux, Rouen, Moulins, Orléans, Caen, La Rochelle, Franche-Comté and Montauban.[13] Admittedly there is some danger in extrapolating from these 13 generalities to the whole of France. But perhaps the risk is not too great. The sample includes big generalities and more modest ones, some rich and some poor.

In all I have counted 10,547 entries, which gives an average of 811 per generality. That makes, for the 34 generalities as a whole, 27,574 entries. But this figure does not represent that number of noble families. It includes, in fact, not only heads of families but also widows,

Total number of individuals

Generality	Entries	Families after multiplication by 4.5	Total population	%
Bourges	480	2,160	528,424	0.40
Amiens	602	2,709	530,062	0.51
Grenoble	613	2,758	669,812	0.41
Rouen	1,079	4,855	731,978	0.66
Limoges	725	3,262	647,686	0.50
Bordeaux	1,860	8,370	1,393,167	0.60
Moulins	533	2,398	648,830	0.37
Orléans	706	3,177	707,304	0.45
Caen	1,575	7,087	654,082	1.08
Châlons	673	3,028	800,706	0.37
La Rochelle	365	1,642	471,285	0.34
Franche-Comté	613	2,758	707,272	0.39
Montauban	723	3,253	541,294	0.60
Total	10,547	47,461	9,031,902	0.52

Average Generality: $811 \times 34 = 27,574$.

After reduction, 25,000 heads of family, multiplied by $4,5 = 112,500$ individuals.

bachelors, spinsters above all, but also separately endowed wives. Thus the two sources converge. We must give up the high figure of 400,000 individuals, and settle for 110 or 120,000, or about 25,000 noble families in 1789.

If we compare this figure with the 6,500 families who joined the second order in the course of the eighteenth century, it means a quarter of the nobility – a minimum percentage for the reasons we have discussed – had become noble since 1700. In the seventeenth century the trend cannot have been less marked. In 1789 the number of families who had joined the nobility in the last two centuries of the old regime must have represented at least $\frac{2}{3}$ of the total. Feudal nobility was no longer anything but a memory. How many of the 942 'presented' families, with proofs of nobility going back in principle beyond 1400, were of immemorial origin? And how many could really provide the required proofs? There were plenty of exceptions: great officers of state, descendants of knights of the Holy Spirit, holders of offices in the Royal Household, not to mention numerous contraventions permitted to the rich and powerful, and the king's caprices. It is true that members of the parlements rarely lent themselves to the ceremony of presentation to the king. Yet certain families were entitled to this honour, not taking it up for reasons of protocol that they thought below their dignity: the king made a point of not kissing their wives! But in fact these were exceptions. So were the difficulties encountered by provincial noblemen in getting presented and riding in the king's carriages, which came less as has been claimed because the ceremony entailed costs they could not meet, than as a result of their inability to put together the necessary proofs. In the end all this is secondary. The nobility, at the end of the old regime, was a social group that was young and on the rise. Most of it was made up of the elites produced by the third estate in the course of the seventeenth and eighteenth centuries.

It is therefore essential to be clear about where in the third estate the constituent elements of the nobility were recruited from. François Bluche has shown the pool from which the parisian parlementaire nobility was drawn. An examination of the letters of merit and files on the King's Secretaries in the grand chancery, some 2,500 cases in all, taps the most massive and richest source for the study of origins. The King's Secretaries are the subject of a collective study by the Historical research centre of the *École des Hautes Études en Sciences Sociales*, and while it is inappropriate to go into its details, I can outline here some of its conclusions.[14] The generation of holders of these offices was made up of a varied range in which hardly any of the social levels making up the middle classes were unrepresented. In front were financial and economic activities: these ennoblements gratified the social ambitions of a good part of the kingdom's economic activists. After that the liberal professions made up the most important contingent. The others came from the law courts, from administration and also from the army, where certain military men found the purchase of 'soap for scum' a way of getting round the wait for ennoblement stipulated in the edict of 1750. If we turn to the generation of the fathers of King's Secretaries, the same preponderance of economic and financial activities is found. But the number of high flying financiers and great merchants goes down, while that of traders and petty financial officers increases. The tax-collector replaces the farmer-general. The liberal professions are poorly represented and the most prestigious (advocates) are absent. Petty office-holders make up a considerable part of the contingent. In administration the great appointments are replaced by the lesser functionaries of the king's household. There are even craftsmen: masons, husbandmen, wine-growers. So there was a clear gap between fathers and sons, indicative of rapid social ascent. The generation of the grandfathers confirms and emphasises it: most King's Secretaries had none, or none who mattered. In some cases however the ascent followed a gradual progression, roughly taking a century.

If for some of the King's Secretaries their rise had been very slow and progressive, above all in the categories linked to small offices and civic dignities, for the categories linked to commercial activities, the world of finance and the liberal professions, it was on the contrary rapid and sometimes brutal – in certain cases two generations were enough to reach the fullest form of ennoblement.

Take the case of Edmé Didier de Laborne, whose father was a farmer at Saint-Nom-La-Bretèche. In 1779 he was 44 and acquired an office of keeper of the king's cloak. Son of a comfortably-off, if not rich, husbandman, he belonged to a peasant family which had already set its offspring on the road to the Royal Household. Present at his baptism was an officer of the king's pleasures, and his godmother was daughter of another member of the Household. Also born at Saint-Nom-La-Bretèche, Jean-Claude Peron was 44 too when he was received into the company of King's Secretaries on 22 April 1774. His origins were the same, but he had risen more gradually. It had taken two generations – a father and grandfather in the Royal Household – for their heir, first a notary at the Châtelet and then an advocate at the parlement, to reach the prestigious company. Claude-Martin Goupy, son of a master mason, a master mason himself, benefited from the protection of an architect uncle 'in the confidence of the duc de Penthièvre', and of a flattering marriage; having become builder to the king and the prince de Condé, he was able to marry into the family of a Treasurer of France, and was welcomed by the company in 1779. Often the journey was slower, straddling several reigns of honourable but obscure service. The grandfather of Ange Saussoye was an attorney at the parlement under Louis XIV; his father held the office of receiver of the capitation tax for almost the whole reign of Louis XV. He himself was a tax receiver when in 1778 he entered on the course which should have brought him in 20 years to possession of perfect nobility. Sometimes too one, indeed two centuries of 'bourgeoisie', notability, came before the acquisition of the 'soap'. The route was, clearly, variable and full of contrasts. There could be explosive arrivals for many reasons – sudden enrichment, protection in high places, exceptional merits or the chances of a lucky marriage – or a protracted climb up a century-long slope. There was no model, no one way. Even so, meteoric arrivals remained exceptional. The social rhythm moved by the century rather than the generation.

Ennoblement by office allowed notable families of plebeian origin to penetrate the second order on a massive scale. This process opened up an automatic, and in a sense impersonal, route from the most favoured levels of the third estate to the nobility. But the aspiration to rise left the gap between the orders intact. Newcomers were so rapidly integrated that they were unable to act as a bridge to make the transition from one order to the other more flexible. Since the disappearance in the sixteenth century of theoretical ennoblement by fief-holding and the profession of arms, ennoblement by office alone could be seen as a relative closing up even though the increase in the number of offices had seemingly made up for the shortfall. Above all it reduced the flexibility of the system, favouring the urban middle classes, talent of course, but above all liquid wealth. Through offices the nobility renewed its blood, maintained its substance but remained based on the exclusive principle of royal service.

Even more: whilst with the development of the Enlightenment an original theory of elites was slowly emerging, the nobility remained a world open in its recruitment but closed in its ideology. Once a noble, the commoner at once lost his cultural bearings, and took on as his own the whole of noble culture. He gave up middle-class values and assumed the ethic of the second order. The gap that he should have filled, the link that he should have formed, were so many empty illusions. And this was still the case when already Enlightenment society was looking for a new solution which, beyond orders, would bring about the union of elites at the highest level, that of the moral person. If offices showed themselves inadequate in meeting this aspiration, the crown traditionally had an effective instrument to hand. Ennoblement by office, a collective and automatic process, was beyond the sovereign's control. But he could ennoble whoever he liked. Letters of ennoblement allowed the king to reward fidelity and devotion. They could also be the instrument of a considered policy on elites, a way of transforming the content of the idea of nobility, of modifying the composition of the second order in whatever way seemed best, or in tune with the evolution of an opinion whose attitude towards the weight of tradition was being slowly reshaped by intellectual audacity.

It was by this personal, individual form of ennoblement that a genuine revolution overcame the noble mentality in the eighteenth century. It promoted the emergence of a modern elite that the members of the Constituent Assembly would try to institutionalise.

Nobility was traditionally rooted in a very strong notion derived from an ideological and social complex which impregnated the outlook of the order and overflowed widely into the collective consciousness at every level of the social hierarchy: *honour*. This notion implied a diverse and complementary range of values: hereditary superiority, or claims to a biologically transmitted excellence; historic origins, another claim to excellence as conquerors; and exemplariness. These were all signs of 'quality' compounded in a claim alien to the non-noble: *worthiness*. This notion of worthiness – and its moral complement, *honour* – was the gap which separated nobility from the third estate and made any cultural identification impossible between two worlds enclosed in mutually exclusive value systems. In the second half of the eighteenth century, more precisely from 1760 onwards, the crown tried to break the cultural isolation whereby nobility and middle classes found themselves confined in two closed worlds, at the moment when the spread of the Enlightenment was tending to bring together elites who were both poised to take a step in each other's direction.

From 1760 onwards the notions of worthiness and honour, which until then had defined what was special about nobles, were overtaken by a new notion: merit, a middle class value, typical of the third order, which nobility took over, made its own, accepted and officially recognised as a criterion of nobility. From that moment on there was no longer any significant difference between nobility and middle classes. A noble was now nothing but a commoner who had made it. This notion of merit admittedly took in a certain number of noble criteria, such as military worth, but these blended with middle-class virtues like work, assiduity, competence, utility, benevolence. And so the standards implied by noble status were turned upside down. What was important henceforth was that nobles and middle classes could recognise each other by the same definition of quality. This was a decisive step. This evolution, resulting from a common education, the same intellectual formation, from a community of interests, activities and behaviour, was one of the most coherent signs of the disappearance of the ideological gap which set nobility and middle classes against one another. Reference to merit as a hallmark of the noble elite expressed at one and the same time in conceptual terms the cultural identity of the two orders, and in practical terms for the first time in history the opening of the nobility to the middle classes. Not, of course, that commoners had not become nobles before 1760. But once they had crossed the barrier into the order, they changed nature through the magic of an ideological transmutation: the break was total, and they were baptised and born into a new life. They entered a universe ruled by worthiness and honour after the entire abandonment of their middle class trappings at the end of a process of total cultural loss. Now however all was changed. The cultural impetus was in the opposite direction. Middle class ideology pushed back and supplanted noble ideology. From now on the newcomer was someone who, so far from renouncing his identity, had come closer than his peers to achieving perfection in middle class merit.

Letters of ennoblement illustrate this phenomenon perfectly. They visibly show, in preambles less stereotyped than they first appear, the gradual rise of merit and the contamination of the notion of nobility by the progressive integration of middle-class values.

These letters, like offices, applied to the higher reaches of notability, but their range is wider and they reach much lower down the hierarchy of wealth. At the end of the old regime an office of King's Secretary cost 150,000 *livres*. A decent competence was not therefore enough, and only the rich could tie up such a sum in an investment without return. Letters of merit were in principle independent of wealth, even though registration duties amounted to 6,000 *livres* and an investigation was required to see that the recipient could maintain himself and would not swell the ranks of the penniless nobility. Letters of nobility were at the sole disposal of the king, who took account of the merits and the titles of candidates but also, it is true, the quality and the influence of their sponsors. Letters had a double advantage: they got round the mechanism of venal ennoblement which benefited only the richest for purposes that were essentially, indeed exclusively, fiscal; and they avoided a dangerous immobilisation of capital when the recipient was economically active.

Of the thousand or so letters issued in France in the eighteenth century, 476 were registered in the court of aids of Paris between 1712 and 1787.[15] They provide a sample important in size, but relatively unsatisfactory in that it is not entirely representative of the average recipients of these letters; the Court is heavily represented and this modifies the very content of the notion of merit. Here it was frequently a matter of favour. This leads us to take special note of these grace-and-favour ennoblements, even though merit did not necessarily play no part in them.

In this category we can put the king's bodyguard (46), the officers of the Royal Household (30), and all those whose grant of letters resulted from exceptional circumstances: mayors and civic officers who won this mark of royal gratitude when a member of the royal family visited their town during their term of office (22). To this group can be added about 50 newcomers who owed their rise not to any particular service or any notable deeds, but merely to their wealth and positions attained.

For all the others, entry into the second order was justified on grounds of merit alone. They were spread fairly evenly among the various professions of the upper reaches of the middle classes:

Agents of central government	29
Intendants' subdelegates	11
Advocates	15
Doctors	35
Merchants	50
Financiers	17
Judges in lower courts	52
Soldiers	76
Engineers	12
Artists and intellectuals	22

Although there was a slight predominance of the public sector, the private, with 139 ennoblements, held its own fairly well. In any case its weight increased with the evolution and transformation of royal ennoblement policy, bearing witness to a new attitude in respect of certain professional categories and certain social groups. The most immediately striking thing is an acceleration. Ennoblements increased after 1760. Until that date, over 48 years, 167 have been counted, but 309 in the 27 years after. But this quantitative increase is not the most important thing. Down to 1760 the most significant ranks were those drawn from bodies of distinction: the army, the judiciary, the bar, or civic office (the representation of mayors is almost entirely confined to this period, with 18 out of 22).

1760 marks the start of a growth in the third world of ennoblement: the number of administrators ennobled went up fourfold, but that of merchants went up twelve times, and that of artists by five. First intended to reward above all military worth and success in public office, after 1760 ennoblement became a prize for personal merit and an official recognition of various sorts of service hitherto enjoying little or modest esteem: economic services, administrative, scientific, etc. But what changed most was the tone of the sovereign and the motivations he expressed. In the first half of the century, most of the letters spoke less as if they were actually ennobling than 'recognising' or 'maintaining' nobility. Their words are explicit: 'We believe', declare the preambles, 'we have a duty to grant to subjects worthy in themselves the advantages accruing to them from the actions of their ancestors and to restore that which by the vicissitudes of time or even circumstances relating to the service of the State has become lost to them in terms of standard proofs.'

When it was impossible to resort to such a fiction, a certain precision became necessary, especially if the main merit of the recipient lay in his offspring; this was the case with François Poisson, father of the king's mistress. Then, a diffuse dialectic was adopted blending, so as to drown the fish (*poisson*), every service deserving royal favour: judicial office, military employment, trade. But of course a case like this was naturally exceptional. Most often the royal declaration proceeded less from the personal merit of the recipient than the aura of his family, the presumption of nobility. It was not an exemplary commoner who was deemed worthy to enter the second order. It was rather a question of reparations granted to a noble who had been unjustly excluded. The time had yet to come when middle class values, and primarily ability, would become values of nobility. In these circumstances ennoblement, far from helping to close the gap which separated nobility from middle classes, could only accentuate it by clearly stating a difference in nature between nobles and commoners.

It was this fundamental rift which caved in after 1760. Henceforth the nobility sought to define itself by middle class criteria, whilst references to traditional values were progressively abandoned. The preamble to the letters of Briansiaux (1765), a Dunkirk merchant, still stresses the military aspect of his activities: by fitting out privateers he had rendered great services to the royal navy. But by 1769 the ennoblement of Louis de La Bauche, a Sedan industrialist, was laying stress on the particularly middle class qualities of his industrial and commercial activities: 'No services are more important for us to encourage by rewards than those of a merchant.' The letters of Jean-Abraham Poupart (1769) were even more explicit in alluding to 'citizens whose industry can win homage from the opulence of nations, and swell the fame and power of the state'. The same year the ennoblement of Pierre Feray, merchant of Rouen, gave the king the occasion to explain that it was 'among his duties to extend his care to all that can make trade flourish'. Here was a recognition of the eminent dignity of the middle class which echoed, in reverse, Saint-Simon's 'base trade'. It would appear that the debate on trading nobility, in which the abbé Coyer had found pathetic tones to exalt the dignity of trade, had borne fruit. It had already probably inspired the edict of 1765 which granted honorific privileges to merchants, such as the right to carry a sword and arms; all of which, at least in outward show, brought them nearer to the second order.

The same evolution appears in a new attitude with respect to artists and scholars. Louis XIV had ennobled Lebrun, Mignard, Rigaud, Boullongne. Down to 1760 however ennoblement of artists remained the exception, and the most numerous rewarded the king's architects. From 1760 to 1780 we can count a score in the court of aids of Paris alone. There were a lot of musicians, architects like Soufflot, painters (Van Loo, Vien), scholars, inventors, planners. In 1718 the preamble to the letters of Antoine Coypel can be situated essentially in the tradition of princely patronage: 'Those who have excelled in painting have in all ages been most favourably treated in the courts of the greatest princes and their works have served to embellish their palaces.' After 1760 the tone changes. The sovereign's good pleasure gives place to public utility: 'The study of the sciences and the practice of the arts make essential contributions to the glory and felicity of the State.' 'We cannot see the useful discoveries that some of our subjects make in the sciences and the arts without feeling moved to show them our satisfaction.' And again: the nobility which we grant them makes them all the more distinguished 'in that it takes its origin from the union of virtue and knowledge'. In this there is a new tone that I shall revert to.

Elsewhere we read, before 1760, that ennoblement 'is the surest means of inspiring virtue'. This clearly implies that if ability precedes ennoblement *virtue*, a noble value, is its immediate consequence. After 1760, on the other hand, ennoblement is simply the official confirmation of the personal merit of those 'who combine virtue and the sentiments which make up the character and the source of nobility'. It could not be said more clearly that nobility is not a matter of birth.

Throughout the century doctors had been ennobled. Consultants to the king before 1760; then doctors often without any links at Court, like Grassot or Levacher. Ability alone henceforth dictated the king's choice. Letters talk about 'talent', 'zeal', 'evenings spent in study'. The king's aim is to 'make illustrious the merit born of personal qualities'. What in fact is recognised is the eminent dignity of merit, its ability to pick out the exceptional man, to place him outside the ordinary run, and to justify ennoblement as a pure formality and ratification of an existing fact. One set of letters declares that the king grants the honour of nobility to those of his subjects 'whose actions and sentiments put them in the ranks of nobles'; or again, 'We regard it as a reward to which their claim is all the better insofar as their actions, arising as they do from the true principle of nobility, have earned them the grant of its rank and appurtenances.'

In this way the theoretical assertions of thinkers who justified nobility on biological grounds[16] or, like Boulainvilliers,[17] by a theory of history, were shattered. Henceforth nobility was officially justified by ability and merit, defining itself by middle class virtues. And so the ability of the elite of the third estate to constitute the second order was solemnly stated. Nor – and this was the decisive argument – was it only a matter of compensating for the fate of birth. Letters which state that nobility 'takes its *origin* from the union of virtue and knowledge' go much further than that. The purest nobility is not therefore of the blood, but takes its principle from moral worth and professional ability.

In this way a rejuvenated elite was defined in keeping both with monarchical tradition and Enlightenment ideology. It was a great success for the middle classes who thus integrated nobility into their mental world and made it in a way their own, and their supreme ornament. Henceforth there would be no more *bourgeois gentilshommes* but everywhere *gentilshommes* who were bourgeois. Reasons for hostility between the two orders, now complementary rather than competitive, were therefore much diminished and the middle classes found themselves physically and ideologically blending with the second order.

There can certainly be no doubt that a cultural model more open than the nobility had hitherto conformed to had carried the circles closest to the king, those who were closely or distantly involved in the outlook of the established order and in its policy-making. Yet whether we have any proof of the generalisation of the new directions formulated mainly by royal policy, and of the extent to which the nobility, the second order as a whole, accepted the results of this development – this is the question that we shall next have to answer.

The grievance lists of the nobility, drawn up in the feverish and impassioned atmosphere of the spring of 1789, speak to us here as elsewhere with exceptional freshness, and are a testimony, on the problem that concerns us here, to the conversion of noble society to the middle class cultural model. They leave no doubt that merit had definitively won the day. For the nobility as a whole, it had become the only criterion of choice within the order, the commanding and exclusive criterion which ought alone to mark out those most fitted to command. This expressly implied the abandonment, which is insistently demanded, of standards of promotion which rightly or wrongly had been traditionally thought predominant: long lineage, the prestige of a name, royal favour. Some went further and leaped across the Rubicon of privilege. For a minority more liberal, or perhaps freer of the overwhelming weight of prejudice, the overturning of the barriers established by the constitution of the orders was already accomplished. Eschewing all reference to personal status, they demanded, even insisted, that henceforth merit should be the sole criterion of selection.

But what is most interesting is what was happening within the order. Assertions of the equality of all nobles led to a stress on merit in promotions and so to a devaluation of all racial and hereditary considerations. This democratisation of the order, this rejection of hierarchies based on birth which was a constant demand of noble *cahiers*, was nothing less than a denial of hereditary superiority. Membership of the noble order was consequently nothing more than a sign of different status. The son of an ennobled commoner need no longer blush for his genealogy or pale before the daunting display of his old-established neighbour's eight or ten degrees of nobility. Judicial status, privilege, still separated noble from commoner; but nothing now divided noble from noble, a Montmorency from a Le Chapelier. From here, the last step was a short one. Some would take it even before the Estates met.

The claims shaded one into another. The most timid *cahiers*, seemingly a step behind history, confined themselves to demanding the abolition of all venal forms of ennoblement, often including that by office. And insisting, as they did in Poitou, that nobility should only be granted henceforth to 'rare merit' and 'useful talents'. A grant of nobility would be an even more noteworthy boon if 'it should only be given for merit' (La Rochelle, Caen, etc.). Merit, we should note, was protean, it could be used in very varied ways and could be demonstrated in very diverse conditions as the nobility of Châlons emphasised when it recommended the grant of letters for 'services rendered to the state and the country by soldiers, magistrates and citizens distinguished by their merits and their virtues'. But to allow merit as ground for promotion from the third estate was of limited importance. Far more significant was the desire to give merit a special status within the order, and to abolish all distinctions based on family or lineage. This was in fact – and what a revolution ! – to bring down the privilege of blood, heredity itself. Heredity was embodied in a perceptible and bitterly resented way in the reversion of offices which favoured old court families. So this practice was universally denounced, and the reasons were clearly expressed: 'Suppress reversions which make favours hereditary and deprive the king of the means to reward personal merits' (Périgord). Lineage? No ! What distinguishes one noble from another is merit exclusively. 'It should be by merit and not by favour or older pedigree that all military ranks should be given' (Senlis). 'Talent, merit and service should make all noblemen eligible for all ranks and dignities' (Toul). Heredity, that was the enemy for the nobility of 1789 !

Certain cahiers sharpened the logic of the argument to the limit. Since merit was now the only standard, to keep the elite of the third estate out of the fellowship of the talents any longer was quite arbitrary. Although many still held back on this, wavering in weak or contradictory stances, others launched themselves towards the inevitable conclusion. Thus the nobility of the Vendômois demanded that 'all military men without distinction should be able to aspire to the highest military ranks through their virtues and their talents . . ., neither wealth, a great name, nor favour should ever exclude merit from honours, rank and dignities'. For the nobles of Perpignan the terminology itself was out of date, and they put forward the significantly new proposal that the demeaning term *officer of fortune* should be replaced by the more honourable *officer of merit*, and that these commoner soldiers should be eligible for the highest dignities. This was no matter of linguistic refinements; it was a real social revolution.

So by the end of the reign of Louis XVI, the nobility had accepted for itself what some of its members still denied to the third estate: equality of opportunity. Some were aware of this contradiction and resolved it positively. Going beyond the strictly noble debate, they drew the final conclusions from the demythologising of the hereditary idea by establishing competition between the orders. 'Members of the third estate', demanded the cahier of the nobility of Peronne, 'should be admitted to military commissions and ecclesiastical dignities', and these would be granted 'by merit rather than favour or pedigree'. 'Through merit', Sarreguemines explained, 'the third estate should be entitled to the king's bounty by admission to clerical benefices, the judicial bench and military rank'. The leaders of the third estate went no further, and Bergasse called in the same terms for 'the opening of free competition to all orders and merit alone to be considered'.[18] A considerable part of the nobility still fought a rearguard action. But a powerful second wind took the others far ahead. All in all the resistance was less lively than the trend, and the third estate shoulder to shoulder with the liberal nobility was ready to take the step that would tip the scales finally their way. The Constituent Assembly would not have to force the course of history; all it would need to do was sanction a completed revolution.

In 1789 the nobility were no longer the second order of traditional France and no longer wished to remain imprisoned within a rigid and outmoded definition. They were aspiring to become the leading class in the kingdom, the great assemblage of all the talents, the academy of merit. They renounced a part of their most important privileges (the fiscal and judicial ones); this was a decisive reorientation which cut the notion of an order down to honorific proportions. They opened – still timidly, but the line was crossed – their monopoly of power to third estate competition, thereby destroying the medieval justification of the three orders in terms of three functions. At the same time, the socio-economic criteria which gave the order its own material character had been carried away by the evolution of capitalism: next to rents – partly feudal, but mostly taking physiocratic or agrarian capitalistic forms – industrial and commercial profits weighed more and more heavily in noble incomes. But that was not the most important thing. The nobility had discovered the virtues of communication. They had come out of their moral isolation, their aristocratic marginality, and had allowed themselves to be seduced and then contaminated by the culture of the century without any reference to the fundamentals of their order and isolationist values. The eighteenth century had confirmed the change – not sometimes without resistance, as a thought for the next century's outbursts will show – from the culture of an order, apart, inward-looking, based on difference, continuity and historic coherence, to a class culture, based on real and universal social cohesion.

Profoundly altered in its substance, rejuvenated in its blood, stimulated by the intrusion of capitalism, released from isolation by the absorption of the integrating notion of merit, the nobility had become the chosen instrument of a revolution in social elites. The work of the Constituent Assembly, very largely, would be its work.

3

Plutocrats and paupers

The old regime is commonly defined as one in which a hierarchy of orders existed together. So there is a strong temptation to think of the nobility as a homogeneous, structured and unified whole. However, a mere glance at the lack of cultural homogeneity and the bitterness of the antagonisms that seethed within the order leads one to wonder whether, as in the case of the third estate, the term order does not take in – even juridically – circumstances so different as to be irreducible to a single definition. The rights of a lord high justiciar, or those of a great officer of the Crown, should in no case be ranked with the slender and often theoretical privileges of a petty squire. Nor did either side mistake matters: there was no equality between them, and perhaps no sympathy or solidarity either.

It is true that in France there was no popular nobility, and the definition was the same for all. There was nothing like the nobility enjoyed in Poland by every man who had remained free when serfdom was generalised, or like the nobility of the Basque country which was based on the absence of Muslim forebears. However, a petty nobility did exist and they were aware of their individuality and apartness: it would be ludicrous to confuse them with the high nobility which never mingled its blood with theirs. This in fact was a decisive characteristic; different levels of nobility did not mix. It was far easier – and examples are numerous and well known enough for it to be unnecessary to prove it – for the daughter of an ennobled commoner to marry a man of high birth than for a country squire to win the hand of the daughter of a great house. Marriages were made not so much within the order as inside recognised groups within the order. These groups, unacknowledged officially, nevertheless existed and marked off different types of noble.

Even so the second order served as an infrastructure. As a necklace joins up finer and finer and larger and larger pearls from the clasp all the way to the central one which is the supreme adornment, so nobility,

43

by an invisible thread, linked individuals of increasing importance and power all the way up to the dazzling elite of the Court which reflected the king's splendour. Drab or glittering, rich or poor, men of power or outsiders, all nobles, however far they were from each other and from the royal sun, together made up the second order of the realm; and the king, closing the circle that marked off their special quality, continued to attribute to himself the title of first gentleman of France.

To be noble was to be in a position to provide proofs. This meant producing titles justifying membership of the order. Proofs were of different types: authentic legal deeds describing the person in question as noble and confirming that his ancestors had enjoyed noble titles and privileges (divisions among heirs, homages, acknowledgements, fief censuses, marriage contracts, etc.); title deeds (provisions to offices and letters of honour, letters-patent of ennoblement); certificates (of knight-service, membership of the order of the nobility in the Estates-General, exemption from the *taille* tax, etc.). The latter were the least reliable, allowing a fair number of renegades to join the nobility, for they did not constitute positive proofs; but they were employed. Those, and only those, who could produce one or other of these titles formed part of the nobility. The laxity of the authorities did allow usurpers to slip into the second order, but reforms, like those ordered under Colbert, were designed to return impostors to their true rank with heavy fines. However, a final way of providing proofs allowed quite a few to get into the nobility through patient obstinacy: if over several generations a family managed to keep itself exempt from commoner taxes, that made it noble.[1]

Juridical unity should not however make us lose sight of the real differences which put one noble in a different class from another in the noble hierarchy. Could privilege make for unity? Yes and no. Some privileges, the most important among them, were common to all – fiscal privilege for example; others, such as certain judicial privileges, only extended to part of the order and went far beyond the world of nobility. The right of *committimus*[2] was shared by broad categories of the third estate, fiscal privileges extended to non-nobles – commoner office-holders, postmasters, etc. – thus robbing privilege of its link with a specific order. Above all, inequality was the law governing the second order. The kingdom's grandees, particularly dukes, enjoyed privileges which they shared with no other noble. Court privileges – high offices in the royal households, presentation to the king, access to his carriages, hunting with him – that is to say the right to be near the king and receive his grace and favour – were in principle only granted to the oldest nobility, able to produce proofs going back to 1400, which right away excluded most noblemen. The latter were not part of the Court, not from 'this country' (Mme de Pompadour's term); they could not claim to share the royal cake.

These rifts, big with consequences, did not however succeed in blotting out the illusion of noble unity. The least younger son of a country squire, although aware of the distance between himself and a lord of the Court, felt a deep affinity with him. The call for equality among nobles was on the one hand an old cultural inheritance going back to the time when the king himself was no more than the leading baron, and more recently the first knight, peer and heroic model in the Francis I mould, which had left the fiction of the king as first gentleman. And on the other hand it was a modern trend towards egalitarianism linked to the rise of individualism, which tended to deny the virtue of heredity in favour of personal merit. Because of this the unity of the whole nobility rested on opposed principles: one demanded it in the name of tradition, the other in the name of Enlightenment, philosophy and progress.

Nobility was defined as much by what it could not do as by its privileges. Most often the prohibitions were theoretical. This was the case with certain occupations deemed incompatible with the dignity of the order but which in fact many nobles followed without losing rank. Here moral prohibition was stronger than the letter of the law, which was often unclear, but was frequently flouted through need. In a very theoretical sense professions provided another element of unity. The army, the clergy, the judiciary were preferred activities for nobles, and careers there might be more or less totally reserved for them. But many commoners did very well in them, and above all there were not enough positions in them to offer outlets to the entire nobility. Many were left out. Nor was it simply the discrepancy between supply and demand, but rather requirements that many noblemen could not meet: personal wealth, adequate talent and knowledge, were obstacles which eliminated the least qualified. These, for lack of money, credit, distinction or cultivation, found themselves to some extent downgraded. Military careers, that noble profession *par excellence*, were more a source of discrimination between nobles than a source of unity. Rank was set by favour rather than merit, and many ranks could be bought with a sack of money.[3] While upstart stripling colonels enjoyed rapid and brilliant careers, petty nobles without wealth, unknown at Court, unprotected and unsupported, were forced to limit their dreams of glory to a lieutenant's or captain's commission won with great effort after 15, 20, or 25 years of service. The cross of St Louis would be their field-marshal's baton, and the reward for their devotion a pension of a few hundred *livres*. They would never attain the high ranks reserved for Court favourites. And yet they could count themselves lucky to have this modest career. How many like them, unfortunate enough not to have resources beyond the pay which the king stingily allowed them to keep up the relatively costly garrison lifestyle, and too poor to kit themselves out when campaigning began on the promise of a distant and always uncertain repayment of their costs, were forced to give up all hopes of serving. And of course a judicial career was closed to such men for even stronger reasons. To buy an office was costly, one needed to be educated to it, and be a university graduate. Perhaps a quarter of the complement of the nobility had no hope either of a civil or a military career, unless they enlisted in the ranks, or the lower grades of the revenue service, became tax-collectors or lived on their wretched estates and themselves cultivated the few perches surrounding the family house which was often little more than a half-ruined shed. Younger sons who gave up hopes of family life and obtained a half-decent living in the church were the lucky ones.

So unity was purely theoretical, and other factors still to be analysed increased the disparities even further. There was however one common feature which, while not making one noble the equal of another, cut all those who were noble off from those who were not. After all, nobility like everything else was defined by what it was not. Nobles were not commoners. This feeling of apartness, in which the biological theory of genetic superiority was one element, was in the last analysis the firmest cement of unity, if not of solidarity (an idea which was to develop out of revolutionary misfortunes). It bound together a nobility whose picture of its identity was blurred, and although lofty, ill-defined before its slow refinement over the nineteenth century following the adversity which began in 1789. The difference could be measured in snobbish terms, and it manifested itself visibly in the right to add turrets and dovecotes to a house, to carry a sword as the humblest nobleman did even as he pushed his plough, to sit in a separate pew in church, and other distinctions flattering to vanity but which above all were symbols of social distinction. To be noble was to be distinct, and a way of appearing distinct. It was also a way of life, which explains the special moral code recognised by all, a particular feeling of descent, of honour. Honour! Admittedly the middle classes and the people also had their honour; but it was individualistic, and therefore common. For a nobleman honour could not be a personal possession; by himself he was nothing. Only his ancestors gave him existence, consciousness and honour. But lineage itself promoted and reinforced inequality. It was defined by age and distinction. Much less strictly than in Germanic countries, lineage was calculated – because it was of course social arithmetic – by degrees in the male line and not by quarterings.[4] Proofs were not required from women, and in strict noble law there was no such thing as a misalliance. To receive the honours of the Court women only needed their husbands' proofs. On the other hand, women could not pass on nobility, and even in Champagne in the eighteenth century there was no longer any 'ennoblement by the belly'; throughout France only the male anatomy retained this privilege.[5] The number of degrees allowed jurists and genealogists to classify nobility. Four degrees, or about a century, made for nobility of race. If it went back beyond 1500 it was called nobility of old extraction; with no known origin, immemorial nobility. Social relations in this hierarchy were expressed terms whose shades of meaning, from 'man of quality' to simple 'gentleman' via 'person of condition', delicately ran the gamut of distinctions which rendered to each what the conventions allowed him.

In the eighteenth century these rifts took on, at least in law, particular force. An edict of 1781 required four quarterings from all candidates for military commissions, and another of 1787 in principle reserved the highest ranks to nobles of extraction who at least in theory alone enjoyed the honours of the Court. In practice other factors came into play to soften this rigidity. The recent and undistinguished nobility of families like the Chamillarts, the Le Telliers, the Phélipeaux, the Colberts, the Mazarins and the Fouquets outshone the old distinction of Créquys and Montmorencys at Court. The Crozats, descended from a *capitoul* of Toulouse at the beginning of the century, produced an officer of the king's order, a president in a sovereign court, a lieutenant general, and a duchesse de Choiseul. Service and wealth could in fact make up for lack of distinction. Of course, not everybody was descended from Jean-Baptiste Colbert, and the Crozat riches were among the greatest in the kingdom. But the will or caprice of the king allowed many to get round the regulation of 17 April 1760 stipulating proofs required for access to the royal carriages. On the one hand great officers of state, descendants in the male line of knights of the Holy Spirit, and holders of office in the Royal Household were not required to provide proofs. And ministers! The Peyrenc de Moras, Bourgeois de Boynes, Villedeuil and still others had been ennobled in the eighteenth century. Besides, it seems that Louis XV thought absurd a regulation that forced a gentleman to come and 'waste his money at Court and make a fool of himself for lack of the right education, however high his birth', whilst others were deserving of access to him, although of modest origin, on account of their, 'fine conduct'.[6] So Louis XV allowed whoever he wished to be presented to him.

Nevertheless, the difference in treatment between various sorts of nobles remained. About this there are some revealing stories. One is of a nobleman stuck in the rank of lieutenant. While on leave he visited a distant aunt at Avignon and, to pass the time, went up into her attic. There he found old parchments which provided him with irrefutable proofs. He dashed to Versailles, had these deeds verified by the king's genealogist, received in one leap the honours of the Court, rode in the king's carriages and . . . was appointed to a command! Even if the story sounds too good to be true, it is a fair illustration of what we know in other ways.[7] Without being exclusive, genealogical constraints remained strong.

A further factor of discrimination, or at least of diversity, was professional. From the middle ages, and more precisely from feudal law, the nobility had inherited the notion of service. The overlord gave protection; and in exchange the vassal owed him a certain set of obligations. The early modern nobility still acknowledged three of them: service, military aid and counsel, which meant Court offices, active service in the royal army, and the exercise of justice in connection with certain political prerogatives. Service in the Household, whose importance grew in the absolutist Court, became ever more codified, and ritualised as a noble function, from Francis I down to Louis XIV. But not all the nobility served. Neither the army – especially in peacetime – nor the parlements offered more than a quite inadequate number of positions to meet the demands and the ambitions of the whole noble body. Moreover, time spent in the army was often very short. After a campaign, many officers returned home, demobilised by reductions of numbers, or disgusted with the lack of promotion prospects. Nor should we forget or minimise middle-class competition; commoners were not excluded from the army, even after the restrictive edict of 1781. Posts available to the nobility were accordingly reduced. Broadly speaking we could say that hardly more than half of the nobility were serving at any one time. But many more had doubtless served at one time or another in their lives. So a first dividing line was between those who had and had not served. Yet even this was artificial in the sense that the individual counted for less than the family, and there were hardly any without at least one member who was serving or had served. It was just as important to have a brother, uncle or relative with the colours as to be there oneself. It was always an advantageous distinction.

To serve, which was one of the essential defining principles of nobility in the eighteenth century, was everybody's ambition, or almost everybody's. Those who did not serve, with few exceptions did so not by design or desire not to be involved, but because it was impossible or because they had tried and failed: they lacked money or promotion prospects. The right to serve was considered an essential privilege of noble status and partly explains noble hostility, however relative and ambiguous, to commoners in service. To serve the king was at one and the same time a right, a duty and an honour, and a nobleman could not avoid these moral obligations. Only poverty, limits on recruitment and the injustices of the system kept some in inactivity.

What was true of the army was even more true of the magistracy. Offices a noble could occupy were not very numerous and their cost was high. Those within reach of them most often disdained them and those who would have liked them were not within reach. If all noblemen had received a domestic education which had effectively to one degree or another prepared them for the profession of arms – they learned the first elements of arithmetic and geography in the regiments, where they were sometimes placed very young – many knew next to nothing. Their education had been confined to basics taught by village priests, their mothers, or old maiden aunts. In these circumstances they could not dream of becoming advocates and then magistrates. The judicial nobility was mostly recruited from its own ranks or those of the closest middle classes. Others lacked wealth quite as much as education. So that there was a sort of demarcation between a sophisticated nobility, often with recent commoner origins, which took all the civil offices, and a frustrated nobility, locked by circumstances into military careers.

Was, then, the opposition between the nobility of the robe and sword merely a matter of economic and cultural differences? Except at the level of the high nobility, where family specialisation was clearly visible in what amounted to the political class – made up of the old flower of the nobility and ennobled middle classes who shared ministerial and administrative functions, Court offices, provincial governorships and field ranks – it had no other meaning. Many magistrates made their sons soldiers; financiers, so close to the robe nobility and the elite of the Court, took the same course; and cases of very old nobility who never left the robe were not uncommon.

Nevertheless it remained true that the oldest, if not the most famous, stock disdained the judicial robe and only entered the parlement wearing their swords, as peers. The Harcourts, the Choiseuls, the Montmorencys, the Brancas, the Brissacs, the Fronsacs, the d'Aiguillons never wore the judge's cap. The duc de Saint-Simon could find no words too humiliating to savage men of the robe, but they still got many a ministry, bishopric or high command. Yet as a whole the world of the parlements was largely a closed one, with its self-perpetuating dynasties. But sword nobility and robe nobility did not form, and could not form, two closed and hostile worlds. They interpenetrated. It was easy to go from the parlement into the army, from robe to sword. The other way was less common for the simple reason that outside the world of the parlement a young noble did not inherit the ability, knowledge, culture and tradition that were indispensable for a magistrate, and the education he received did not prepare him for such a course. A century later heredity would still weigh heavily in the recruitment of the judiciary, and the Séguiers, to name only one family, would still have a bright future in the nineteenth century. Beyond that, careers were just as difficult. The same proofs were required, and sometimes the magistracy was more lofty about this than the army. They were in fact two parallel worlds, often intermingling but separated by cultural barriers which sometimes bred misunderstanding.

So the unity of the noble world was largely a theoretical concept, an ideological invention spawned by the ideas and the solidarity engendered by misfortunes undergone in the Revolution. Before 1789, nobles were much more conscious of what divided them than of the elements of unity which they could only be vaguely aware of.

Stronger than the theoretical contrasts between robe and sword were three complementary levels of division: economic, cultural, and ideological.

A quantitative study of the wealth levels of the French nobility as a whole is a difficult proposition, but not impossible. One source, fiscal in origin, allows us to get an overall view which can be refined and sharpened by information from various other quarters: the capitation tax, which reveals incomes. Every Frenchman except the heir to the throne and paupers was subject to it. Fortunately for us, the nobility was separately listed. Noble capitation was assessed by the intendant of the generality with the nominal assistance of a nobleman. In the eighteenth century it was established that the nobility paid a capitation of 1/90 of income.[8] In practice, nobles were not hard hit. It was easy for them to pull strings and lobby ministers, intendants and subdelegates. They regularly appealed against their assessments. Thus in 1788 baron de Marguerit had half his capitation remitted by the intendant of Montpellier.[9] Another wrote to the intendant of his generality: 'A sensitive heart will never allow a father of my rank to be subject to a strict twentieth tax like an ordinary father.'[10] In Rouergue 'it had always been the practice to grant nobles reductions in their capitation''[11] Capitation was paid at the place of residence. Rich landlords with estates in several generalities, sometimes far off, and those who lived in Paris or at Court were in the best position to evade it. Proportionally, the richest were those who paid the least. The princes of the blood only paid 188,000 l. in twentieths: they should have paid 2,4000,000 l. ! And the duc d'Orleans flattered himself that he set his own tax rate: 'I work things out with the intendants; I pay more or less what I like.'[12] In these circumstances, what use is the capitation as a gauge of wealth? Despite its drawbacks it is an indispensable document. First it enables us to make comparisons: with it we can establish an order of magnitude for noble riches. It is also an indicator of wealth. Despite all the drawbacks to be borne in mind, it does have a rough value. Leaving aside the occasional very great lord of the Court for whom there is no reliable information, it can be used for all the others. Nobles living in the provinces were subject to a capitation levied at a rate very close to that put forward by Dupont de Nemours: 1/100. Admittedly there were marked inequalities. A favoured few only paid 1/200. For others, less fortunate, it was 1/50. At Aurillac, M. de Miramon paid 300 l. on a taxable income of 31,327 l. M. de Caissac, with an income of 12,653 l. only paid 80 l. as did his neighbour d'Anjorry who only enjoyed an income of 9,099 l. With nearly 4,000 l. Passefonds de Carbonnet was assessed at 25 l. along with Pelamourgue who only had 1,000 l.[13] At Laon, Vairon de Doigny paid 360 l. on an income of 40,000 l. and Rillart d'Epourdon 72 l. for an income of 12,000 l., whereas Viefville de Presle paid 96 on 6,000 l. Levesque de Champeaux, with 18,000 l., only paid 42 l., but de Noue paid 30 l. on an income of 1,000 l.[14] Despite these flaws, it is still a source that can be used, and the assessments at 1/100 of income are broadly correct, even though the highest levels are generally underassessed. The richest were those who had the most influence with administration. But for the poorest the Revenue sometimes proved astonishingly lenient. M. d'Hédoubille with his income of 600 l. only paid 12.4 s., and Villelongue 1 l. on 700 l.

Out of the 34 generalities of the kingdom, the capitations of 13 have been recovered, that is, the rough taxable income of 38 % of nobles or just over 10,000 (mainly heads of families, but also unmarried women and wives enjoying their own property). The estimates are certainly not always reliable: yet we can still say that 100 l. capitation represents an income of 10,000 l. There is no absolute uniformity, for fiscal inequality was the rule within the order. But overall the differences in treatment cancel out . . . It should not be overlooked that we are talking about minimum incomes, above all for the greatest fortunes. To these should often be added annuities, pensions and allowances (in any case taxed at source) which were not taken into account in assessing the capitation. The 13 generalities we do know about were very diverse in extent, population and wealth. They offer an excellent sample for France as a whole, and conclusions about them can fairly safely be drawn for the entire kingdom.

In terms of levels of wealth the nobility can be divided into five groups:

1. Those paying over 500 l. in capitation and enjoying at least 50,000 l. in annual income. They were a tiny fraction: 24 in 13 generalities, or around 60 for the whole kingdom. We can add to this group perhaps 100 families living at Court, established at Versailles or in Paris, with incomes often over 50,000, 100,000, 200,000 and more. Or, in all, 160 or perhaps 200 families, who effortlessly dominated the whole nobility of the kingdom by their luxury and standard of living. To them can be added around 50 high-flying financiers (a few farmers-general, treasurers and receivers-general of taxes) who were nobles too and whose wealth equalled or surpassed that of the greatest lords. This means at most 250 families, the majority living in Paris, making up the plutocratic kernel of the second order.

2. The second group comprised rather more than 3,500 families over the whole country. With incomes between 10,000 l. and 50,000 l., they represented the rich provincial nobility, including the members of the sovereign courts. In Paris their situation would have seemed quite modest, but their incomes guaranteed them a lavish lifestyle in the provinces. They made up 13 % of the nobility.

3. Between 4,000 and 10,000 l. came easy circumstances: 7,000 families, or a quarter of the nobility, had reached this level. They could lead a comfortable, even a spacious life, entertain several times a month, keep a number of servants and five or six horses.

4. Modest circumstances appeared below 4,000 l. The 11,000 or so families (or 41% of the total) with between 1,000 and 4,000 l could still live decently provided they avoided extravagance, confined themselves to one or two maidservants, were frugal, and shunned lavish expenditure on clothing and other outward show. Those who lived in the country could still allow themselves a few lordly airs and graces.

5. Below 1,000 l. we reach the level where noble life became straitened. Over 5,000 families lived at this barely decent level. Half of these had less than 500 l.; some had 100, or even 50 l. Then it was no longer a matter of proudly-borne misery, but real poverty. Some paid no tax at all and remained on the noble capitation lists prior to being finally struck off and rejoining the people. Already they were indistinguishable from peasants; some were even worse off and lived a wretched life of dependence on alms (see p. 63).

The plutocratic kernel. At its heart were the courtiers: those who lived at Court, held office and lodged there, and only lived for and through it. They were only therefore a tiny fraction of those who came near the king, those who had been 'presented' – most of whom only came to Court occasionally, if indeed they ever set foot there on more than the one occasion when they were presented, never reappearing after that. Courtiers brought together numerous sources of wealth: income from their estates, Court offices, pensions, part of the income of the clergy, high commands, provincial governorships, ministries and diplomatic postings.

Their landed revenues almost always reached a very high level. Without mentioning princes (whose incomes were measured in millions), courtiers often had more than 100,000 l. Among dukes the Saulx-Tavanes (whose rank was recent, it is true)[15] were small stuff with 90,000 l.: the duc de Mortemart had 500,000, Grammont 300,000, Chevreuse 400,000. Other lords, though less well-endowed, enjoyed incomes of similar size in which the royal bounty often made up a considerable part. Eighty-six lords, all great dignitaries at Court or in the army, ministers and diplomats, shared almost 3 millions. All were in receipt of more than 20,000 l. The highest pension, 80,000 l. went to Jules-François de Polignac, brigadier and hereditary First

Equerry to the queen. The wife of maréchal de Mirepoix, lady in waiting to the queen, got 78,000 l., maréchal de Broglie 70,000, the ex-Comptroller-General Bertin 69,000, lieutenant general the prince d'Anhalt 40,000, maréchal de Contades 33,000, François de Croismare, commandant of the petty stables, and lieutenant general the duc du Châtelet 28,000 l. each; the wife of maréchal du Muy was paid 42,000 l., and the First Equerry to the king, he duc de Coigny, 50,000 l. Other courtiers enjoyed a share of the 483 pensions of the second rank, between 8,000 and 20,000 l., representing a total sum of 5,608,268 l.[16] This same privileged class also drew the wages, emoluments and indemnities attached to offices in the Royal Household, and the households of the queen and the princes. The office of grand master of France, held by Louis-Joseph de Bourbon, brought in 139,800 l. a year. The four offices of First Gentleman of the Bedchamber (held by the ducs de Villequier, Fleury, Richelieu and Duras) were worth 12,760 l. to each holder, but the First Gentleman on duty received 27,850 l.[17] The Grand Master of the Wardrobe (La Rochefoucauld-Liancourt) had 31,590 l., the High Steward (Charles Alexandre de Péruse d'Escars) drew 134,968 l.; the governess to the Dauphine (Mme de Tourzel, *née* Croy d'Havré) 43,200 l., and the lady in waiting to Mme Elizabeth (Diane de Polignac) received 21,058, as did those to Mme Adelaïde (Françoise de Narbonne) and Mme Victoire (comtesse de Chastellux). The 13 lady companions to Mme Elizabeth, Mme Adelaïde's 10 and Mme Victoire's 9 got 4,000 l. each.[18] In practice the fringe benefits of these offices made them lavish sinecures: according to Mme Campan the resale of candles alone made the lady companions small fortunes, and 'pushed up the price of their offices to more than 50,000 l. each'.[19]

All these offices besides represented important capital investments whose return was often shared between several courtiers. For on taking up an office one had to pay off one's predecessor and his or her heirs. 800,000 l. for the office of Lord Chamberlain, 600,000 for that of Master of the Horse, 400,000 for captaincies of the guards, 500,000 for First Gentleman of the Bedchamber, 475,000 for Grand Master of the Wardrobe.[20] In all, the offices of the Royal Household alone represented a capital value of 33,761,000 l. Louis Bruno, comte de Boisgelin, who drew a pension of 8,000 l. from the Treasury, and 5,400 l. worth of emoluments for his office of Governor of Saint-Mihiel, was appointed in 1760 to an office of Master of the Wardrobe vacant after the resignation of the comte de Maillebois. He was obliged to give the latter a credit note (*billet de retenue*) of 480,000 l.; he had borrowed 400,000 l. from different lords who thus had claims on the income from the office: 20,000 l. from the marquis de Saint-Chamans, 30,000 l. from Turgot, 50,000 l. from the comtesse of Gisors, 20,000 l. from the comte de Montboissier, 90,000 l. from the comtesse de Gisors, 90,000 l. from the comte de Thiard, 8,750 from the duc de Valentinois, etc.[21] The great favourites of the king and the queen obtained gifts that even astonished the Court. The princesse de Lamballe had 150,000 l. in fees, 200,000 as Mistress of the Household, a 600,000 l. grant from the taxes of Lorraine, and the prince de Carignan her brother had 54,000 l. The Polignacs had received 2,500,000 l. in cash and piled up 437,900 l. in pensions and salaries. François-Camille, marquis de Polignac, First Equerry to the comte d'Artois, drew a salary of 24,000 l. but the perquisites of his office took its yield to 20,000 l.; as a knight of the Royal Orders he drew 6,000 l. and, from 1772, enjoyed a pension of 12,000 l. From 1784 to 1788, he received 1,230,000 l. in cash from the extraordinary fund for the royal stud farms, of which he was the director, and in 1789 he was pensioned off with 12,000 a year. Jules-Francois, his nephew, created a hereditary duke by a warrant of 20 September 1780, was hereditary First Equerry to the queen, and had a salary of 80,000 l. and a pension of the same amount entailed upon his wife, granted on 8 September 1783; in 1784, he received in addition a gift of 100,000 l., and 800,000 l. on 8 January 1786 in compensation for estate duty of one eighth owed on the fief of Saint-Paulin, plus a bearer-bond of 1,200,000 for the price of the domain of Fenestrange. The duchesse de Polignac (*née* Polastron), governess to the royal children, was paid 7,200 l., the same for services rendered to the Dauphin, plus 14,400 l. under various heads. Louis-Héraclius Victor, vicomte de Polignac, former ambassador to Switzerland, received an ambassadorial pension of 20,000 l., and 3,500 as Governor of Puy-en-Velay. His daughter the comtesse de Polignac, lady-in-waiting to Mme Elizabeth, was not forgotten either: a salary of 7,200 l., 4,500 under various heads, and a pension of 1,900 l. Auguste-Apollinaire, son of the comte de Polignac, a Cluniac monk, had a 9,000 l. pension from the Abbey of Saint-Germain des Prés from 1777. Camille Louis drew 25,000 l. as bishop of Meaux and 30,000 l. as Abbot of Saint-Epure. The Polignac wife of the duc de Guiche enjoyed a pension of 6,000 l. granted as a jointure. The Saintonge branch of the family was no less favoured: Guillaume Alexandre comte de Polignac and his daughter Mme d'Aspect in 1784 received gifts totalling 400,000 l. and in addition drew annuities of the order of 60,000 l.[22] And this was just the Polignacs!

Bishoprics and rich abbacies made up part of the bounty which the king dispensed to his intimates and their families. The bishop of Strasbourg (Rohan), the archbishops of Sens (Luynes), Toulouse (Brienne), Narbonne (Dillon) or Rouen (La Rochefoucauld) drew enormous incomes of several hundreds of thousands of *livres* from abbeys. For laymen the Treasury was a bottomless source of salaries and sinecures. They took the 37 great and 7 small provincial governorships (not to mention governorships of particular places which brought in less but still a fair amount) and the 13 governorships of the Royal Households. The governorship of Paris was worth nearly 70,000 l., Berry 35,000 l., Languedec 160,000, Guyenne 100,000, Burgundy 150,000, leaving aside the perquisites they carried.[23] The major foreign embassies, like that at Madrid, brought in up to 200,000 l. while a secondary station like Parma was worth 60,000 a year to the comte de Flavigny, before expenses and fringe benefits were included.[24] Ministries carried important remuneration. In 1789 the Chancellor got 120,000 l., the Keeper of the Seals 135,000 l. Secretary of State Villedeuil had a salary of 226,000 l. Admittedly ministers had enormous expenses and had to keep simultaneous open house both in Paris and at Versailles.

Great landowners in France, and so recipients of fat rent-rolls, royal favourites who could pile up favours in the form of pensions, gifts, grants and salaries, courtiers also sometimes drew considerable income from diverse sources such as the general farm of the taxes where there were sometimes important 'rake-offs',[25] industrial and commercial ventures,[26] and bribes paid for their favour and influence with the king and his ministers. Another gold mine was colonial wealth. I am here talking about great adventurers like Lally-Tollendal, who took risks and paid for their enrichment at personal cost and sometimes with their lives. I mean plantation owners who most often had never crossed the sea to set foot in their overseas estates. The great planters of Saint-Domingue, often poor younger sons who had gone to the West Indies in the hope of making their fortunes, blended in with the greatest aristocrats of the mother-country. By marrying their daughters the Rouvrays, the Galiffets, the Menous, the Vergennes, the Reynauds, the Paroys, the Osmonds and the Maillés became in turn rich planters. The marquis de Gouy d'Arcy inherited plantations valued at more than three millions from his wife, a creole called Bayeux. The duc de

Brancas, the Noailles, the Lameths, the Rohans and the Castellanes alos
enriched themselves by West Indian marriages. The great landowners
of Saint-Domingue were people like the duc de Choiseul-Praslin, the
comte de Magallon, the marquis de Perrigny, Montholon, the marquis
de Rostaing, the comtesse de Choiseul-Meuse, the comtesse de Poulpry,
the comte de Vaudreuil, princesse de Berghes, the marquis du Luc and
some sixty other lords, who all owned sugar cane plantations and coffee
estates.[27]

For these favourites of fortune money came in from all quarters.
But they spent it prodigiously, lavishly, frenetically. For every one
who saved part of his annual income, two had trouble balancing their
budgets, and a fourth went into debt. The comte de Choiseul-Gouffier
was of the first sort. His gross income of 247,795 l. 15 s. 4 d. was made
up of 150,943 l. 8 s. 4 d. from his estates (17,950 l. 4 s. 2 d. in seig-
norial dues) 26,759 l. 14 s. from annuities, and 50,092 l. 14 s. from
houses, shops and properties in Paris and at Pierrefitte.[28] After deduction
of outgoings (twentieth and capitation taxes, gamekeepers' wages,
stewards' fees, agents' salaries, debts, pensions and gratuities) amounting
to 80,056 l. 6 s.; a net income of 167,739 l. 9 s. 4 d. was left. The up-
keep and wages of 17 servants (2 secretaries, a butler, 2 valets, 5
footmen, 3 chambermaids, a nanny, a coachman, a postilion and a
groom), maintenance of ten horses and carriages, boxes at the *comédie
française* and the Opera, and an allowance of 10,000 l. for the comte
and comtesse de Choiseul (their pocket money) came to a sum of
36,223 l. 9 s. 3 d. That therefore left 131,516 l. 0 s. 1 d. After deduction
of household expenses, food, clothing, and luxuries the balance was
still in credit.[29] Prince de Robecq, though maintaining a dazzling lifestyle, was a good manager of his money since he was able to save
something each year. His income of 214,233 l. 8 s. 7 d. came from his
landed estates in Flanders and from his principality of Robecq, his
lordships in Touraine, Burgundy, Brie and Holland, from money lent
out, and from his wife's dowry which yielded 15,000 l. His offices
and military commissions brought him in a third of his income:

Order of the Holy Spirit – 3,000 l.
Governorship of the town of Aire – 12,048 l. 6 s. 4 d.
Military governorship of the provinces of Flanders, Hainault, and
  Cambrésis – 46,433 l. 4 s.
Emoluments from the Estates of Lille (payable to their commissioner)
  – 7,500 l.

His food bill amounted to over 58,000 l. and his wardrobe cost him 3,450 l. a year. Wages and salaries to the officers and servants of his household came to 17,406 l. In 1787 mourning for the wife of maréchal de Luxembourg brought extraordinary expenditure of 3,868 l. Theatre tickets, newspaper subscriptions, concert subscriptions and sums spent on books and prints came to 2,054 l. The prince's Paris town house cost 12,627 l. and the one he had in Lille 1,438 l. In all, he spent 208,674 l. 16 s. 9 d. and so saved little in 1787. But he had the advantage of a credit balance of 64,542 l. 12 s. 10 d. from the previous year.[30]

Sometimes landed income barely now accounted for the lion's share. The revenues of a great officer of the crown like prince de Lambesc, peer of France and Grand Equerry, were divided almost equally between landed income (176,620 l.) and Court salaries, grants, and gifts (137,300 l.).[31] The comte de Béthisy enjoyed an income of only 67,799 l., but despite debts of 241,000 l. he lived high and kept 13 servants costing over 10,000 l. a year.[32] The duc de Coigny was one of the ones who did not keep careful accounts. He spent beyond his income irrespective of the loud protests of his business manager. In 1774, with revenues of 80,000 l., he spent 138,800: 36,000 l. on food, 15,000 on personal expenses, and the same on horses. But he knew he could count on unanticipated income. In 1790 his revenues had risen to 110,000 l. His inheritance remained intact thanks to exceptional windfalls.[33]

Incomes like these could only promote prodigality, in an age that could certainly be called carefree and in which fashion and snobbery could easily bring to ruin intrepid millionaires like Prince de Guéménée or great financiers like Saint-James. There are plenty of good stories of colourful extravagance. Mme de Guéménée owed her shoemakers a trifling 60,000 l., and Mme de Montmorin's tailor was owed 180,000 l.! The young duc de Lauzun had debts of two millions and Mme de Matignon gave her hairdresser 24,000 l. to style her hair in a different way every day of the year. Even if some of this is exaggerated, there are still some striking examples of prodigality. But after all most of them could afford their eccentricities. Some lords certainly ruined themselves without a thought. The marquis de la Bourdonnaye filed for bankruptcy in 1789 as had the marquis de Gouffier earlier with debts of more than a million.[34] There were also many who sold off a part of their patrimony in order to obtain ready cash. Yet many still had intact fortunes in 1789 and even the Revolution was not to take them away. Great lords of the Court resurfaced in force under the

Consulate and the Empire: they were still the greatest landowners in the country. In most cases these were inherited lands, although some, like d'Aguesseau, did not miss the chance to round off their estates by buying national lands. Under the Empire the duc de Choiseul, a great landowner in the Côte d'Or, was the richest landlord in the Sarthe and the Seine-et-Marne; Montmorency was the biggest taxpayer in the Eure, the duc de Mailly came at the head of the great landowners of the Haute-Loire and among the greatest of the Saône-et-Loire; the duc de Luynes was among the handful of the three richest in the Somme, Seine-et-Oise and the Sarthe. The duc de Luxembourg came at the top in Seine-Inférieure; the marquis de Serrant and the duc de Cossé-Brissac were the two richest landowners in Maine-et-Loire, followed by the marquis de Maillé who had acquired a tenth of his property during the Revolution. The duc de Noailles was the greatest landowner in Eure-et-Loire and a Montmorency was at the top in Eure where the grandson of Chancellor Maupeou had been the main buyer of national lands.[35] In the Sarthe, around 50 noble families rounded out their estates by acquiring national lands, led by Choiseul-Praslin who took over 13 farms, 2 mills and 5 lakes making 570 hectares in the district of Sillé.[36] Almost the entire Court nobility turned up on the lists of the greatest landowners under the Empire, along with the odd farmer-general, a group which had not done so well under the Revolution, but which was happily represented by Legendre de Luçay, the leading landowner in the Indre. He had acquired national lands for 150,000 l. and, as Prefect of the Indre, a new career.[37]

The rich provincial nobility. The 60 or so provincial families enjoying incomes over 50,000 l., although not courtiers, or only occasionally, still belonged to the plutocratic kernel of Versailles. If they had chosen to live in the provinces for much of the year, it was by choice, out of spite, or by order of the king. But in his exile at Chanteloup Choiseul built up a court around himself, more Parisian than the *salons* of the capital and quite as fashionable as the mansions of ministers in office. Everything bound these exiles, eccentrics, or originals to the Court nobility.

Much more numerous were the true rich provincial nobility, with at least 3,500 families, making up 13 % of noble numbers and in fact rather more since the magistrates of the parlements, taxed on separate capitation rolls, were numerous in this category. Here incomes ran from 10,000 to 50,000 l. Some of them lived months of the year in Paris, many went to Court from time to time, and among them prestige spending, although sporadic, was still considerable. Many were senior officers and generals, or members of the sovereign courts. They had some access to Court bounty. All pensions of the second class (8,000–20,000 l.) which were not cornered by courtiers went to them, as did a great part of pensions in the third class (2,400–8,000 l.; in all 9 millions worth of them!).[38] Those who lived in or near Paris appeared regularly at Court: to remind the king of their existence, badger ministers, and keep up links with the favourites. Ferdinand de Schömberg and his wife, Dumouriez' sister, drew 3,900 l. from investments and 5,000 l. from the domain of Corbeville (near Orsay), or only 8,900 l. in all. But Schömberg's salary (18,000 l.) when he was promoted to staff rank in 1777 tripled their resources. While her husband was in Corsica (until 1783), Mme de Schömberg lived at Corbeville; but she made trips to Versailles where she had taken lodgings for 800 l. and to Paris where she had bought a house for 70,000 l.[39] The Schömbergs belonged to those 'presented' families, which, by assiduity at Court, managed to progress well – Schömberg retired in 1783 with the rank of Lt General – if slowly, but their resources put them in no position to live permanently under the king's eye and win a wider share of his bounty. Others only came to Court even more exceptionally, either because their birth kept them away, or because it did not interest them. The comte d'Antraigues was not allowed to enter the king's carriages since his credentials were inadequate and the king refused to make an exception. Between 1780 and 1790 his income came to 38,068 l. a year. In the Gard, the baron d'Assas had over twenty thousand a year.[40] In Provence the marquis de Sade had 17,500 l., in Montpellier the marquis de Saint-Maurice had 16,098 l. in 1786 not counting interest from loans to the province of Languedoc;[41] the comte de Vinezac and the marquise de Londre had similar incomes, as did the 12 presidents and several counsellors at the court of aids.[42] The rich provincial nobility was very unevenly spread throughout the kingdom. They were numerous in rich generalities and in the seats of sovereign courts. In Guyenne they made up only 12% of nobles as a whole, or rather less than the national average: this resulted from the imbalance between the rich elections of Périgueux and Bordeaux, and the poor elections of Condom and Sarlat. In Caen, they made up over 18%, as at Grenoble. In very poor generalities like Châlons or La Rochelle they did not exist (0.9 and 0.5%).

These sumptuous squires, rich provincials, lived lavishly. When Arthur Young visited the château at Nangis (Seine-et-Marne) belonging to M. de Guerchy, he noted that to live there with 6 manservants, 5 maids, 8 horses, a garden, and 'a regular table' without ever going to Paris, 25,000 l. a year was needed.[43] That was the normal lifestyle of the rich provincial nobility living far from the capital. Those near to a large town kept a house there, and only spent the fine months in the country. In Toulouse, Aix, Amiens or Rennes mingling in town society had its duties. Much was spent on entertaining and clothes. Visits must be made to the intendant, the governor and the presidents of the court, invitations must be returned, guests and travellers of note put up. The theatre, balls and receptions lent well-heeled provincial society a metropolitan air. The provincial nobility was quite happy to play the game of imitating Paris and following fashion. When the governor passed through he would bring news from Court, and his wife would have the latest hair-style; everyone had to copy them, and in this rush to imitate the whole nobility lived as it were in Paris at one remove. Yet without quite losing its own character. To live in the provinces, on a large income, was an existence, a way of life that had been deliberately chosen. There was a certain scorn – not untinged with envy – for the attractions of Paris and for the courtier who had lost some of his openness when he abandoned his local roots. Doubtless it was here that the most representative nobility was to be found, a model for the second order; and it was often from among them that its representatives were chosen in 1789.

The disinherited of the second order. The category whose incomes ran from 4,000 to 10,000 l. made up the upper crust of the squirearchy, and about a quarter of the nobility. They spent little time in town where living was dear, but led a comfortable life on their estates. They would have a country house, simple but well appointed, a manservant, two maids, three horses and a gig.[44] They would entertain their friends in the district, and might have rooms in town; their womenfolk had riding habits and the men would keep hounds.

Below 4,000 a year lifestyles became modest. Many nobles were in this position: 41%. However, in the country with this sort of income one could still hold up one's head. Provided one was frugal, avoided entertaining, and reduced luxury and display to the minimum. This made for decent gentry without needs, who divided their time between estate management and hunting. Many of them had seen military service. A captain's pension was a valuable asset, and a mark of distinction.

Beyond the 1,000 l. threshold poverty was quickly reached. There were plenty of noblemen below this danger-level: more than 5,000. Half of them had less than 500 l., and some had 100 l. or indeed 50 l. or 25 l. The best-off were peasants, and those most in need were beggars. Although this was not a sociologically defined poverty,[45] it was genuine, and in some cases really wretched. In their demands of 1789 the nobility were much preoccupied with the state of these unfortunates (optimistically setting the threshold of poverty at 1,200 l.): in fact it was only below 300 l. that conditions of life became dramatic. Above that figure, a noble who poached, sold his trout (or his neighbour's) rabbits and gamebirds, could manage to get by.[46] But there was worse. Some were so poor as to pay no capitation. There were lots in poor provinces, like Champagne. Many of them fell into the most abject ranks of the people. In Villefranche de Beaujolais it took an exceptional event, the calling of the Estates-General, to uncover their hidden miseries: a family of old stock had fallen into such extreme poverty as to move the nobility; they decided to make immediate provision for 'the necessity of this family within their order' until they could recommend it to the good offices of the Orléans family.[47] According to the English traveller Smollett, some noblemen around Boulogne made do with only one meal a day; they never issued invitations and, having no money to breed dogs or buy guns, had nothing to entertain themselves except cards.[48] Obviously such people did not have *châteaux*. What they called the big house was merely a humble farmstead, sometimes a hovel, with at most a large general room whose sole luxury would be a chimney-breast emblazoned with the family arms.[49] In Normandy they shared the hard life of the peasantry. At Saint-Flour, they took leases of land.[50] In the Angoumois, Antoine de Romainville led his own oxen and ploughed his own land. When he died he left his son a few straw-bottomed chairs and many debts.[51] Too poor to serve in the army, they had no military prospects; too ill-educated for the church, they could not even hope for a slender benefice. They were more than lucky if they managed, like Antoine de Romainville, to find a wife among the middling sort of the countryside who brought in a dowry of a few hundreds. Jean-Etienne de Chabannes, a small-time nobleman descended from a King's Secretary, left 5,060 l. in all among his six children. After paying his brothers and sisters their legal entitlements, the eldest had nothing left to live on.[52] Some took service under better-off nobles. Châteaubriand tells us that La Morandière became agent for the *château* of Combourg. Others become gamekeepers or clerks in the revenue service; in Soissons there

Numbers assessed for the capitation on separate noble lists

Generality	Over 500 L.	200– 499	100– 199	40–99	30–39	20–29	10–19	5–9	Under 5 or unable to pay	Total
Amiens	1	22	77	192	49	55	96	51	60	603
Grenoble	4	52	99	174	96	61	88	29	10	613
Limoges[1]	1	38	99	206	80	72	78	23	14	611
Bordeaux	3	56	186	581	197	286	324	156	76	1865
Caen	10	88	187	412	175	163	260	151	138	1584
Chalons	0	0	5	97	60	87	193	116	101	659
Moulins	1	9	45	168	51	71	88	44	55	532
Rouen	2	35	120	286	126	156	213	83	60	1081
Bourges	0	20	49	115	49	61	71	43	71	479
Orléans	0	8	38	171	64	132	175	73	52	713
La Rochelle	0	0	2	25	8	26	78	70	144	353
Besançon	1	13	28	140	45	106	138	82	58	611
Montauban	1	27	67	149	83	79	91	82	142	721
Total	24	368	1002	2716	1083	1315	1893	1003	981	10425

[1] For information: 114.

were noble tax-collectors. Many, as Châteaubriand says, went back to the plough, took up a trade, and rejoined the people. They could even be found in the poor-house.[53] In Poitou in 1789 seven noblemen appeared: dressed like peasants, without swords, they explained that their daughters were looking after their sheep. The assembly subscribed to pay for their accommodation. In 1781 the marquis de Vaudreuil recommended to Ségur a captain descended from one of the oldest families in Normandy; his 80 year-old father lived in penury with his wife – their income was 220 l.[54] The Tribunal of the Marshals of France uncovered even more affecting wretchedness. Duvallier de la Combe, imprisoned for debt, was unable to help his wife who was living without servants in a garret with her two children.[55] Many petty nobles were in prison for debts of 40 or 50 l. which they could not manage to pay off. History is quite willing to stress the misery of the third estate. The ostentation of the greater nobility and the comfort of the rich provincial nobility have too readily obscured the deplorable state of part of the second order; without financial resources, unemployable for lack of money and education, marooned by prejudice in inability to redeploy themselves, they were doomed to extinction. How many went this way in each generation is impossible to say exactly. But the constant renewal of the order shows by implication that it happened.

There was more than one nobility; the range of wealth proves it. Money divided what law united. Education emphasised these gaps, and deepened the rift. Separated by lifestyle, nobles were even further divided on cultural grounds. Within the privileged order equality of opportunity was not a reality, even if the dream of it led to the creation of military schools reserved in principle for the most needy.

4

The fundamental divide: culture

At the end of the old regime divisions according to length of nobility or its degree of dignity, which so obsessed Saint-Simon, were in fact negligible beyond a certain social level. At Court, newcomers mingled with members of the oldest houses and the highest in dignity. The quarrels over precedence which had taken up so much of the time of dukes and peers at the Court of Louis XIV were now only exceptional occurrences. The hierarchy had stopped measuring itself by exclusive reference to divine right.

With the defeat of *polysynodie*[1] the peerage was forced to give up any ambition to control the state, dukes confined themselves to positions of honour, and the secretaries of state, those 'petty persons' or 'nonentities' (that is, holders of recent nobility), recovered the power they had wielded at the height of Louis XIV's reign. The Court had lost its heavenly image: the Father in the full splendour of his glory, the princes of the blood-royal standing as the model of the Son, sharing His being, and the peers, the elect, mediators and grateful intermediaries between the Father and his people. This Court, at once medieval and modern, presented a Biblical picture of a King-Father who was lofty and an object of fear, but who was humanised and as it were democratised by the glory he had granted to the peers of his realm, chosen by his will alone from among the most trusty and deserving of his people. In this celestial Court at which divine right assigned each to his place, the peers alone escaped the inevitable. They alone could be called upon to share in the glory of the highest blood, even though not of it themselves. Through them the whole nobility and the people were shown to share in the monarch's glory, and through them too they were shown to share in and theoretically to limit royal power.

But over the century matters had changed. Just as the king's image had become less terrible, the peers lost their splendour, and their privileges came into question first from the whole nobility in the name of the equality of nobles, then from the entire Nation in the name of popular sovereignty. Thus the Nation was born through the slow erosion of the peerage's privileges. Divine right then became blunted by a new sort of legitimacy, and rights of blood retreated before those derived from ability and success. The Court ceased to be the altar where a divine liturgy was celebrated, and became somewhere for the conflicts of profane society, and the revolutions that could happen in its midst.

Somewhere, above all, where hierarchies crumbled and social mingling occurred.

At the same time as divine right began to weaken, privilege based on blood began to ebb. It was no longer henceforth enough to be 'well born': social success demanded other qualities. The evolution of marriage patterns reflected changes in custom which called the whole social theology into question. Misalliances, which were still the exception in the seventeenth century, became so common that they no longer attracted notice, and ceased to seem unusual. Remember the indignation of Saint-Simon when he heard about the marriage of the duc de Piney's daughter:

It cannot be borne to see him marrying his daughter to René Potier, she being a maiden of such high birth who, should her only brother die without issue, might bring all the goods of that great house, and the dignity of a duke and peer, which is yet rarer, to her husband . . . René Potier was son and elder brother to secretaries of state . . . his father was a counsellor in the Parlement and his grandfather the mayor of Paris, and his father in turn an official of the mint, and beyond him nothing to be seen. It should not therefore be thought that misalliances are so new in France, but in truth they were not then common . . .[2]

In the eighteenth century, marriages between equals in dignity shared the stage with fashionable marriages of convenience based on wealth, education and power. Marriages were made with families of secretaries of state whatever their 'lowness' or the 'grime' of their origins, and those of rich financiers were also in demand. Villars, Choiseuls, Sullys, Aumonts, Béthunes and many others made alliances with Crozats, Peyrencs, Bonniers, Pâris. The flower of the nobility and those cleansed by 'soap for scum' could live very well together and nobody was outraged to see it.

The wealth which blurred one sort of rank produced another within the second order by its cumulative effects. For it was this, in fact, which very generally dictated levels of education and culture. In a century that was well ordered, learned and brilliant, the pretensions of armigerous rustics were much reviled. To be able to produce one's proofs, and to belong to the best nobility, was not enough to be fully accepted and make a mark at Court. But a highly educated first-generation nobleman was at once at home there. A nobleman from a great family but lacking in fashionable ways and cultural standards was only allowed in through pity and did not remain. M. de Pentavic, from good Breton noble stock and a sea-captain, wished to be presented to the king. He had 'all the elegant ways of Brest or Toulon, and all the graces of a courtier of Neptune, which were none too strikingly close to those of Versailles'. He had a long wait before 'breaking bread with his master', but came away delighted, like so many others whose 'whimsical faces amused' courtiers who went to no lengths to be pleasant to provincials.[3] Much was made in fact of a fine bearing, worldly wisdom, good speech and cultivation. Learning and the arts elevated a man, made him sought-after and valued. In this refined and knowledgeable society, what hope of success had someone who could not get the superior education of the elite? This is a fundamental point that should be strongly emphasised: not all nobles by any means set out with the same chances of success, the same indispensable requirements for a career either in high society or in professional life. The theoretical equality of the second order did not imply equality of opportunity. In practice cultural divisions were even more marked than those based on birth, and they were dictated largely by wealth. It was because they had received, in family, convent or the world at large, the same education as better born girls, that the daughters of rich middle-class businessmen and of all recently ennobled financiers, were able to marry dukes and not be out of place in the society this took them into; a society forever closed to daughters of nobility that was old but poor and neglectful of their education.

Wealth, education and culture brought together the two extremes of noble society, dignitaries and newcomers. Sénac de Meilhan, like so many others, was aware of this confusion of ranks. One man's stepping-stone was another man's barrier. A rift was opening up between those who enjoyed all these advantages and those without them, between those to whom all doors were open and those who, from the outset, were condemned to outer darkness.

All nobles did not receive the same education. A large income was essential for access to the education dispensed by good schools, academies, good teachers and fashionable convents. The free entry granted to poor pupils at the military school was a numerically negligible palliative.

Segregation by education cut off an elite from the body of the second order, and imposed a rank on those left behind.

For daughters, education was as serious a business as wealth, a guarantee against spinsterhood in a society where the only alternative to marriage was the nunnery. It was not enough to have a dowry. It was also essential to have acquired worldly ways – that is, a whole cultural underpinning which allowed them to appear to advantage in polite society and not lack any of the knowledge valued in such circles. It required a long, private apprenticeship, open only to those privileged by birth or wealth. Whichever model was chosen – and in the eighteenth century there were at least two – a girl's education, if she was intended for a great marriage and a brilliant position, was very costly. If the new fashion of education at home, introduced in the second half of the century, was followed, the best teachers had to be employed who would guide their young pupil into the world. This was the sort of education received by the future marquise de Lafayette and Mlle Randon de Malboissière, from a financial family. They were found the most esteemed geography, mathematics and dancing masters.[4] They had boxes at the opera and the theatre. Nothing was spared to achieve the most all-round education. Sometimes neglect or unorthodoxy lent a touch of eccentricity. It then added all the more charm. Lucy Dillon, niece of the archbishop of Narbonne and future marquise de La Tour du Pin was given at the age of seven a tutor called Combes, an organist from Béziers. Engaged to teach her the clavichord, M. Combes, who was well-educated, gave her a taste for reading; at twelve she was impressively well-read. Full of curiosity, she learned everything that came her way, from cooking to the chemistry she learned from an apothecary. The gardener's wife, who was English, taught her to read that language. But she hardly knew her catechism because there was no chaplain in the archbishop's house![5] She was destined for a brilliant future at Court, where she astonished the courtiers by introducing the handshake favoured by the British: 'Avez-vous shake-and avec Mme de Gouvernet?' Mlle Ducrest, later famous under the name of Mme de Genlis, learned to read from the schoolmaster of her village. She was accepted at seven as a canoness in the noble chapter of Alix, and there had a governess called Mlle de Mars who was a musician, but besides music also taught her history, the catechism and the first steps in reading.[6]

If the preference was not to break with tradition, there were plenty of convents: 43 in Paris alone. The most famous took girls destined for Court. Pentemont Abbey, or l'abbaye aux Bois took in Mlles de Choiseul, Montmorency, Châtillon, Bourbonne, Lauraguais, Caumont, Saint-Chamans, Lévis, Chabrillant, Aumont, Talleyrand, Damas. There were famous provincial convents too, and that of Fontevrault brought up Louis XV's daughters. But this superior education was exclusive. The whole nobility could not take advantage of it. Fees were 600 l. a year at Pentemont, 500 at l'abbaye aux Bois, 400 at the Conception in the rue Saint-Honoré, 400 at La Madeleine du Traisnel, not including lessons, clothing and various extras. Many noble families did not even have incomes on this scale. Admittedly there was no lack of convents for poor girls. But fashionable education was neglected there, and the nuns did the teaching themselves. They produced girls who were modest and became good mothers, nuns, or retiring spinsters destined to live in the shade of an elder brother. The luckiest ones got into Saint-Cyr. But they had to prove 140 years of nobility. They received a solid education, but not a fashionable one; it was provincial life for them.[7]

If education was important for girls, it was even more so for boys. It largely dictated their careers. Three great routes were open to young noblemen: college, military or page school, or the academies. For rich children the preference was for college, after spending the earliest years in the hands of a tutor or schoolmaster. Thus the marquis Ducrest was sent at five to the famous establishment at Le Roule run by M. Bertaut, who had devised a method of teaching reading in six weeks. Clermont and Harcourt colleges took in the greatest aristocracy and the upper magistracy along with sons of the middle class. Clermont educated princes of the blood, foreign princes, and dukes. There one found names like d'Albret, La Rochefoucauld, Beaufort, Croy, Rochechouart, Noailles, Montmorency, etc. They sat alongside members of great legal families: Lamoignon, Ormesson, Feydeau, Le Pelletier de Saint-Fargeau, Nicolaï, Turgot.[8] Harcourt drew on the same groups: Talleyrand, Choiseul-Gouffier, Gouy d'Arcy, Hérault de Séchelles.[9] These were the really aristocratic colleges, which educated young courtiers-to-be, those who would get commands, administrative and ministerial posts, and sit in academies. The high fees (900 l. at the Oratorian college at Juilly) excluded lesser noblemen. At the end of the old regime the latter, who traditionally took up the profession of arms, could go to the twelve military schools which prepared pupils for the one in Paris.[10] Although impoverished gentry could get into these schools, the number of places was limited, especially as they were soon attracting the best young people. For non-scholars fees were 700 l. at Sorrèze. Among its pupils were Castellanes, Turennes, La Tour du Pins and Mauleón-Narbonnes.[11] So there were not many places for young people with little money. Between 1776 and 1787 the military schools took in a total of 1,592 nobles destined for the Paris military school, for prestigious cadet regiments, or for the navy. But 438 out of this number failed in their studies or left college prematurely.[12] It was true that many of the pupils at military school did not have scholarships. Comtesse de Chatelaillon paid 1,500 l. to the treasurer-general of the royal military school for 9 months' fees for her son from 18 April 1784 to 18 January 1785.[13] On leaving college the luckiest ones went on to the page school. This was reserved for those of the highest birth: proofs must be provided going back beyond 1550 with no known ennoblement. Fees of 400 l. a year also had to be paid. Supervised by the Grand Preceptor, the First Preceptor, and others their education for all that was quite lax; riding and worldly polish replaced learning. But serving the persons of the king and the princes gave them a head start for promising careers.[14]

Take the education of a young accomplished nobleman from one of the oldest families in Normandy, Alexandre de Tilly. His father's marriage to a girl 'of distinguished rank though of quite a modern family', but very rich, had restored his family's hopes. He was educated at first by his father, who then put him in the hands of a tutor. At nine he went to La Flèche where Antoine-Louis Séguier, future advocate-general at the Grand Council, the marquis de Turbilly, later a famous agricultural writer, and comte de Rohan-Polduc were also educated. The studious tastes shown by young Tilly allowed him to take full advantage of teaching which he was nevertheless critical of: 'La Flèche was now merely a shadow of that seminary of doctrine, learning and literature that the Jesuits had made it, but an excellent college for all that'. At thirteen, his contacts got him appointed page in the Queen's Household, which he left with the rank of sub-lieutenant.[15] Or take Lauzun, who was brought up 'at the knee of the king's mistresses'. He was given the most fashionable teachers, but also a tutor whose sole merit was a great talent for calligraphy and reading aloud, a talent he passed on to his pupil. This neglected education made him however indispensable to Mme de Pompadour, who kept him close so that he could read to her. 'It was still the same for me as for all children of my age and condition', he said. 'I went out in the prettiest clothes, but died of hunger at home.'[16] But at twelve he joined a guards regiment whose command the king promised him when it fell vacant. 'I knew at that age that I was destined for immense wealth and the finest position in the kingdom, without needing to take the trouble to behave myself.'[17]

For those who did not go to college or who left early, those who did not get into military schools or the page schools, there was still a glittering but expensive solution: an academy, where entry was at 15. In the eighteenth century there were those of Dugard, Jouan and Villemotte at Paris, and one at Angers in the provinces. There were less well-known ones at Versailles and at Bordeaux. Attending an academy was very costly. Among pupils at Angers were the comte de Bourmont, the chevalier de Maillé, the son of the Breton president Cornulier, the marquis de Walsh-Serrant, an Amelot de Chaillou, a La Rochefoucauld, and the prince de Salm. In Paris the fees came to 4,000 l. per year for a boarder. Among subjects taught were riding, fencing, military exercises and dancing.[18] The son of the baron de Schömberg, a general officer, attended an academy at Versailles where, in addition to riding and dancing, he was shown how to draw up plans, and taught languages, history and mathematics.[19] Others avoided academies and used their contacts to get into the army very young. Young François-Marie d'Arod was only 15 when he was posted to a company. He wept when his captain reprimanded him! Military life was a continuation of school: young nobles learned on the job, standing guard and joining exercises, but going as well to teachers of languages, mathematics and geography.

So much then for the luckiest and the best-off. But even all of these had no guarantee of a distinguished career. They would become lieutenants; but as soon as it came to promotion to captain there was great competition. The career of the chevalier de Franchelein, who eventually became a senior officer, shows the difficulty of becoming a captain very well. Joining the first company of musketeers in 1741, he had to chase promotion for years with frenetic tenacity, getting Barjac, Fleury's valet, on his side and paying him 200 louis, paying court to Breteuil and then d'Argenson, winning the favour of the prince de Dombes and, on top of all that, paying out 15,000 l. to buy his company! Even modest success was therefore extremely difficult for those whom a decent fortune gave access to a careful and specialised education, but easy for those who had gained entry to the great colleges, distinguished academies and the royal Court.

But what about the poor? For poor noblemen were numerous. Military schools only offered a limited number of scholarship places. The education of the rest was by comparison very inadequate. Without money a college or academy education was closed to them. They often received, with other village children, an elementary education from the parish priest, who might if they were lucky given them a little Latin, or they would be taught the rudiments at home by their mother or a maiden aunt. At best, a poor tutor might give them a passable education. Even in relatively comfortable families the education of children could be lax. Châteaubriand, an unloved younger brother, was left to his own devices: 'I grew up, without studying, in the family circle.' He spent his time among the louts of Saint-Malo, and at night with his sister's help he repaired the clothes he had torn during the day. Young Antoine de Romainville, whose family was almost penniless, was sent to board at Angoulême with a solicitor at the presidial court who asked 150 l. per year for food and lodgings. He was sent to a schoolmaster who took 12 s. a month: at sixteen, the young man was still learning to write! It is true that he became an officer, but his career was to be a limited one.[20] This was the normal fate of much of the petty nobility who got no proper education, no instruction, no cultivation, and were destined to be good junior officers but with no hope of distinguished careers. The chevalier d'Oisilly, who could write, became secretary to a high court judge.[21] Some enlisted in the ranks, like Claude Harenc, grandson of a gentleman of the Royal Household.[22] Laurent de Belchamp, who was educated at a Jesuit seminary in Pont-à-Mousson where the fathers failed to satisfy his aspirations, offered his services to an advocate after giving up the church[23] Threadbare squirearchy was far removed from the mighty who gathered around the sun. Truly, it was a different world.

And so, everything made for two distinct nobilities: wealth, education, culture. Education was an unbridgeable divide which ran right down the middle of the second order. Most had an education that was mediocre, haphazard, and uncertain. At best it produced junior officers, and often uncouth squires who were kept out of the army through incapacity or lack of means, passing an unrewarding life alongside peasants hardly more rustic than themselves. At worst, it produced beggars and social drop-outs.

For the elite, on the other hand, education was organised to cultivate the mind and impart solid knowledge, to lead to great things in the army, administration, the law or the financial world, and to give the worldly accomplishments and polished outlook and manners that opened the door to the Court and success. To have access to this education was not strictly a privilege of birth, but rather one of wealth. The rich middle classes also took advantage of it, and in the best schools the sons of tax-farmers rubbed shoulders with the sons of dukes and princes of the blood. In this way a cultural elite emerged in which old stock mingled with new blood and magistrates-to-be with officers-to-be.[24] Accordingly the Enlightenment was not the product of a typically middle-class culture: the nobility played more than a preponderant part in it. After all, if Voltaire, Diderot and Rousseau were commoners, Montesquieu, Mably, Jaucourt, Condorcet, Condillac and Vauvenargues were nobles.

In fact, much of the intelligentsia were recruited from the nobility. Or rather it was more as if the nobility, in this age of doubt and self-questioning, was seeking to redefine itself as an intelligentsia in order to escape the threat of extinction and refound its existence with a new identity. But not all the nobility by a long way was involved in this cultural process. Daniel Roche, who has studied the provincial academies, has estimated that out of 6,000 academicians over the eighteenth century, 37%, or 2,200, were nobles. Even so that represents somewhat less than 10% of adult male nobles. Was there culture beyond these circles? There were not many subcriptions to important books or journals. Out of 400 subscribers to Expilly's *Geographical historical and political Dictionary of France* just over 200 were nobles:[25] 400 nobles took the *Mercure de France*, or 47% of subscribers. Similar proportions of nobles are found among the correspondents of Voltaire (50%), Diderot (25%) and Rousseau (30%). In comparison with the national average, therefore, the nobility made up a cultural elite. But within the order only a minority took an active part in the advancement of knowledge (about 30 nobles wrote for the *Encyclopédie*) or even read enough to share high cultural levels. Here again wealth and privilege went together. Only the richest possessed libraries. All the magistrates who were members of the Academy of Toulouse were worth over 250,000 l. At Rouen counsellors at the parlement had over 6,000 l. a year and all the noble members of the Academy of Montauban paid over 200 l. in capitation. In the Parisian academies the proportion of nobles was of the order of 35%, and 50 of the members of the French Academy had received the honours of the Court. So the part played by the nobility in the elaboration and spread of ideas – and in particular reforming ideas – was considerable. Almost all the great literary or political *salons* where ideas were first launched or books foreshadowed were held in aristocratic houses. Nobles' names were frequent among the very great figures of Enlightenment thought. How could we overlook, in addition to those mentioned already, Buffon, Helvétius, Lavoisier, and the great economists, physiocrats like Quesnay (an ennobled doctor), Turgot and Mirabeau, or mercantilists like Véron de Forbonnais?

The nobility as a whole do not seem to have been great readers. A great proportion of them had no books, and it is at least probable that reading rooms and public libraries were patronised more by those who had books of their own rather than those who had none. Jean Meyer has established that in Brittany the important book collections were those belonging to magistrates or courtiers, and that half at least of the nobility did not even own the beginnings of one.[26] The reading nobility, with libraries worthy of the name, was confined to members of the parlements, the rich provincial nobility and to courtiers. With obvious differences between categories as to their character: a provincial magistrate did not read the same things as a courtier. The members of the parlement of Rennes were solidly grounded in literature, law and history, but seemingly read little of the philosophy of the eighteenth century.[27] At Montpellier the reading habits of the magistrates of the court of aids were much the same. Courtiers, on the other hand, were greedy for novelty, both victims and initiators of metropolitan culture. If we analyse the library of a magistrate, and then of a courtier, we get some idea of this contrast. One will be classical in character, the other up to date, more fashionable and also doubtless more rebellious. Of course it would not be correct to push this too far. Many members of the parlements, above all in Paris but also in the provinces, had grown up in touch with the ideas of the Enlightenment. People like Dionis du Séjour and Hérault de Séchelles, or Guyton de Morveau at Dijon had not distanced themselves from the trends of their age. Many magistrates, however, clothed in the austere gravity of their calling, seemed to be unaware of, or to shun, bold and perhaps subversive new ideas, and it showed in their cultural life. This remained the case in the second half of the century when they lost some of their gravity even and perhaps too some of their awareness of their professional status.[28]

At the end of the century, a provincial magistrate like president Claris of the court of aids of Montpellier had inherited a tradition rather than created a personal culture. His library, obviously inherited since the number of books published after 1750 was tiny, comprised 1,576 volumes making up 632 titles, whose subject spread was as follows:

Theology	37.34%
History	12.02%
Literature	26.58%
Law	5.85%
Records and memoirs	3.63%
Geography	1.42%
Science	2.05%
Education	1.25%
Various	9.81%[29]

The importance of theology, and strongly Jansenist theology too (all the works of Nicole, Pascal, Arnauld, the Montpellier catechism and about 30 volumes on the Bull *Unigenitus*) was doubtless his father's work rather than his own, but pious reading made up a striking proportion of his purchases: Pradale's *Lent* (1779), the Abbé Paule's *Sermons* (1778), Father Neuville's *Sermons* (1776), *Christian Instruction* (1780), *The Spiritual Director* (1761) *Christian Reflexions* (1768), and so on. Law was represented by only 37 titles, not a lot for a magistrate's library. If history was better represented with 76 titles modern ones were rare, the most recent purchases being *Considerations on the Greatness of the Romans* (Montesquieu); Abbé Gelly's *History of France* (1775), and Lauris' *History of France before Clovis* (1786). Literary works pointed to a culture revolving around the classics, whether ancient or seventeenth century French. The eighteenth century only featured incidentally with Mme de Genlis, a few works by Voltaire, but two editions of the *Spirit of the Laws* and the Neuchâtel edition of the *Encyclopédie*. This then was a library reflecting a solid classical education and a profoundly religious outlook, but a lofty indifference to – if not indeed a fierce rejection of – the thought of the age and its poisonous boldness. Was this outlook a dated and worn-out one or was it a militant rearguard action?

Here now is a courtier's library. What a contrast! Louis Bruno de Boisgelin de Cucé was Master of the King's Wardrobe and colonel of the Lorraine Guards Regiment. His wife was Catherine de Boufflers. He had rooms at Versailles, and it was there that he kept the books he acquired. Nothing here was inherited. It was all his own choice. Its makeup was very characteristic:

Literary works	61 % (268 titles)
History	20 %
Politics	6.37 %
Science and Geography	6 %[30]

Law, military matters, etc. made up negligible percentages.

Physical and chemical sciences were Boisgelin's favourites: the works of Lavoisier stood beside Nollet's lessons in experimental physics and Ozanam's mechanics. Medicine, in its modern and slightly fashionable aspect, features with Gatti's reflexions on inoculation.

The literary fare of this courtier, who could read English, consisted of the great authors of the eighteenth century. The whole of eighteenth-century English literature was there: about 50 plays, and Dryden, Shaftesbury, Addison, Pope, Swift and of course Locke. All the great works of the French eighteenth century with the (accidental?) exception of Rousseau were there in this very 'Parisian' collection: the whole of Voltaire (over 40 volumes), the philosophic works of Diderot, *Of Man* and *Happiness*, by Helvétius, Buffon, Montesquieu, the works of La Mettrie, of d'Holbach. Economists, with Dupont's *Physiocracy* and various works on the grain trade, stood beside history, much of it philosophic in character: Raynal and Mably were prominent, without however totally crowding out traditional history, where England, Russia, the Empire and America were better covered than France.

This collection was inventoried in 1787, which was just too early to take in all the political pamphlets which came before the calling of the Estates-General. But, alongside classics on the English constitution, Boisgelin had collected numerous books and pamphlets on public finance and taxation and political broadsides. Finally there were several anti-religious books (*Treatise on the Three Impostors, Of Priestly Imposture, or Collection of Pieces on the Clergy, The Philosophic Soldier, or Difficulties put to Father Malebranche by an Officer, The Cordeliers' Koran* . . .) but no works of theology or piety. Boisgelin was certainly no bigot.

All this is a long way, then, from president Claris' library. Boisgelin was a courtier, a great devourer of novelties, a man of the Court but also of the *salons*. In other words he was, by calling, up with the very latest in intellectual and metropolitan life. His was a fashionable culture, not always unserious, and steeped in the new outlook; Boisgelin was a creature of the Enlightenment, Claris rather a man of the *grand siècle*. This contrast was to an extent one between courtier and magistrate, but even more between Paris and the provinces. To be sure, many provincial nobles had not stood apart from the trends of the age, as they showed by flocking in droves to become freemasons. But insofar as it hardly went beyond the rich nobility, the new culture remained profoundly Parisian. Many a provincial nobleman stood revealed as steeped in the spirit of the Enlightenment, and a petty noble from the Vivarais, such as d'Antraigues, might show himself in 1788 to be as progressive as Sieyès: but he was a man of the Paris *salons*. Insofar as culture ran up against economic limitations, a great part of the provincial nobility could only have come across the new spirit at second or third hand. The cultural unity of the elites was an established fact at the highest level; the cream of the middle classes read the same things as the richest nobility. But within the second order there remained marked differences, between both types and levels of culture. And yet Robert Darnton's analysis of the distribution of philosophic works in the provinces suggests that the Enlightenment reached the petty nobility at least superficially.[31] The reforms they called for in their *cahiers* of 1789 reinforce this impression. Freemasonry may have played a not unimportant role in this process. Although it only appealed to a minority of the nobility, it was still a wider group than that of the culturally aware. At least 3,000 nobles were members of masonic lodges. Among them many were courtiers, financiers and magistrates. But numerous military lodges led to the initiation of the petty nobility who were officers and made up the largest contingent at 46%.[32]

Only a minority of the nobility, perhaps 10%, was in touch with the higher cultural levels; their interests were more modern and progressive in character among courtiers, with all sorts of gradations and striking exceptions. The bulk of the nobility stood outside the cultural world, whereas the elite of the order made up an important proportion of the creators and consumers of the Enlightenment. The latter, however, in the form of a sub-culture, had a fairly wide influence among the ranks of the nobility, above all among soldiers; ideas circulated in masonic lodges and in garrisons. Country squires had no such chance to taste these crumbs. The comte de Tilly, when forced to stay with an uncle in the provinces who spent the whole day in looking after his estates, buildings and domestic affairs, was astonished at how little this countryman who was falling asleep by ten had to talk about. With his aunt, all conversation was on pious topics. Her nephew's first talk of love brought threats of being sent to his confessor! The library?

Nothing. A few mystical works, a few novels, 3 volumes of Corneille, a large work on gardening and a French cookery book was all there was. Luckily (Tilly added) there was also Pascal's *Provincial Letters* and – amazingly! – an edition of Buffon too.[33] The movement of thought held little appeal for these provincial gentry of slender means, entirely taken up in the management of their estates.

Balzac painted a striking portrait of the baron du Guénic, a wild Breton who came through the Revolution and the Empire without the new age modifying in any way his character and his behaviour. Although a literary portrait, it could easily describe many an old regime nobleman:

His appearance, though somewhat heavy, had like all the Breton faces gathered around him a wild quality, a blunt calm recalling the impassiveness of the Hurons, a touch of stupidity . . . Thinking occurred seldom to him . . . He had beliefs and sentiments which were so to speak innate, and which saved him from reflection. Institutions and his religion did his thinking for him. We must confess that the baron du Guénic was completely unlettered, but unlettered as a peasant is: he could read, write, and count up to a point; he knew about the military arts and heraldry; but, beyond his prayer book, he had scarcely read three books in his life.[34]

Balzac clearly understood that elementary education, which was often the only sort that the penniless petty nobility had, did not rule out a 'culture' made up of respect for institutions, religion, and sincere faith too, which brought such squires close to their peasants. They were limited but upright characters, strong in their beliefs and their loyalties. And for such naïve souls but stout hearts, rooted in what they knew, the Revolution could only be an outrage. For those of their peers moved by the breath of the Enlightenment, though not totally won over to the point of wavering in their deepest convictions, a little revolutionary boldness was enough to bring the old character out from behind the superficial sheen.

And so, as soon as the Estates-General met, the nobility was to split in two. So far from making up a united bloc, they took two divergent courses. Loyal to their upbringing, those who had grown up and lived sheltered from the contaminations of the age showed from the outset their hostility to innovation. The others welcomed the boldest reforms with enthusiasm and often proposed them, although some would back-track for reasons hard to explain – the conversion of d'Antraigues is the most spectacular case – unless perhaps they were upset by the impact of new ideas on characters brought up to accept and live comfortably within the tested and reassuring traditional scheme of things.

Fundamentally the nobility had always been cut in two. But it took '89, the pressure of events, and the necessity of making choices, to bring the contradiction fully to light, and make some fall back upon a blank refusal to accept what had been done; while others, headlong, proclaimed their faith in the new values that had slowly matured over the century, and tried by peaceful means to impose a new society born from long discussion that had begun with the dawning of the crisis of the nobility and had slowly been extended to the whole Nation. If one part of the nobility remained locked into an old-fashioned cultural outlook, living on through largely discarded ideas, and rejected the integration that was now necessary, a whole different segment rejected cultural apartness and joined in and often took the lead in the national initiative. As splits opened up within the nobility, a part of it would cement an alliance with the Nation in order to build a new France in which the reconciled orders would recover their dignity in a society more just, free to make its own way, and liberated from the arbitrariness of a power henceforth to be checked, rationalised and humanised. I repeat: the nobility was not all one. Wealth, culture, outlook had created rifts which long remained unnoticed. The need to take sides, at a moment of decisive choices, brought the contradictions out. It serves no purpose to try to place the nobility as a whole on one side or another on the basis of a few individual examples. Nobles joined both sides with the same enthusiasm, and in both cases stayed loyal to the choice they had made. Although nobles often initiated some of the boldest moves, they also by their very nature checked initiatives. This dualism was to weaken the nobility, but also open it to suspicion. It was unable to offer a united front to detractors determined to destroy it. But was it not in this a reflection of the whole Nation itself, divided in its aims, divided by an ideological gulf that nothing would ever succeed in bridging?

There is still one point on which, without claiming to throw much light, it is nevertheless possible to reach some confident conclusions. Throughout the centuries noble society had always thrown up its deviants. In the sixteenth and seventeenth centuries, above all in times of trouble and insecurity such as the wars of religion or the Fronde, delinquency in its most brutal forms, whether piracy, brigandage, or murder, was a very widespread phenomenon among the nobility. Sometimes it was linked with uncertain economic circumstances, but also there was a pathological deviancy, a falsification of the noble code of values, and at that time it assumed alarming dimensions. There is the well-known case of captain Guilleric who terrorised the western provinces. The plays on words 'gent-kill-men' or 'gent-steal-men'[35] reveal more than a popular taste for puns. During the Fronde, and at the beginning of the reign of Louis XIV, above all in Auvergne, a badly-policed region, the *Grands Jours d'Auvergne* have immortalised noble brigandage on a considerable scale. Tyrannical petty squires pillaged and terrorised their peasants. The lords of la Motte–Cannillac and Massiat d'Espinchal were the most grimly celebrated. However, the government's stern measures, the effective action of the intendants and the progress made in administration and policing stamped out this spontaneous brigandage. In any case, it was in troubled periods above all that morality lapsed, even in the upper classes. The eighteenth century was spared such upheavals and offered no favourable occasion for collective delinquency to reappear within the noble order.

However, in more individual and different forms noble delinquency did not disappear. First there was violence. Challenging religion and morality, scorn for vulgar prejudices and sexual violence were frequent. Crimes of dissipation replaced marauding expeditions in which whole regions were held to ransom while nobles played war games or hunted. Above all robbery, confidence-trickery and blackmail seem to have been favoured on certain fringes of the nobility.

Cruel and thoughtless tyrannising itself had not entirely disappeared. The little-known case of Pleumartin is perhaps a unique one, and in any case a throwback to former times. The age did not lend itself to these sorts of exploits on the border between rebelliousness and a pathological condition.

Victor Ysoré, marquis de Pleumartin, lived in mid-century in his castle on the borders of Berry and Poitou. He was son-in-law to the marquis de Bonnac and a nephew of the duc de Biron. He liked rather cruel games. If monks came to his door in search of hospitality and a bite to eat, he would lock them up without food. One of his favourite sports was to dangle peasants from the top of a tower and threaten to let them drop. All this seems not to have brought the law down on him, and after all it was nothing terrible. But one day he took it into his head to murder someone, and was rash enough to choose an official victim. He overcame and shut up ushers who had come to seize him, and killed some policemen. He was arrested and condemned to death, but died in prison before execution.[36] The right to carry arms and the country habit of going to the tavern on fair days to get drunk increased the risks of the trouble; homicide was quite widespread, and even when the courts passed severe sentences, those convicted often obtained reprieves. Duelling was frequent but always pardoned, as numerous letters of pardon show, but neither that nor fighting between officers were enough to quench the violent inclinations of many nobles, as is shown by many condemnations for murder.[37]

Such dissolute violence shows that in the midst of a well ordered society there were still people unable to conform, who needed an outlet for their primitive impulses. No doubt the clemency which the government too often showed in distributing letters of pardon gave them the idea that they could get away with it, and encouraged behaviour that was no longer acceptable.

Less dramatic violence seems to have been above all the province of the penurious petty nobility, often on the brink of wretchedness, whose behaviour was attributable as much to their lamentable conditions of existence as to the ill-controlled brutality of unpolished individuals.

Young nobles, guards, officers and others often joined in violent pranks whose favourite victims were priests or lawyers' clerks. The Tribunal of the Marshals of France dealt with this mischief when it sometimes went wrong; it stemmed from youthful high spirits and the certainty of impunity. Some behaved freely but loosely too. The comte du Lac ingratiated himself with a 'worldly lady' – a prostitute in fact – whose attention he had caught 'through the picture of his circumstances and his misfortunes'. He made up to her and she generously came to his assistance. In short, she kept him, he cleaned her out, and eventually she threw him out. Our happy warrior did not admit defeat. He came back with some high-spirited friends, sacked the house, and only agreed to go when the neighbours complained. He took with him the contents of her desk![38]

Robbery and swindles seem to have run deeply into the lives of certain unbalanced and unscrupulous characters who hoped to get away with it thanks to all-too-easily-made contacts with the great through which they hoped to make their fortunes. The criminal outrages of the marquis de Ganges' circle, and those of Mme de Valois de Saint-Rémy, comtesse de La Motte, the central figure in the diamond necklace affair, are too well-known to be mentioned again. But if these were indeed isolated characters, they remained common enough to think themselves above any law, and to have lost all sense of self-respect. In 1774 Julie de Fauris, wife of a president in the parlement of Aix, was interned under a *lettre de cachet* for forging promissory notes in the name of maréchal de Richelieu. Jacques-Luc de Pillotte de la Barollière, later to become a revolutionary general, forged discount bank notes in 1787. The chevalier du Petit-Thouars was convicted in 1783 of fraudulently obtaining goods and papers. It is astonishing the number of noblemen who were condemned to the galleys or to loss of rights in the years just before the Revolution for false pretences, passing forged notes or swindles. Among them we find the names of the baron de Fages-Chaulnes, the chevalier de Saintré, Le Roy de la Poterie and baroness de Norbreck.[39]

The low doings of these abandoned nobles were sometimes colourful: for example there were fraudulent marriages. In 1789 Jean de Bette d'Etienville, a military surgeon, Joseph-Guillaume, baron de Fages-Chaulnes, Life Guard to the king's brother and François Duhamel, comte de Précourt, put together a promising scheme. They went to a goldsmith called Jean Locques with the story that there was to be a great marriage between rich heiress and de Fages. The tradesman handed over a load of jewellery and refused to talk about price. Précourt, who seems to have been duped by his friends, was acquitted. The others were merely sentenced to return the goods and were bound over 'on pain of exemplary punishment'.[40]

We should of course remember that to rob a prostitute or swindle a tradesman could seem like a smart trick in certain dissipated circles. The nobility as a whole condemned such dishonourable deeds. Life in the capital, the money needs of certain ill-endowed nobles, or the luxurious lifestyle demanded in Paris and at Court, made some weak-willed gentlemen forget themselves. But the moral decay of certain noble circles brought strong reactions.

Flouting established morality was condemned far more severely than swindles, towards which a certain indulgence was shown. The marquis de Sade is the most striking example of deviants rejected by their order, as indeed by society as a whole. All those who contravened sexual morality were punished by *lettres de cachet* and condemnations. In 1771 Antoine Nicolas d'Acary was sentenced to be beheaded for indecent assault with violence upon a girl he had no intention of marrying whom he had raped and then tortured.[41] Sexual perversions were especially severely punished. The comte de Solages, nephew of the founder of the Carmaux mines, was shut in the Bastille in 1784 for 'atrocious crimes for which life imprisonment was not too harsh'. Was it homosexuality or sexual violence? Debauchery, often flagrant, was common among certain young nobles. The comte de Besons, grandson of a marshal of France, a brutal, unscrupulous master blackmailer, was the crony of a wastrel who was to become notorious during the troubles of the revolution – the marquis de Saint-Huruge. The latter was – and how many others were there of the same stamp? – a small-scale version of de Sade or the marquis d'Antonelle, rakes but men of the Enlightenment, both of them sharing the same sexual deviations, but who judged their own times in a critical spirit formed by the philosophy of the age. Both of them, deep down, espoused the Revolution. Sade became secretary of the Pikes Section, Antonelle was a member of the Revolutionary Tribunal and collaborated with Babeuf.[42] Sade vehemently rejected a society that had used him cruelly, a judicial system that had condemned him, and a religion he spurned. He wrote what the philosophes did not say or dare to say. Justice? 'Any poor woman without connections or protection will get a very summary trial in a country where virtue is believed to be incompatible with misery, and where misfortune is conclusive proof against anyone accused.' God? 'An absurd phantom.' Christ? 'A rogue.' Priests? 'Knaves draped in lies.'[43]

So there did exist a whole range of nobles, on the fringe of respectability but numerous, of whom the 'divine Marquis' was only the most brilliant example, in whom contempt for existing institutions and morality, sexual confusion, revolt, contempt for God and religion were all mixed up, foreshadowing in some degree the overthrow of a whole society and the values on which it was built. Sade was more than a raddled philosopher: he was the cancer within a society which no longer believed in its own legitimacy.

5

The nobility and capitalism

The Revolution is often interpreted broadly as the victory of progressive forces over the dead weight of the past. The latter was made up of political conservatism, a retrograde force standing in the way of economic expansion, the rise of the productive classes and the freeing of capital and enterprise from juridical and social constraints linked to a 'feudal' structure of society, production and exchange. This interpretation sets up a dichotomy both suggestive and yet unreal between the opposed nobility and bourgeoisie, a 'feudal' economy and a 'bourgeois' one.

This analysis is particularly persuasive in that it has the appearance of logic on its side and fits in with intellectual patterns that have come down from the Hegelian-Marxist dialectic. To challenge it is therefore to call in question a doctrine that is not the monopoly of one school or party, but which has affected and dominated the whole of modern historical thinking. The result is well known. It gives the French Revolution its meaning and its legitimation. The bourgeoisie, embodying all the productive forces of the future but held back by the constraints of monarchical tradition and blocked by the resistance of a socio-economic system with a vested interest in the maintenance of pre-capitalist structures, was called by an irresistible logic to destroy the type of society whose existence was tied to the maintenance of forms of production passed down from the feudal system. It formed the major obstacle to the rise of early modern capitalism, which in order to flourish was only waiting for the establishment of a bourgeois society in place of the retrograde society which perpetuated beyond their time outdated and retarding forms of production. To overthrow the monarchical order was to release initiative hitherto sterilised or held back, to go in one leap from an archaic feudalism to a modern type of capitalist economy. Marxist historians have refined this picture to the point of caricature, happy to run the risk of having to explain

84

the Revolution's failure to keep a promise of success always just around the corner.

And nobody would surely deny the strength of the obstacles of all sorts put in the way by the very forms of monarchical society and the weight of privilege – which we should not forget often favoured the bourgeoisie, as commercial and industrial monopolies for example show. But there was also a fiscal policy whose inadequacies, together with the system's financial anarchy, made it necessary above all in the last quarter of the century to draw dangerously on the kingdom's capital reserves by an unparalleled level of borrowing.

Beyond these basic points, we still need to assess how far economic transformation had been made impossible, and how far the aristocratic structure of society prevented new departures. In other words, was the nobility, as one of the main beneficiaries of the kingdom's net income, doomed to sterility, and was the arrival of the bourgeoisie the necessary precondition for the unleashing of modern productive forces? What we shall find is that those who are usually blandly held responsible for all the problems – doubtless through not investigating their links with government – were no less concerned than the bourgeoisie to be rid of restraints and checks on economic expansion. This was because they were themselves a rising class, even a revolutionary one.

As they thought of themselves in the eighteenth century, nobles were far from a class of lightweights, flippantly and jadedly waiting in polite resignation and suicidal indifference for the end of a rule that they knew was at hand. On the contrary, they were a dynamic class, confident in the future and well aware of the opportunities offered by the decline of a faltering, unrespected monarchy, the stimulus of burgeoning political thought, and technological changes whose rapid progress they followed with interest. The nobility was a reformist elite, if not indeed a revolutionary one, and in the second half of the eighteenth century it was preparing to press for changes that would break open the constricting straitjacket in which it accused the monarchy of trying to keep the system forever locked.

As I have already suggested, the mistake lies in presenting the monarchy and its nobility as a single entity linked together by interest and ideology, and thereby giving the country a legal definition opposed to the rest of the Nation. For if the nobility did identify with the king, and not the whole of the monarchical system, it was the result of a confusion which made the king the first gentleman of the realm and not the head of a monarchical bureaucracy with which the nobility as a whole felt nothing in common. Nobles took the justifiable view that they constituted a progressive force in the kingdom. And they proved it in the Spring of 1789, when in their *cahiers* they proposed radical reforms identifying themselves more with the Nation than with the king and deliberately renouncing some of their most substantial real privileges. But, it will be asked, why in these circumstances did they stubbornly oppose so many of the reforms sought and pursued by the reforming ministers of Louis XV and Louis XVI? The stock answer is that they were systematically hostile to all questioning of the advantages they had gained, and any change likely to affect the existing state of things. An analysis of the *cahiers* undermines this hypothesis and enables us to explain, as I shall shortly do, this apparent last minute change of attitudes. In fact the nobility could not allow ministerial despotism, that constantly-denounced bugbear, yet further to subject the Nation as personified by themselves to its arbitrary power, when they thought of themselves as the last redoubt of liberties against the omnipotence of government departments and their ministers. On the contrary, from the moment that the announcement of the meeting of the Estates-General gave the Nation back some basic guarantees, the nobility no longer hesitated to give up what henceforth was no longer a defence against arbitrary power, but an obstacle to the Nation's freedom to subject all its citizens to a common law. So long as reforms were imposed from above by ministers, for nobles to accept them was less to lose material advantages than to give up the last remnants which kept up the tradition of, and desire for, freedom among a minority at least. Seen from this viewpoint, the resistance of the privileged – while certainly including an element of low calculation on the part of some – takes on the character of a struggle against despotism.

Among the economic elites the nobility, which in political terms represented one of the lines of resistance to kingly absolutism, stood in the first rank of the most dynamic minorities, and in terms of innovation and modernisation nobles were among the leading activists. What makes this all the easier to demonstrate is that the upholders of the 'feudal' interpretation have up to now been happy to assert it with no backing: it was enough to bring in the dialectical machinery in which a necessarily progressive bourgeoisie took over from a no less necessarily reactionary nobility after eliminating it. Neither of these pictures is convincing. In the economic sphere as elsewhere, nobles showed themselves often more advanced than more cautious, less innovatory bourgeois; the middle classes showed less flair and more conventionality than a nobility that was sure of itself and often more aware than the bourgeoisie that it was a force for regeneration, boldness, and looking forward.

Their economic behaviour was often exactly the same. Over a whole range of activities and enterprises nobles, either alone or in association with members of the greater business bourgeoisie, showed their dynamism, their taste for invention and innovation, and their ability as economic leaders: by which I mean their ability to direct capital originating in land or government stock into productive activities, to choose investments according to their productiveness and their modernity, and in fact, during the last decade of the old order, to transmute the forms of production into an industrial revolution by starting great metallurgical complexes on the model of Le Creusot. It is true that this revolution was premature and that its failure to spread was perhaps inevitable so long as there were no instruments of credit which freed the founders from the weight of financing it entirely from their own resources; but it showed clearly enough that there was no incompatibility between the monarchical society of the eighteenth century and development towards industrial capitalism, and that there was no need for the Revolution to free the productive forces of a bourgeoisie supposed to be the sole possessor of initiative.

In fact, in the last 20 years of the old order the traditional nobility, working often alongside their more recent fellows, were involved in all the most important mining and metallurgical enterprises, ones which overturned the traditional forms of family exploitation, both financially in drawing on enormous combinations of capital, and in terms of production and productivity by using improved plant and the most modern technology, and by recruiting the services of engineers and well-trained specialists. They were also able to open new avenues in the decelerating field of large-scale trade, often in association with greater merchants and traditional bankers.

There will be at least two objections to this interpretation. It has been said and will be said again that noble involvement in capitalist activities was negligible in scale. I am in no way claiming that the number of firms managed or financed by nobles was greater than the mass of middle-class business activities. The opposite is true for commercial companies and even manufacturing firms, with the exception of metallurgy. The nobility only realised quite late that they had a business vocation, and only a few of them were involved in this trend. Provincials, partly out of natural hesitation, partly for lack of capital, only joined the new movement timidly. But – and this is the decisive test – nobles stood for the most innovatory, the most dynamic and the most modernising trends in the business world. The second objection is equally invalid. This one points out that only those recently ennobled, who had been involved in productive activities before their elevation, are to be found in the ranks of the great capitalists. We shall see that this was certainly not the case. The high nobility was very well represented, as was the rich provincial nobility. It is in any case very odd to count ennobled commoners, or sons or grandsons of such people, as members of the third estate while at the same time being prepared to exclude from the third in other contexts holders of privileges, offices and others who were linked by their offices and their contacts with the established system. People like the Wendels, whose nobility was recognised and confirmed in 1727, or Baudard de Saint-James, grandson of a King's Secretary who had died in 1714 (and whose descendants were thereby ennobled from that moment), or Sérilly the grandson of a Court usher, nephew of an intendant of Auch and son of a counsellor at the parlement of Paris, cannot be considered as representative of the third estate without irony. They were fully and legitimately integrated into noble society, and this is in any case underlined by legal documents in which the most prestigious names of the traditional nobility are found among their relations and friends.

Now it is true that the order as a whole was not involved in the commercial vocation which affected only a part of the nobility. And this is where we find the fundamental distinction which drew a very clear demarcation line right through the order.

On the one hand there were the numerous nobles who only knew the harsh life of the countryside, often poor, ill-educated, endlessly reliving in their cramped manors and halls the old dreams of glory, and for whom the king's service seemed the only option, for the very good reason that they had not been fitted or trained for anything else within the narrow horizons of their daily activities. How could a grandfather, uncle or distant cousin, back home with the cross of St Louis after 20 or 30 years on active service or garrison duty, not seem a model hero whom young men thought of following in the future? Neither their social environment nor their cultural world led them to think of anything different. To serve the king was at once a duty, an inspiring adventure and the expression of an asceticism which had long been accepted and absorbed. For among the nobles whom contemporaries and historians alike often misunderstood, there was a willingness to sacrifice themselves that was well captured by the chevalier d'Arc, the king's bastard son and a stern and haughty lord, in his dream of a society where luxury would be banned and the nobility, thinking only of serving, would be endowed with a quite unrealistically austere and grandiose moral code. This idea of spartan virtue illuminates and lends profound significance to the measures of 1781 which tried to give legal substance to the aspirations of the old petty nobility to a monopoly of military commissions. It was a rejection of contamination on the part of an elite that was ready for any sacrifice on condition that no alien element likely to spoil its self-imposed ethic should be allowed in. Only officers risen from the ranks, who had long shared the same outlook, were excepted. This makes it easy to understand the rejection by this sort of noble of the idea that they should look for employment, security and promotion opportunities in other activities. That was the importance of the conflict between the abbé Coyer and the chevalier d'Arc.

As soon as more ample resources began to open up wider horizons, nobles no longer placed all their hopes in military service. Going occasionally to Paris, or in any event to the nearest town, confronted them with a world quite different from what was familiar. At one level of wealth further up, the noble lifestyle took in the provincial capitals. There, they came into contact with the most diverse circles, attending masonic lodges, agricultural societies, learned societies, and rubbing shoulders with magistrates, financiers and merchants. This less hide-bound world was more receptive to the arguments of the abbé Coyer than to those of the marquis de Lassay, of Montesquieu, or of the chevalier d'Arc. But by deliberately twisting his meaning, they used his ideas for their own advantage, as did the high nobility who went furthest in this direction. Coyer was seeking a solution to the problem of the poor nobility. Given that in normal times the king could not offer employment to more than 15,000 officers, not all nobles could serve him. Instead of languishing in degrading, wretched idleness, those who were left out, Coyer thought, could find an honourable career in commercial activities which, by enriching them, could put them in a position to serve worthily in the next generation. Coyer's suggestion was to 'Turn idleness into activity and set indigence on the road to riches.'[1] Very few petty nobles took it up, but it struck a chord among the higher nobility and the rich nobles of the provinces.

It is difficult to assess the impact of Coyer's arguments on noble psychology. He himself lived in circles won over to the idea that the nobility would gain strength from engaging in all sorts of activities, and he was doubtless the mouthpiece of a Parisian circle where great French lords mingled with foreign aristocrats, and in particular the influential Jacobite group which was one of the first to throw itself into great seaborne trading enterprises. The latter brought in, against French prejudices, the example of their homeland which Voltaire had so vaunted, and proof that one could take up activities other than military ones without dishonour. Thus it was not the petty nobility which benefited from this transformation of outlook, limited as it was. It was the richest nobles, often too the most illustrious, who ran the least risk of being taken for members of the world of trade.

This choice also reveals differences in cultural and political attitudes. I have already pointed out that the greater nobility was not content to be imprisoned within the definition of a functional nobility, with a precise but limited purpose within the Nation – that was the ideal of other nobles. The great saw themselves as an elite with a whole range of vocations. In the economic sphere, this manifested itself by massive involvement and flourishing initiative, whose forms we must now examine. It is clear that the whole of the nobility was not involved, but only the part that can be considered its natural elite, either on account of its long-standing position or because of its wealth, its talents, and its openness to the progressive tendencies of the age.

In quantitative terms the noble contribution remained modest though far from negligible. Its real importance is to be gauged by its quality. It was only quite seldom that nobles competed with the commercial middle classes in traditional activities. The family-based trading business was not their strong point. On the other hand, they made a strong showing wherever the early forms of modern high capitalism were emerging. Here they enjoyed a sort of monopoly.

As we have seen, the psychological barriers which might have stood in the way of these inclinations only lingered on in one part of the nobility. The latter could only imagine industrial or commercial activities in conjunction with the economy of rural estates. And so, despite their numerical importance, titled mine-owners and ironmasters played no role in big companies, and their innovatory power was non-existent. They played no part in the rise of modern large-scale capitalism and often obstructed new approaches by standing in the way of the big noble capitalists. There were plenty of instances of this rivalry. For example, in mid-century there was a conflict between Antoine-Paulin, marquis de Solages, from an old Albigeois family, grandson of a president in the parlement of Toulouse, and himself a former royal page, and a group of mine-owners at Carmaux led by a petty noble, Joseph Méjanes, who opposed the exclusive permission Solages had obtained to mine in the area. Mines were the main source of income to these needy squires. They were furious, and Méjanes fought like a lion; but the intendant had to dismiss their pleas, however sympathetic he was, because although they had combined in great numbers, they were quite unable to put together the necessary capital, and the mines had remained unexploited.[2] In 1789 many *cahiers* would still be calling for the revocation of these great concessions.

At the other extreme, legal barriers which might have impeded noble commercial and industrial ambitions had been steadily removed, even though they did not overcome the disinclination of the majority, as we can see from the frequency of laws which abolished prohibitions in the seventeenth and eighteenth centuries, and from the behaviour of the petty nobility. But among the upper nobility, increasing numbers of marriages into the world of the financiers – nobles of recent origin whose drive dominated capitalistic activity – promoted their absorption into the business world.

And so, in the second half of the century, conditions came together which allowed part of the nobility to become capitalists, businessmen and entrepreneurs.

There can be no question here of drawing up a list of all the economic activities in which nobles were involved in one way or another. Partnership deeds are lost in notarial records, where they can only be sampled. The archives of the Paris commercial court have disappeared. Company archives, where they survive, are not always clear about the status of shareholders. The poverty of the sources is made worse by the way nobles often disguised their involvement for obvious reasons, and by the use of pseudonyms or straw-men to hide the true identity of many of them. Perhaps, however, a list of this sort might not be of great use. I suspect that it would not help to widen the circle of known noble entrepreneurs. For in practice they were drawn from a numerically limited group; at least when we are talking about the great capitalistic undertakings. It was different with small businesses of the traditional sort where noble dominance is beyond doubt, such as iron-founding where the noble contingent was substantial, or glass-making and other manufacturing which did not demand huge investment, or revolutionary equipment, or operatives familiar with new methods. What interests us here is the noble contribution to the development of capitalism, the noble role in the transformation beginning at the end of the eighteenth century from traditional capitalism to industrial capitalism. Even so a sketch will be worthwhile: it will show the range over which nobles were active.

Contrary to a widespread opinion, nobles were not forbidden to engage in trade and the crown, above all from the time of Colbert who complained of not being able to find investors for his overseas trading companies, had issued and reissued edicts designed to encourage nobles to turn to commercial activities. The edict of December 1701 was re-iterating previous policies in allowing any noble to trade without loss of status, provided it was 'in bale and bond', that is, wholesale. They were forbidden to open shops, but they might sell retail at the place of manufacture and at fairs.³ However, before 1760 the reluctance of the nobility to trade was so obvious that the declaration was reissued several times, was discussed at the council of commerce, and formed the subject of an enquiry among the provincial intendants in 1755.⁴ A new edict of 1765 confirmed the right of nobles to trade freely, with the exception of holders of judicial office. Two years later came the corollary. On 30 October 1767 a decision of the council laid down the privileges, exemptions and prerogatives to be enjoyed in future by wholesale merchants: ennoblement for two merchants a year, and the right for all to carry a sword and arms when travelling.

So only retail trade remained forbidden to the nobility. But infringements were not infrequent. Nobles were not always aloof from it. However, it did have certain demeaning associations – not to mention the risk of loss of status – which prevented them from taking to it openly. Thus the duc de La Force created a veritable scandal, although at a time that was none too fastidious, when in 1721 he opened a grocery under a straw-man's name. This custom never died out. In mid-century the comtesse de Frinc owned a trading house at Nice under the name of Widow Reynaud, and in Brittany many noblemen, who were often involved in overseas trade, sold retail a very varied range of commodities, from grain to cloth or sardines, under their wives' names.⁵

Banking, though not among the commercial activities permitted to nobles by any edict, also attracted some of them. It seems probable that nobles were often sleeping partners in banking firms like that in which the comtesse de Sabran, the duc de Nivernais or the comtesse de Boisgelin were involved. Founded on 30 October 1784, this company under the title Douzard and Co. brought together Joseph Douzard, a banker of the rue Sainte-Anne, François de Treillars de Catry, his nephew Benoît, the comtesse de Sabran, Marie de Boufflers the wife of the comte de Boisgelin, and the duc de Nivernais. Its capital was fixed at 450,000 l.; between them the last three partners alone put up 300,000 l. Nor did the company confine itself to banking. It traded in brandy and tea at Roscoff with Jean Drot and Co. of Morlaix, and sent a ship, the *Duchesse de Lauzun*, to Senegal, under the care of M. Thirion, secretary to the chevalier de Boufflers.[6]

If certain sorts of business were more or less successfully disguised, land speculation went on openly. Professional businessmen, like Joseph Laborde the Court Banker or the farmer-general Bouret de Vézelay, who gave such a boost to this sort of speculation, especially with projects like the Chaussée d'Antin, were not the only ones involved. Many lords too, from the duc d'Orleans downwards, were not afraid to register companies for this purpose and to manage their operations themselves. The company set up at the office of the Parisian notary Quatremère on 13 December 1778 is a typical example and was the complete opposite of most current practices. It brought together Louis-Henri de Villeneuve, marquis de Trans, colonel of the Roussillon Regiment and premier marquis of France, and the chevalier Gabriel de Fageolles, in a speculative enterprise over lands at Le Roule. Heedless of soiling his hands, Trans declared himself 'head of the company' and in this capacity undertook to manage sales. The Roule land had been bought by the marquis de Trans for 1,130,000 l. cash and annual instalments of 10,710 l. To finance the undertaking, he had tapped commercial sources of funds. Philippe Richer, a merchant grocer, lent him 74,600 l. The company's aims, described as 'a new sort of speculation', were 'the disposal, resale and traffic which the parties intend to effect retail of the different parts of this land that the marquis de Trans has bought wholesale'.[7]

This sort of enterprise, limited to a particular purpose and put together afresh on each occasion, can be found in other activities. Thus the marquis de la Rianderie and Jacques-Eugène de Villy, gentleman, formed partnerships in 1784, 1786 and 1787 in order to sell horses, La Rianderie providing all the capital. Villy bought the horses in England, and his partner undertook to resell in Paris.[8] Quite often nobles lent their capital to fellow nobles or to the middle-class possessor of a 'secret' or a royal privilege. Thus on 21 September 1782 Jean-François marquis de Vichy, a cavalry captain living near Clermont in Auvergne, formed a partnership with Jean-François Fabre, lord of the barony of Le Bousquet, who had a secret way of turning wines into vinegar, to make money from spoiled wines and turn them to good use. Another partner was Charles Perreaud de Fontermand, the king's procurator at the town hall of Cognac. Fabre's contribution was the process, but he put up no capital. His two associates financed the scheme and undertook to establish three trading houses, one near to the estates of the marquis de Vichy, another at Cognac under the management of Perreaud, and a third at Bordeaux.[9] The wine trade appealed to the nobility. On 25 March 1785 the marquis de Drenenc and the marquis d'Asse set up a company in which they became sleeping partners of Jean-Baptiste Perrot, a Châlons merchant, 'for the purpose of buying and selling Burgundy wines'. Drenenc put in 100,000 l., d'Asse 200,000 and Perrot 100,000 l.[10] During the 1780s the nobility was struck by an unprecedented entrepreneurial fever, schemes proliferated, and they threw themselves into all sorts of different and unpredictable activities. The marquise de Marigny, *née* Choiseul, the marquise de Paysac, *née* Rastignac, the chevalier Savalette de Langes, former counsellor at the parlement of Paris and guardian of the Royal Treasury, and Joseph Ferrand, freeman of Paris, set up a company with a capital of 100,000 l. to exploit a concession from Monsieur, the king's brother, of the marshes in his apanage.[11] It was the marquis Colbert de Chabanais who, together with Jean-Baptiste Rouillé de Fontaine, chevalier de Saint-Louis, André Bietrix de Saulx, the banker Jean Abée and Laurent de Leutier, a merchant, established a company in 1780 to buy two lots on the rue Coq-Héron for a trading venture.[12] Finally we could mention a company for producing lamp-oil and street-lights for Paris, Versailles and the provinces, which brought together, along with Fabre du Bousquet and the ubiquitous financial office-holders (Sanlot, gentleman, a farmer-general; Millon d'Ailly, gentleman, general administrator of the royal domains; Millon d'Ainval, gentleman, receiver-general of the finances), the marquis de Lort, the comte de Baillon, the chevalier de Bonnard and the marquis de Rasilly.[13] We could go on with such examples. Even so, only exceptionally did they deal in really big capital sums.

By contrast, overseas trading in the second half of the century involved a broad segment of the Parisian nobility. This trend was at its fullest in the Breton ports and at Nantes, under three influences: Breton noble traditions, the presence of foreign nobles, and the involvement of financial office-holders. Jean Meyer has demonstrated the importance of nobles or those recently ennobled (though earlier in the century and now completely integrated into the second order) in the trade of Nantes; the Luynes, the Montaudouins and the Walshes were among the leading merchants.[14] Whatever Necker might claim, ennoblement did not lead to the abandonment of commercial activities, and the Picot de Closrivière family, who had been ennobled at the beginning of the century by an office of King's Secretary, remained in trade throughout the century.[15] In any case, merchants' letters of ennoblement most often specified that children should not give up their fathers' profession on pain of annulment. For their part, in mid-century financiers launched large companies of shareholders designed to restore the trade of Nantes and take over from the run-down Indies Company. This is how Paris-Montmartel brought into being the Angola Company, or how the Guinea Company was formed, backed by a group of ten farmers-general put together by another, Dupleix de Bacquencourt, brother of the Indian governor. An extra push was given by the Jacobite aristocracy. Not sharing their French counterparts' prejudices about trade, needing in any case to remake their fortunes, and standing well at Court, they were the most influential 'colonial' group, and they played a major part in the management of the Indies Company and the running of colonial establishments which gave the French aristocracy a model and a taste for commercial investments. The Rothes, who were also serving army officers, were the first to organise expeditions to Indo-China out of Pondicherry, and subsequently specialised in the China trade which they took over from the Indies Company after its liquidation in 1769.[16] As great foreign aristocrats, but recognised in France and naturalised, the Jacobites were fully integrated into Parisian noble circles, and French marriages were common. So contamination was inevitable.

It was from 1770 onwards that the nobility began to be massively involved in great overseas trading companies, which they sometimes founded. Between 1769, when the Indies Company was liquidated, and 1785, when a new company was set up, the two most important overseas trading companies were the Senegal Company and the Northern Trading Company. There was also a company of a rather special type in that the shareholders, without putting up any of their own money, stood surety together for a loan of 1,200,000 l.[17] This was the company for the exploitation of the privilege of seaborne communication between France and the colonies, founded on 27 December 1781; its intention was to fit out ships in the various ports of France to transport 'letters, official packets, and the king's cargoes' to the colonies. The shareholders, almost all of whom were nobles, divided up between them the 60 *sols* that made up the company's portfolio; Charles-Armand, prince de Rohan-Rochefort, lieutenant-general, took seven *sols*; Louis Drummond Earl of Melfort, a Jacobite and another lieutenant-general, seven *sols*; Louis-Charles, comte du Hautoy, seven *sols*; chevalier Lambert, counsellor of state, seven *sols*; chevalier de Berge, four *sols*; a doctor of medicine, Charles Guiraudet, four *sols*; François Renaud de la Grelaye, four *sols*; and a solitary merchant, André-Louis Fournier, a Nantes shipper, two *sols*. The company distributed the 18 remaining *sols* among its new secretaries, only one of whom is known: prince Frédéric de Salm-Kribourg, who in 1782 acquired two. Although far from negligible, this company was much less important than the French Guiana Company.

In 1763, the government decided to make Cayenne the most important French holding in America. The 500,000 l. that were spent there each year produced no result. It was then that Dubucq, the senior clerk in the colonial office, was authorised to set up a company with a capital of 1,200,000 l., divided into twelve share blocks, to establish a plantation and a trading-house in Cayenne. Dubucq's company was very soon making a loss, and it surrendered its rights to a consortium which, after several fruitless experiments in 1771 and 1772, established itself in 1774 under the name of the West Africa Company to launch a trade in goods and Negro slaves on the coasts of Africa and in the interior. On 6 January 1776 an order in council authorised this company's directors, the comte de Jumilhac, governor of the Bastille, and Charles de Mazière, Jean-Baptiste Herenc de Borda, and Jacques Paulze, farmers-general, to set up in French Guiana 'establishments for the cultivation and exploitation of articles of subsistence necessary to the Windward and Leeward islands of America . . . under the name of the French Guiana Company'. The company was granted numerous advantages. It received lands situated between the rivers Oyapock and Approuague, use of the buildings owned by the king along the Oyapock, fifty Negroes belonging to the king but due to be replaced from the slave-trade within a year; and on top of all this, the company would receive a bounty of 300 l. for each European man or woman which it should convey to and establish anywhere in its concession, 200 l. for each boy or girl and 100 l. for every child following its father or mother. The king also granted a premium per head on each batch of Negroes, to wit 150 l. for the first 1,200, 100 l. for the next 1,200, but 200 l. for those coming through the trade with Mozambique, all this on condition that these slaves were employed in ground-clearing;

there was also to be a warship fitted out at the king's expense, either to take possession of them, or to carry the first batches. The company was authorised to begin trading as it saw fit with the coasts, islands and interior of its lands, posts and establishments. It also received preferential treatment for six years in provisioning French posts on the coast of Africa. In September 1776 it was granted too the privilege of supplying provisions to troops stationed in Cayenne.

So the company's aim was threefold: as a colonising venture, it was entrusted with the peopling and opening up of Cayenne; as a trading company, it basically undertook to procure black slaves; and as a supplies contractor it cornered the provisioning of troops in Guiana and Africa.

The company issued 1,000 shares valued at 500 l. each, divided between 24 shareholders. The list is notable for the absence – exceptional though this was – of experienced men, being exclusively recruited from the nobility and the circles of army officers and farmers-general:

	shares
Duc de Duras, peer and Marshal of France	30
Jean-Baptiste Gaillard, baron de Beaumanoir, captain of dragoons	121
Charles Mazière, gentleman, farmer-general of taxes	37
Jacques Paulze, gentleman, farmer-general of taxes	30
Jean-Baptiste Lemoyne de Belleisle, knight, chancellor to the duc d'Orléans	52
Geneviève Lemoyne de Belleisle, widow of the chevalier Lejaulne	12
Claude-Louis, marquis de Saisseval, army officer	30
Claude-Henri, comte de Saisseval, army officer	30
Antoine-Joseph-Marie, comte de Jumilhac, former governor of the Bastille	25
Antoine-Laurent Lavoisier, gentleman, farmer-general of taxes	30
Jean-Antoine Clément de Barville, first advocate-general at the court of aids	60
Jean Herenc de Borda, gentleman, farmer-general of taxes	34
Jacques-Mathieu Augeard, gentleman, farmer-general of taxes	30
Pierre Rousseau, administrator-general of the King's Domains	20

Henri Lefèvre, commendatory abbot of Chartreuve   shares   22
Prosper Tassin de Vilpion, intendant of finances to
   the duc d'Orléans   30
Etienne Serre de Saint-Romans, comte de
   Fresserville, master ordinary in the chamber
   of accounts   144
Elisabeth-Marie, marquise de Mesnilglaise   20
Alxis-Janvier de la Live de La Briche, Introducer
   of Foreign Ambassadors   30
André-Marie Clairval, knight of Saint-Louis   25
Marie-Philippe Taschereau de Baudry, widow of
   André Potier de Novion, marquis de Grignon,
   honorary president in the parlement   3
Pierre-Constantin Levicomte, comte de Blagny   30
Jean-François, Marquis de Rochedragon, infantry
   colonel   20

The company was dominated by the traditional nobility, followed by
farmers-general, officers of the King's Household and those of the
princes, and widows, that indispensable element in any joint stock
company. Not a single merchant. When the capital proved inadequate,
a further thousand shares were issued. They were acquired by existing
shareholders and by several newcomers:

> André-Marie-Gautier de Montgeroult, knight of Saint-Louis
> Pierre-Louis Taboureau, knight of Saint-Louis
> Marie-Thérèse de Mondran, widow of Jean-Joseph La Live de la
>   Pouplinière, farmer-general of taxes
> Palteau de Veymerange, intendant of the royal armies
> Barthélémy-Jean-Louis Le Coulteux de La Noraye, knight, king's
>   counsellor
> Antoine-Jean Amelot, Marquis de Chaillou
> Jean-Pierre Loliot, secretary general of the cavalry of France
> Sylvestre Richer, treasurer of the revenue from offices
>   (*parties casuelles*)
> Théodore Maron de Montjuzion

On 14 April 1777 the company obtained an extension of its rights in
the form of the exclusive privilege of provisioning the island of Gorée
and its dependencies from Cape Verde to the Casamance. In practice
the Guiana company seems not to have put much effort into making

Cayenne yield dividends. It chiefly concerned itself with trying to corner the exclusive trade in black slaves for Saint-Domingue and the Windward Islands. A hostile document accused it of taking annually 2,200 blacks from Juda and 400 from Gorée, but not sending them to Cayenne, which was in no state to absorb them. 'Cayenne', it was said, 'is the place it is least concerned with.'

Nevertheless the slave trade became too heavy a weight and the company asked to be allowed to abandon it. This request was granted by an order in council of 28 December 1783, in which the king took account of the services it had rendered at the time of the conquest of Senegal and the heavy losses it had undergone, and in compensation granted it the monopoly of the gum trade and allowed it to undertake whatever trading ventures it saw fit. The company immediately reconstituted itself under the name of the Senegal Company.

The deed of partnership of 24 May 1784 stipulated a capital of 3 millions made up of 3,000 shares of 1,000 l., to which were added the 2,000 shares of the Guiana Company, whose holders would be entitled to two fifths of the profits of the new company. The former partners would sell to the Senegal Company the goods, ships and slaves of their posts in Senegal as well as all their lands in Guiana together with their buildings and plantations, furnishings, supplies, etc. for 1,000 shares in the new company. The former partners bought up most of the new shares, so that although its name had changed, the company had not changed shareholders. The duc de Duras acquired 90 shares, the marquis de Saisseval 120, the marquis de Chaillou 90, the chevalier de Belleisle 156, de Montgeroult 75, the comte de Blagny 90, the marquise de Mesnilglaise 60, Saint-Romans 216, Vilpion 90, and Veymerange 33. A few new faces appeared, but possibly they had been involved in the previous company: one Sylvestre Gougenot de Croissy, gentleman, the duc de La Vrillière, Mme de Langeac, the comte d'Ailly (as heir to the comtesse Le Camus), Président de Noiseau, the princesse de Lamballe, and Dangé d'Orsay.

It has been well worthwhile to dwell on this company, it is the characteristic type of a great joint stock company whose managers and entire body of shareholders were nobles. Such companies seem, in the closing years of the century, to have had more appeal in noble circles than the traditional sleeping partnerships in commercial ventures.[18]

This was a case of a very large undertaking, and almost unique in this last decade of the old monarchy when warning signs of an economic crisis of unusual intensity were building up. The only comparable enterprise at this time also owed a good deal to noble initiative and capital. But here there was no shortage of practical men, and financiers (although they too were an integral part of the noble world) were represented in the central role played by Claude Baudard, baron Saint-James, treasurer-general of the Navy. This was the Patriotic Northern Trading Company.

This venture illustrates in more ways than one the dynamics which led the traditional nobility and the financial nobility in to the renewal of French seagoing traditions. The Atlantic, West Indies and India trades, with their established patterns and reliable returns, attracted merchants of the ports who had little inclination to depart from well-trodden paths. To open the Baltic trade to France was to run huge risks and they were reluctant to become involved. It is not without signifi-cance that men bold enough to take over from the foot-dragging commercial middle-classes, and give impetus to a commercial sector which was vital for a kingdom hitherto dependent for provisions on neutrals, should be found among the nobility. On 10 August 1776 the navy ministry concluded a treaty with the royal Prussian government for the delivery of wood to Hamburg. Dutch transporters initially undertook to convey it to French ports. After England declared war on the United Provinces (December 1780) Danish and Swedish flags were used. In 1782, the navy used the services of a trading company established at Stralsund under the management of two Swedes and two French noblemen: Simon-Léon Casauranc de Saint-Paul and Laurent-Guillaume Fraissinet de Larroque. But by the end of the year the ministry, which was dissatisfied with the supplies it was getting, was thinking of breaking the contract. It tried to interest the merchants of Bordeaux in the northern trade, without success. It was then that two French entrepreneurs already involved in this area under the neutral cover of the Stralsund company, Saury and Casauranc de Saint-Paul, secured a contract under which they undertook to deliver to French ports the shipbuilding wood that Prussia was supposed to supply. The activities of this company, which merged on 2 January 1785 with a venture to supply the royal navy run by Ferber, brother, and Co., have already been studied, and I shall not go into details that are already well known.[19] What is interesting here is the character of the shareholders.

The Northern Trading Company was financed by two Perigord nobles, Joseph de Coustain, comte de Bourzolles and François-Antoine de Laverie-Vivans, comte de Siorac, who put up 400,000 l. for buying the first vessels for the company. This was a provincial intrusion into the more normal recruitment of commercial investors among the Parisian nobility. Behind the Ferber brothers, on the other hand, were Parisians like Paul-Juste Harmensen de Polny, gentleman, administrator of the Discount Bank, and Claude Baudard, baron Saint-James, treasurer-general of the navy. The latter was led to invest larger and larger sums in the company, amounting by 1787 to 2,400,000 l. And so, thanks to two provincial nobles and a representative of Parisian high finance, the French flag managed to establish itself in the North Sea and the Baltic, and France avoided a dangerous dependence. It was one more proof that, while the commercial middle classes hung back, imaginative capitalism was developing within the second order.

If the part played by the nobility in commercial capitalism in the eighteenth century was substantial, and even decisive in certain sectors, this supposedly 'idle' class became involved even more prominently, especially after 1770, in the development of manufacturing and, to call it what it was, industrial capitalism.

Here, alongside the traditional nobility there often appeared the recent nobility of the financial office-holders. But we should be careful how we interpret the term 'recent'. It has often been claimed – quite wrongly – that if nobles were to be found involved in capitalist activities, they must have been newly-ennobled and not have shaken off their original bourgeois activities, to which they often owed their ennoblement. Yet in most cases they were not recently ennobled; they were servants of the king, entitled to call themselves *chevalier*, and able to prove their lineage back through two, three or four degrees of nobility and a similar number of financial or judicial offices which long before had freed them from their commoner origins and cut them off from their beginnings in trade. That was the case with the Sérillys and the Baudards who were of the first importance in this field. But their involvement in the conduct of the royal finances cast a confusing veil over the form of their rapidly-developing capitalism. How can we speak of industrial capitalism when some of the capital was fiscal in origin? And of course we know what confusion there was in the funds of the government's leading accountants and bankers between public moneys and the financiers' own resources. But I do not see in this any major impediment to the development of industrial capitalism. Just because revenue was sometimes used to finance some manufacturing venture – which was in any case quite rare because treasurers were most often pledged in advance rather than in funds – it did not make for a situation much different from that of today when the state subsidises a sector of industry in order to boost it, or grant it tax advantages.

Among the enterprises in which nobles were involved it is essential to distinguish between those which were a simple extension of estate management, and capitalist ventures unconnected with land-ownership.

In the first category, alongside mines and foundries which almost all nobles, from the comte d'Artois down to the merest Couserans squire, set up on their lands, we should place manufacturing establishments set up within the confines of estates and which were funded, with or without privileges, from a landlord's own capital. Manufacturing had some famous backers. The king set an example at Sèvres. Following him greater nobles threw themselves enthusiastically into manufacturing. The duc d'Orléans had glassworks at Cotterets and Bagneux[20] and establishments producing printed cottons at Montargis and Orléans. The comte d'Artois set up the chemical works at Javel and owned a porcelain works.[21] The prince de Conti owned a factory near Soissons, the marquis de Caulaincourt made muslins in Picardy, the comte de Custine employed 400 workers in his fine china works in Lorraine. The duc de La Rochefoucauld-Liancourt invested 36,000 l. in a cloth works on his estates and brought workers from abroad for his school for spinning-girls and to instruct apprentices.[22] The marquis de Bullion made artificial soda,[23] Mme d'Areville had a sheeting works at Sedan,[24] the vicomte de Laugest was the owner of a paper mill,[25] the comte de Brienne bought English looms, the comtesse de Laval owned a cloth works and one Monsieur de Lamartine two iron wire factories in the Jura.[26] We could go on with such examples, but they would only show the participation of the nobility in traditional manufacturing and individual enterprises. They do however reveal the importance of estate-based manufacturing, which still awaits tabulation, but whose share of national production as a whole was without doubt far from negligible.

More interesting were the great capitalist companies, joint-stock concerns, which brought together large capital, men of practical experience and new techniques. Examples are the Saint-Gobain works, the Neuville works, or the project for tapping the waters of the Seine linked to the foundry at Chaillot. What they had in common was the linking up of capital-rich noblemen with specialists who provided practical knowledge and sometimes secrets. The oldest firm, Saint-Gobain, at first recruited its shareholders among financial office-holders

and King's Secretaries, before opening up after 1750 to the greater
nobility: Anne de Montmorency, the vicomte de Ségur, La Vieuville,
La Luzerne, the comte de Jaucourt, and the marquis de la Ferté-Imbault
all joined the board.[27] In 1789 the capital value of the venture – which
had huge workshops at Saint-Gobain, in Paris and at Tourlaville –
amounted to 10.5 millions. A less important glassworks was that of
Baccarat, established in 1765 by the bishop of Metz, a Montmorency-
Laval, and the advocate Antoine Renault, which in 1788 gave work to
700 operatives and sent its products to Spain, Africa and the West
Indies. The Royal Manufactory of Neuville (cotton spinning and
manufacture of cotton cloth, muslins and silk velvets on a cotton base)
was made into a public company on 26 March 1782 under the title
François Pernet and Co.. Pernet owned the royal privileges; an English-
man, Milne, was the inventor of the machinery on which the works
would run (English machinery, in fact); and Benoît Allier de Hauteroche, knight, of Lyons, provided the financial backing. This financial underpinning came in the form of 24 shares of 25,000 l. of which
6 belonged to Hauteroche, marketed in Paris by an enterprising notary
called Baroud. The shareholders soon found themselves in complete
control. Pernet died, Milne was bought out, and Hauteroche sold his
interest on 2 November 1783 to the marquis de L'Aubépin. The other
shares were acquired by Jean-Baptiste de Menardeau, knight and former
counsellor in the grand chamber of the parlement of Paris, Jean-
Baptiste-Armand de Menardeau, formerly advocate-general in the
parlement of Brittany, Claude-Etienne baron de Marivetz, Marie-
Henri La Martinière, Claude-Servant de Poleynieux, treasurer of
France at Lyon, and Philippe François Bertaud du Coin, knight. The
shareholders had put up a total sum of 375,000 l. when a new company
was formed in 1785, which added to the old five new members, two
of whom were already well known in the business world: Baroud and
Jacques-Constantin Périer. They brought in with them Joseph-Benoît
du Plain de Saint-Albine, gentlemen of the Royal Household, Louis-
Clair Maurin, court counsellor to the Prince Royal of Prussia, and
Pierre Bonfils, gentleman and King's Secretary. The capital value was
raised to 600,000 l., plus 200,000 l. for the value of buildings and
plant.[28]

The Neuville works opened immense possibilities in industrial
development. It heralded the installation, from which there was no
going back, of mechanised cotton production. The influence of the
Jacobite Holker, a Lancashire gentleman who came over to France

after the defeat of the '45, and later became inspector general of manufactures, was decisive. Under his influence the spinning jenny spread throughout France, and large mills were set up to house Arkwright machines and the mule-jenny. The Milne family, of British origin, was to play a capital role in this push for modernisation. After leaving Neuville, the Milnes secured the support of Calonne, Vergennes and the comte d'Angivilliers for the establishment at Passy of a factory making modified and improved Arkwright machinery. With his passion for the mechanical arts, the duc d'Orléans foresaw all the advantages to be reaped from this new device, and undertook to finance the foundation of large works on the English model. Accordingly he set up two cotton-spinning mills on his estates. But he was anxious to keep the process to himself, and he obliged the Milnes, under a contract (that was only sporadically observed), to build their machines only for him. The Montargis mill, which Jean Milne managed, was equipped between 1788 and 1792 with 18 sets of machines produced in the Passy workshops, and employed 400 operatives. Even bigger was the mill at Orléans, which was placed in 1786 under the management of Milne's son-in-law Foxlox, a cotton manufacturer formerly of Manchester. In 1792 it was equipped with 21 machines.

In 1790 this mill witnessed a new departure which was to have huge consequences for the process of mechanised cotton production. Until then the machines were worked by manual power. Orléans, who had followed closely the experiments of Périer at Chaillot, fitted his works with a steam engine. The first French steam-powered spinning mill had arrived.[29]

The steam-engine, the key innovation in the process of mechanisation, had been introduced to France early in the century. The first one had been set up at Anzin in 1737, and the mineowners from 1777 were using it to pump water out of the workings. It was the duc d'Orléans' circle, however, which explored with intense excitement the various ways of using Watt's machine introduced into France by the Périers. The chevalier d'Auxiron, the vicomte d'Harambure, the chevalier de Follenay and comte Jouffroy d'Uxelles through Orléans met Périer, the marquis Jouffroy d'Albans and the duke's close friend the marquis Ducrest, who had elaborated theories for the maximum use of the new machine.[30] Their contacts gave birth to steam navigation and a company for transporting goods along the Saône and Rhône which was abandoned for lack of money. But the Périers, taking up one of Auxiron's ideas and encouraged by Ducrest and the duc d'Orléans, began to build steam engines in the Chaillot workshops: around 40 were produced there between 1778 and 1791.[31] The Creusot manufacturers used them for drilling and forging; for his part the duc d'Orléans introduced them into cotton spinning, whilst less pragmatic nobles, like the duc de Chartres at Monceau, used them for pleasure, as a means of raising the water needed for irrigating their elegant English-style gardens.

The scheme for piping the waters of the Seine throughout Paris, an offshoot of the Chaillot foundry,[32] is another example of a great capitalist undertaking bringing together specialists (in this case the Périer brothers), the upper nobility and representatives of high finance. The deed of partnership of 27 August 1778[33] enumerates among those concerned a councillor of state, two knights, a knight of St Louis, seven gentlemen, two receivers-general, a farmer-general, seven treasurers-general (including Baudard de Saint-James and Mégnet de Sérilly), a King's Secretary, various officers of the Royal Household and one foreign nobleman and sometime court banker, the comte de Seneffe. All these were rapidly joined (as a minute of discussions on 18 January 1781 shows) by the duc de Châtelet, the duc de La Rochefoucauld-Liancourt, Beaumarchais, gentleman and King's Secretary, Boullongne de Préminville, knight, Colonel Ylverton de Kendall, and the bankers Mallet and Perregaux.[34]

Steam technology and the mechanisation of cotton production linked aristocratic names with the specialists they had helped on, and they had been the first to turn their inventions to industrial use. The mills at Neuville and Orléans opened the way to large scale cotton production. It is true that these were still isolated growth points. But modernisation was on the way to a decisive leap forward with the introduction of the latest technology and the use of a new source of energy. Without wishing to become embroiled in the debate about the validity of the terms industrialisation and modernisation,[35] and confining ourselves to a suggestive sketch rather than a rigorous definition, could we not say that all this prefigured and already in a certain sense was an 'industrial revolution'? Such a concept might appear exaggerated as a description of what happened during the last decades of the old monarchy, and to make a case we should need to take into account a certain number of measures and variables (such as rationality, growth of returns, urbanisation and so on) which are not relevant here.

However, in one sector at least the term does not seem excessive. In mining and metallurgy there did appear an unprecedented combination of factors: an enormous concentration of capital and labour, geographical concentration, a massive demand by capital for skilled operatives, the use of the latest technology and what could already be called 'scientific research'; whilst under the archaic appearances of classic methods of finance there were emerging ways of raising capital that were quite close to those introduced by the merchant banks of the nineteenth century. Here too, in order to cope with the new conditions introduced by the size of giant undertakings, different types of share-holding began to be explored, as older ones showed themselves ill-adapted (less by nature than in consequence of unfavourable political and financial circumstances) to the process of industrialisation. As an industrial revolution it was abortive, certainly. It was too closely tied to the order of things under which it had been born not to be swept away with that order. But this first take-off was not to be in vain, and, beyond the Revolution, an industrialised France would be born from the old regime experiments that Le Creusot or the cotton industries managed to keep going in spite of terrible vicissitudes and ruinous upheavals.

Mining and metallurgy did not necessarily make up an advanced sector of production. Forges, indeed, were an old-established industry in which the individualist and artisan traditions remained strong, and throughout the eighteenth century nobles great and small had won mining concessions. It would be superfluous to list the names of all those who developed mining for coal, copper and silver. But from the duc d'Aumont to the marquis de Traisnel, from the duc de Chaulnes to the marquis de Foudras, from the duc de Charost to the marquis d'Antraigues, the upper nobility, and with it some lords of lesser importance right down to small nobles in reduced circumstances, saw mining as in some way their own special preserve.[36] It was the same with forges, over half of those that have been recorded belonging to nobles.[37] The researches of Guy Richard over several generalities have shown that there the nobility owned between 45 and 86 per cent of smelting workshops, with a similar share of the total production.[38] Mining concessions, glassworks attached to them, and forges, even quite substantial ones, did not lift the nobility from the traditional framework of the normal careful search by landowners for means of maximising their lands' resources. Nevertheless lords with enough influence at Court won concessions embracing complete dioceses and even whole provinces. In the last 20 years of the old order they were not far from monopolising the field.[39]

Many of these nobles worked or managed their own mines and

forges. Some were quite happy to lease them out, but even here they kept interfering, telling the manager what to do, and planning out the workings. The comte d'Artois, advised by his agent Radix de Sainte Foy, leased out his estate at Vierzon to one Bergeron, a naval supplier: the contract stipulated that the lessee should build two blast furnaces, a forge and a foundry, and would enjoy the same privileges as the leaseholders on forges at Clavières and Ardentes which were also in the apanage of the king's brother.[40]

Once again this was nothing new. The late eighteenth century saw the development of an old established trend in the proliferation of ventures whose innovatory scope was limited. It was a different story with mining companies, which on noble initiative established themselves inside and outside France on capitalistic lines. The most important of all was Anzin, with a capital value of over a million in 1789, which brought together a large number of nobles under the auspices of the prince de Croy, the marquis de Cernay, vicomte de Sandrouins and, for the Aniche branch, the marquis de Traisnel.[41] The marquis de Mirabeau was the castigator of the abbé Coyer and the declared enemy of a trading nobility, but his heart was not in his theories, and he had in fact formed a company to exploit the mines of Glange in Limousin with a founding capital set in 1766 at 300,000 l. made up of 300 shares of 1,000 l. They were almost entirely taken up by representatives of the Versailles nobility – the duc de Nivernais, the duchesse de Cossé, the comte de Broglie, Turgot, Malesherbes, the marquis du Saillant, the marquis de Brancas, the comtesse de Rochefort with d'Antraigues from Auvergne.[42] The company for mining coal in the neighbourhood of Paris, set up in 1785, drew its shareholders from the same circles: the greater nobility with Polignac, Montesquiou and Laval; the financial nobility with Saint-James, Sérilly, Sainte Foy; the king, who took thirteen shares, the prince d'Hénin, the comte de Fouquet, the baron de Besenval, the comte d'Espagnac, the marquis de Couey, Wendel and Périer.[43] On 13 August 1778 two companies merged. One was made up of Louis Thomas Richard, knight, his brother, the comte de Buffon and the Paris bankers Sellon and Perrouteau; the other comprised the advocate Carouges des Bornes, du Rotroy the commandant of Saint-Quentin, and three other noblemen. They merged to form a company for processing coal into coke in the provinces of Normandy, Dauphiné, Provence and Languedoc and the generality of Lille and Valenciennes. The capital stock was valued at 1,200,000 l.[44] A scheme for supplying Paris with peat for burning, under a company set up in

1784 and reconstituted in 1786, brought together the same sort of group, where alongside the marquis de Valençay were found the big business financiers Saint-James, Sérilly, Pyron de Chaboulon and Gigot d'Orcy.[45] Broadly based companies were also set up in Brittany. The most important were those of Poullaouën and Chatel-Audren. The latter, reformed into a joint-stock company in 1774 with a capital of 920,000 l. (after a false start as a company with bearer-shares) included among its partners Le Roy de Chaumont, François Rothe, the marquis de Briqueville, the wife of président de la Fortelle, the comte de Blagny, prince Czartorysky, the chevalier d'Arcy, a senior army officer and a member of the Academy of Sciences, and the marquis de Cordouan.[46] The most important of all the mining companies sought success in Spain. The Guadalcanal Company was run by the comte de Clonard, a naturalised Irish Jacobite, and brought together a range of ducs (Harcourt, du Châtelet, La Rochefoucauld-Liancourt) numerous great lords (the marquis de Bussy, de Lévis, des Réaux, d'Houdetot, d'Hérissy), aristocratic ladies of industry (the marquises de Marboeuf, de Cambot, de Boursonne), comtes de Blagny, de Peyre, de Custine, du Hautoy, a foreign noble Count Doria, the comtesses de Ruffey, de La Suze, de Coustin, the vicomte de La Rochefoucauld and president de Vaudreuil. In 1778 the Gaudalcanal Company had absorbed over three million livres.[47]

So noble involvement in the industrial expansion which marked the last years of the old order was massive. But the importance of this involvement is to be gauged less by its scale than by its quality. The cotton sector had opened revolutionary avenues by mechanisation. Metallurgy too had been opened up to new developments. First it was modernised by concentration. Large concerns were established. There were the works of Babaud de La Chaussade at Cosne and Guérigny, bought by the king in 1781 for two and a half millions; the munitions works at Tulle which in 1783 came under the control of the Wendel organisation; the foundry of Ruelle set up by Montalembert in 1753, bought up by the comte d'Artois in 1774 and by the king in 1777; or the colonial forges of the comte de Rostaing at Mondésir in Mauritius.[48] The most powerful concentrations were in the east. The characters who set them up are worth dwelling on for a moment. One of them was to play a decisive part in the establishment of Le Creusot.

The Wendels were a military family coming originally from Flanders. They became involved in metallurgy at the end of the seventeenth century, at first through managing the forges of the baronne d'Eltz at Ottange, and then on their own. Jean-Martin bought the works at Hayange, and the forge at La Marolle from the marquis de La Marolle. The family was probably already noble or considered as such, because in 1727 Wendel received letters of confirmation from the duc de Lorraine. Nevertheless, to cover himself he bought an office of King's Secretary in the chancery of the Metz parlement. His daughter married Gabriel Patteau de Veymerange, and this brought useful links: the son born of this marriage would become the successful advocate of Le Creusot with the minister Calonne. When he died in 1737 Jean-Martin de Wendel left 700,000 l. and five fully working forges. The scale was still modest; but his son Charles enlarged it with forges on the Warndt at Sainte-Fontaine. In 1768 the Wendel forges were producing 1,370 tons of iron and castings annually. Charles' son, an artillery officer, forge inspector and an enquiring and innovatory character, deliberately broke with tradition. He discerned the importance of English methods and planned out a revolution in industrial techniques. In 1769, at Hayange, he and Gabriel Jars achieved the first successful coke-fired casting of iron in France.[49] The Strasbourg banking family of Dietrich gave up their financial activities as soon as these began to seem incompatible with the dignities which came to them over a short period of time: ennoblement in 1761 on the recommendation of Pâris-Montmartel, a barony in 1762, and the elevation of their manors into a county in 1783. As well as being the greatest landowner in Alsace, Jean Dietrich was also its most powerful industrialist. In 1789 he employed 1,500 workers and was producing 3,000 tons of pig-iron, 700 tons of castings and 2,500 tons wrought iron in ingots, rods and sheets.[50]

These concentrations, important though they were, were not enough to bring about a real revolution in the metallurgical industry. Two other conditions were needed: technical renewal, and the use of improved machinery. All these conditions would come together for the first time at Le Creusot. But what gropings, failures, and resounding setbacks lay ahead before achieving the result! The Wendels at Hayange, Buffon at Montbard, and Guyton de Morveau, the learned advocate-general of the parlement of Dijon, had all managed to produce cast iron with coke. But these results were experimental. Commercial exploitation of the technique still lay in the future. Whilst the chevalier Richard was setting up a company for processing coal, another was being established by Count William Stuart, a Jacobite officer now in French service and captain in the Zweibrücken regiment, the baron de Kesling, an officer from Lorraine and former captain in the Nassau regiment, the chevalier Milleville and Jean Roettiers de la Tour, a Paris alderman, to make ordinary coal fit for smelting iron. They bought a forge at Mévrain and a blast-furnace at Bouvier for 125,000 l. in 1776, and then the concession of the Le Creusot mine for the sum of 60,000 l. cash and an annual payment of 15,600 l. They spent 250,000 l. to equip the coal mine and set up plant for making coke and smelting with it. But they had no good technicians, and the venture failed. For coke metallurgy really to take off, bigger blast furnaces than charcoal-fired ones were needed, and more powerful draughts. It took a small Languedoc nobleman, the aptly-named Marchant de la Houlière,[51] an infantry officer and royal lieutenant at Salces in Roussillon, to show the way. With the help of the metallurgist Gensanne he established himself at Alès, and soon saw that the French did not know enough and that their experiments were going round in circles; so he decided to go and discover at source the secret of English methods. Thanks to the comte de Guines, the French ambassador in London, he was able to get into English metallurgical circles, and above all to get to know John Wilkinson, who put his brother and partner William at his disposal.

This was how the future components of the Creusot complex came together. First with the experts: Wilkinson, who was up with the latest English methods, and with him a very worthy engineer, Toufaire, who had built the Ruelle foundry. With this first-rate team, the Indret munitions works came into production. But output was low, and the cannon were small-bore ones. This was when Wendel stepped in. He saw at once the chinks in the armour; old cannon were being recast, a reverberatory furnace was being used, and castings were done in sand rather than clay. Indret needed to be equipped in a different way; it needed blast-furnaces and coke-smelting. He was given control of Indret, and the foundries of Forgeneuve and La Ruelle. All that was now needed was a site for the future works. Wendel, Toufaire and Wilkinson chose Montcenis near Le Creusot, already the choice of Stuart's company. They soon made it the pride of French metallurgy. Montcenis had an annual capacity of 5,000 tons of cast iron. The works were equipped with modern plant: a steam-bellows. Wendel imported from England a rotating machine which transformed the alternating movement of the piston into a continuously circulating air stream. Alongside the blast furnaces and the bellows a forge was set up and a second steam engine to work the hammers.

For such a vast venture to succeed, big capital investment was needed. Necker was approached, but declined to help. The two greatest state financiers of the age, Sérilly (War Treasurer) and Saint-James (Treasurer of the Navy), who were also directors of the Discount Bank, then took a hand in their personal capacities as principal sleeping partners, and they brought in with them Nicolas Bettinger, chief clerk of the General War Treasury, Palteau de Veymerange, former counsellor at the parlement of Metz, knight of Saint-Louis, Royal Intendant of Armies and Posts, Wendel's cousin and a contact with Calonne, who he had known at Metz; and finally Constantin Périer. Wendel brought his skill and authority to the head of the whole concern. After lobbying by Veymerange, in 1784 Calonne persuaded the king to invest 600,000 l. in the enterprise and become one of its main partners.

The company went on growing: in 1785 it bought out the installations at Mévrain, and in 1786 the Montcenis coal mines. Finally the queen's crystal works, which ran on coal but were not doing well where they had been established at Saint-Cloud, were added to its range. They were moved to Montcenis, near the mine, and the Creusot partners put up 200,000 l. capital to finance them. Set up, modernised and equipped in this way, Le Creusot became the equal of the finest English plants. It took 2,400 four-ox carts to move raw materials about the site. Building workers came from Auvergne; the 600 employees came from all over the country. The blast furnaces were lit on 15 November 1785, and the first pig-iron produced on 11 December. Activity now speeded up. Whilst the blast furnaces, the reverberatory furnaces, forges, bellows and steam hammers worked on, the coal pits produced at full capacity, as did iron workings twelve miles away. A steam engine raised the coal, and another worked the great cylindrical piston-bellows. Finally there was the first French railway, another signpost to the future, which linked the coalmine to the furnaces and interlinked the workshops. By 1 January 1787 Le Creusot had absorbed seven million livres, and its success was complete.

Despite this exemplary departure, the upheavals of the end of the century cut short the rise of the French iron industry. Le Creusot was not copied, and stagnated until in 1836 the Schneiders gave it a new lease of life.

Yet what a wonderful technical achievement it was! And what an enormous industrial concentration: Wendel's Le Creusot company monopolised nearly all large-scale metallurgy – the mines at Blangy, Chalency, La Pâture, and Antully, the forge at Mévrain, foundries at

Indret, Ruelle and Forgeneuve. What was more, Wendel also had important interests in plants at Hayange, Charleville and Tulle. Le Creusot, in fact, was the finest enterprise on the continent, and England herself did not have one as huge.

And so two great holders of royal financial offices and an artillery captain, assisted by a British technician and a naval architect, had created the most modern of European industries. Financing had been put together in a less old-fashioned way than the main sorts of people involved might lead us to believe. The great treasurers, Sérilly and Saint-James, royal accountants, were also and above all great cartel-builders; their credit was enormous and they were able to function like modern merchant banks. Advised by Calonne, the only minister of Louis XVI with an economic plan, the king himself was one of those preparing France for an industrial future. And yet the way matters were financed placed all the weight of the venture on very few shoulders, there was little flexibility, and in the long run this was potentially dangerous. That became clear when Sérilly and Saint-James went bankrupt. But they had foreseen the risks. Accordingly, they suggested a transformation of the company by opening it directly to the public with the creation of bearer-shares. The new company was set up on 1 January 1787. But this solution, which would have given Le Creusot a financial structure to put it out of danger, came too late, at a time when other preoccupations were about to relegate the great, momentary dream of modernising the kingdom industrially to the realm of side issues and trifles.[52]

And yet modern heavy industry had been born. Did that mean that the industrial revolution which had succeeded so well in Great Britain had been naturalised? It would certainly be a long time before it would spread in France. More Creusots would have been needed. The revolutionary storm would bring other concerns.

From small scale manufacturing on family estates to large industrial complexes, from small commercial partnerships to great trading companies, nobles were incontestably involved at every level. There were signs of them embracing the new capitalism of the late eighteenth century everywhere. In agriculture, the lord's own domain became more important as production became commercialised. 'Seigneurial' manufacturing establishments were set up by many nobles on their ancestral estates. But it was above all in the pioneering sectors – the mechanisation of the cotton industry and the revolutionary modernisation of metallurgy – that the innovating role of noble capitalism was most vigorously in evidence. The nobility gave proof of ability to throw itself into innovation, to join the ranks of modern capitalism, to throw off the weight of tradition, and to play a part in breaking out of 'feudal' forms of production. Of course, it would be going too far to attribute such dynamic behaviour to the whole order. Is that so surprising? On the one hand we have to remember there were unrepentant conservatives, for whom the unchanging order of things was fixed forever and who, here as elsewhere, opposed everything new in the name of traditions which were usually imaginary but which seemed to assure them of a return to an idyllic past. Men of this sort could be found everywhere, whether among the Court nobility or among petty provincial gentry, among rich and poor, and doubtless among the middle class as much as the nobility. And what about petty squires in comfortable or sometimes obviously impoverished circumstances? Their absence cannot be put down to ideological considerations. What are we to think when we find them naïvely calling in their *cahiers* for the right to pursue large-scale trade which had so long been legally open to them? It is lack of capital that explains why they remained outside a movement which absorbed their more favoured compeers. As we have seen from our less than exhaustive survey, the latter were numerous and varied in background: old nobles, new ones, financial nobles or nobles of merit, but always rich nobles. Whether their nobility was chivalric as with La Rochefoucauld, or recent as with Wendel, they had shown their ability to lead the great attempt to industrialise France, after England certainly, but still at the right moment. In this way they vindicated, in a field of particular significance, their pre-eminence and the ambition they would shortly display of sharing in the kingdom's regeneration. Then, too, they would meet resistance in some quarters and hostility in others. The important thing was that a progressive force, capable of breaking out of decaying structural constraints, had emerged within the nobility; and that, having helped to unleash productive forces, it took its place, and sometimes the lead, among those who were preparing to rejuvenate the realm and give society a new, freer and juster face.

Most important of all, however, was not the fact that in updating its image the nobility played a part in the kingdom's economic activity, even if this part was a stimulating one. The results of noble initiative went far beyond that. Society itself was turned upside down. In place of the old hierarchy in which orders were distinguished one from another by not intermingling and by different functions, where everybody kept to his station and pursued the specific activities of his order, the determined nonconformity of part of the nobility substituted inter-communication, amalgamation and fusion through parallel activities, pursued in close collaboration between orders hitherto cut off from one another. In trading and industrial companies nobles of old stock rubbed shoulders with rich upstarts just up from the third estate, mostly financial office-holders, the most dynamic representatives of the upper middle class, great bankers and commoner merchants. The world of business emerged as best fitted to break the constraints of a socio-political structure ill-suited to the development of a modern economy, capital accumulation and the rise of large-scale industry. It was in this world that the elites were first seen merging in a way that, after the destruction of the orders, would lead to the formation of a class of great notables where the best qualified members of the former orders would henceforth rub shoulders within a ruling class essentially recruited from the business world, on equal terms hardly affected by the uncertain weight of dignities, and paying little heed to social distance. Thus, in the last decades of the old order, thanks to the greater nobility's lack of prejudice, there came together a composite class which dominated financial and economic activity in the kingdom. There is no need to emphasise the corrosive effect, and the dangers to traditional society, posed by this blending of elites in activities which constituted the most powerful influence tending to splinter a system based on distinctions between orders, and the separation of professions and sources of livelihood. From now on nobility was no longer exclusively tied to landed income and the royal treasury. Nobles drew part of their profits from the same sources as merchants; they shared their interests, dipping into the same pot. This was the most profound social revolution that France was to know before the late arrival of democracy in the nineteenth century.

Economic activities contributed to the breakup of traditional society. The absorption of financiers into the nobility accelerated the trend. By involving themselves in third estate ventures, the nobility shattered segregation at the level of attitudes and behaviour. In marrying outside the tribe, the great lords of Versailles did much to obliterate the frontier cutting them off from the elite of the third estate.

Financiers were a group common by origin, noble by recent elevation, whose wealth was based on the manipulation of public funds and on very various banking and commercial operations.[53] They belonged both to the third estate where some of their families were still stuck, and to the upper nobility with whom they increasingly intermarried and shared sinecures and positions of power. Through them the Court and the elite of the third estate came together. The upper middle class and ducal circles now formed a single society; smart, rich, but also powerful. They monopolised ministries, and the Peyrencs and the Bourgeois sat alongside the Ségurs and the Castries. Sénac de Meilhan clearly grasped at the time the importance of this composite group:

Increasing numbers of alliances between families of magistrates, financiers and those of the greater nobility forged links which bound these various classes together . . . The children of financiers raised themselves to judicial honours, and embraced the highest offices and sometimes ministries. The riches of financiers became the resource of great families grown needy, and matches proliferated between the most illustrious stock and the most opulent moneyed interests.[54]

The colonisation of the Court by financiers was the result of a marriage policy which traded millions for titles. The daughters and granddaughters of Crozat the receiver-general joined the families of Evreux, La Tour d'Auvergne, Montmorency, Broglie, Béthune, La Tour du Pin and Biron. The children of Ollivier de Sénozan, receiver of the Clergy, married Montmorencys, Lamoignons, and Talleyrands. The Pâris married into the Béthunes, the Pérusses de Cars, the Fitz-James. Michel, from Nantes, married his sisters to the marquis de Marbeuf and the duc de Lévis. Although he himself was treasurer-general of Artillery, his brother remained in trade. The daughter of the receiver-general Fillon de Villemur married the comte d'Houdetot, while Abraham Mouchard's married Claude de Beauharnais. The rise of Mme de Pompadour brought farmers-general to the top, in the persons of her husband and a first cousin, Jean-Baptiste d'Arnay. One daughter of Jean-Joseph Laborde, farmer-general and Court Banker, became comtesse de Noailles; another, the duchesse des Cars. We could go on with examples, but the point is made. The firm link established by financiers between two worlds, whose deeper unity people are too often reluctant to accept, is clear. Take the case of the Michels: a Nantes merchant becoming brother-in-law to the duc de Lévis. It says it all. The sons of these financiers no longer needed intermediate brothers-in-law to get fully into the upper nobility. They were found in leading positions in the army and in the parlements. Crozat's sons were president de Thugny and baron de Thiers, a lieutenant-general in the army, a rank reserved for Court noblemen.

Dupleix de Bacquencourt's sons were an intendant and a cavalry colonel. They were often found in charge of ministries. The marquis de Moras, Navy Minister and then Comptroller-General of the Finances, was the son of one Peyrenc, a man of dubious reputation who made a fortune from John Law's 'system'. Another comptroller-general, Tavernier de Boullongne, was the son of a farmer-general ennobled by an office of King's Secretary. Flesselles, a merchant's grandson, was the son of a government broker who owed his nobility to 'soap for scum'. Bourgeois de Boynes, minister of state, was the son of a cashier in Law's bank who had made his money like Peyrenc from speculating on the 'system'. Most frequently, the power of financiers was exercised through front-men. They pushed forward their noble relatives and often refused the most prominent positions in order to be more effective behind the scenes, as can be seen from the political role of the Pâris brothers under Louis XV,[55] or Laborde and the Marquets under Louis XVI. After the American war and the peace with England, when Joly de Fleury, a member of a parlement, was made comptroller-general, Marquet de Bourgade was made his mentor and a financial committee was set up to supervise all the ministries. On it sat Miromesnil, Keeper of the Seals, Vergennes, Foreign Minister, and Fleury, which meant Bourgade and Micault d'Harvelay, who were on excellent terms with their kinsman Calonne. In this way they had in their grasp financial supervision of all the ministries and their power behind the scenes became even greater when they were able to get Bourgade's nephew, Calonne, appointed comptroller-general.

For it was at government level that the collusion between the financial world and that of the upper nobility stood out most clearly. Here came together the parties which united them both as ambition and inclination dictated, here came the blending of two already close worlds as they took the state into their grip.

And that was the lesson of a profound change, that the Revolution was to confirm: the elite of the third estate and the elite of the nobility swept away the barriers placed between them by the orders, and brought together their strength and their ambitions in pursuit of the same goal: a monopoly of power.

6

Rites and strategies: the marriage market

Baron d'Andlau decided to pay court to the future Mme de Genlis. Being a man of courtesy, and very attentive, before his visit he sent his best compliments and a little gift: his genealogy. When Monsieur de la Bedoyère married Agathe Sticoti, a showgirl, he was sued by his own family. Mlle de Comminges refused to marry the comte d'Effiat; she thought his family name of Coiffier (hairdresser) too comical. Nor would her sister consider the marquis de Porcelet; the arms of this old-established family showed three wild boars, and made people think of pigs. The marquise de l'Hospital refused the comte de Choiseul, even though he was an eldest son. Of course, she had a sound reason: the count's arms were on a blue field like her own, and red would have gone with them so much better! Maréchal de Richelieu was worried that some might question the length of his ancestry, and so married Mlle de Guise. What he loved were her crosses of Lorraine and her golden eaglets.

Concern for armorial bearings, the search for ennobling wombs, astonishing misalliances. But beyond the anecdotes we can see the outlines of marriage policies. Not all were so eccentric. In the last analysis, those were the exceptions. In a society organised into clans, marriage was as much a matter for families as for the two individuals themselves. Matches were arranged like alliances between two kingdoms. Compatibility and love were secondary to social and economic imperatives. Two people joined their names, their dignities, their credit and their fortunes. Everything counted in these matches, from the handsomeness of their coats of arms all the way to their position in the world, but inclinations and feelings were not entirely left out. They were, indeed, considerations which were tending to become, if not more important than the rest, at least more and more of a priority from the time when, with the growth of individualism, happiness in married life began to count more than anything else. But this happiness was not entirely, and not even essentially, tied to love. The ideal was a golden mean between a sensible marriage and a pleasant one.

Aspirants to a girl's hand set great store by her possessions and her expectations, by her relatives' position in the world, by the past but also the future of her family. Lucy Dillon was niece to the archbishop of Narbonne, one of the richest prelates in France. She had great expectations from him, and was also taken to be the heir to her grandmother.

All those who sought to marry me were much taken with these fine prospects. They knew, in marrying me, that I was destined for the post of Lady in Waiting to the Queen. In those days this had great weight when fashionable matches were being contemplated. To 'be at Court' had all the sound of a magic formula. My mother had been there because the queen had taken a liking to her, and because she was the granddaughter of an English peer and daughter-in-law of another. Lastly because my father, a distinguished soldier, was one of that very small number likely to become Marshals of France.[1]

Wealth taken for granted, famous forebears, a father destined for a brilliant career, and a position at Court: all this made Lucy Dillon one of the most eligible propositions in the kingdom. There were plenty of suitors. But the young lady in question had a mind of her own, and was quite capable of turning down those whom she did not take to or thought inappropriate. Thus the vicomte de Fleury failed 'for lack of wit or distinction', and anyway his was the junior branch of a family of no great renown; as to Espérance de l'Aigle 'I did not find his name sufficiently illustrious.' The next candidate, Frédéric de La Tour du Pin, was son to a former governor of Provence who was now a marshal. He was a cousin of the archbishop of Auch, had the interest of the princesse de Hénin, and was favoured by the queen. A veritable cabal was formed to win the approval of Mme de Rothe, Lucy's grandmother, and His Grace Archbishop Dillon her uncle. Dazzled by the advantages of this promising match, Lucy accepted at once. Then followed the solemn liturgy which preceded a marriage. The two young people had in fact never seen each other. First meetings passed according to established rules. Listen to Mme de Créquy, *née* Froulay, on her first meeting with the husband chosen for her:

—Niece, you have a suitor whom you do not know, and who has never seen you. Your grandmother has decided that you might meet each other without embarrassment in one of the visiting rooms of Penthemont Abbey. He is a young man of high birth, now head of his family, and you only need open the history of the great officers of the Crown to see what the men of the Créquy family are.

—Oh! Aunt, I know their ancestry well; it is a name that echoes like the sound of a trumpet. It is a famous family, and is, I believe, the only one in Europe to be mentioned in the capitularies of Charlemagne. They have produced cardinals and marshals, ducs de Créquy, de Lesdiguières and Champsaurs, princes de Montlaur and Poix. But how can this one not be a duke?

—Apparently because he is indifferent to the idea. After the latest creations, everyone agrees that titles no longer mean anything. Only a name can show nobility. They are the king's cousins, so, my pretty one, tomorrow morning put on your new princess dress with the flowers and be ready on the stroke of eleven. I should like you to put your hair up. We shall be paying a visit to the ladies of Penthemont, to whom I have promised to take you.

The dowager marchioness always took the view that old customs should be observed. Her first interview with my grandfather before marrying him had been through the barrier of a parlour at Bellechasse. It had worked well, and in her eyes it was essential to behave towards M. de Créquy as if I were still not out of convent school.

So there we were at Penthemont inside the monastic buildings, and we began by making courtesy visits to the abbess, her coadjutor and the prioress. The prioress was Mme. de Créquy-Lesdiguières. It had been agreed that her cousin would have her called to the parlour and that care would be taken to have us summoned there at the same time by the duchesse de Valentinois whose lodgings were opposite the abbey.

We found the marquis de Créquy there, in conversation with his cousin at the other end of the speaking barrier, and all he did was bow deeply to us. He glanced several times in our direction with a noble mien, but it was so perfectly judged that young Mlle de Preuilly could have no doubts. One glance at him was enough for me, and my decision was made.

It is true that this was a rather old-fashioned ceremonial for grandmothers still to be insisting on in the eighteenth century for the ironic satisfaction of their granddaughters. In general things were done less severely than behind the bars of the cloister; but still they were subject to strict protocol.

Once the young people had seen and liked each other; after the two families had given their consent – and that was often after long diplomatic preliminaries conducted through intermediaries, relatives and friends – came the marriage, whose celebration fell into three stages: signature of articles, signature of the contract, and church ceremony.

The official proposal could be made either by the father or by a near relation. Once it was accepted, the families would meet together in the presence of a notary for the signing of the articles, a preparatory act at which the future couple were not present. It was only after they had been read that the girl was introduced to and saw her fiancé. From now on the future husband could come freely to visit her, but it was customary for him not to sleep under the same roof. The signing of the contract, which might now take place more or less promptly, was an occasion of great solemnity.

For those most highly placed at Court there were two stages. First, at Versailles, the king, the queen, the royal family and courtiers set their signatures to the contract. The next day or several days later it was signed again by the families of the betrothed, their friends and witnesses. It was often quite a grand occasion, with best clothes, the fiancée in pink or blue - white being reserved for the church ceremony. And finally came the great day. It would have been preceded by visits from kinsfolk bringing presents. Lucy Dillon was pampered. M. de Gouvernet gave her a basketful of jewels, ribbons, feathers, gloves, laces, several hats and decorated headpieces, and gauze mantles. Princess de Hénin brought a tea table complete with a Sèvres service and a tea-pot and sugar bowl in silver-gilt. She was given a travelling trunk, a pair of earrings, a plant table complete with the rarest plants, a small bookcase, and some fine English prints in pretty frames. On the day of the wedding, which was celebrated at Montfermeil, everybody assembled in the morning room. All the guests were there - ministers, the archbishops of Paris and Toulouse, and Languedoc bishops brought along by Archbishop Dillon. In all there were 50 or 60 persons including maréchal de Ségur, the war minister, who had marked the occasion by giving young Gouvernet a month's leave. They then moved to the chapel, where Uncle Dillon performed the ceremony and delivered a very fine address. When the ceremony ended, the bride was kissed by all the women present in order of age and kinship. Before sitting down to the reception there was still one more small formality. It was the custom to give a little memento to each of the guests, and very expensive they could be: sword-knots for the men, hat-bands for the prelates, and fans for the ladies. They could then all move to the dining room. The bride remained in her dress of white crepe finely embellished with Brussels lace and trim, but had changed her veil for a little tocque of white feathers in which she pinned her bouquet of orange-blossom. The meal began at four. Afterwards Lucy made a round of the tables set up in the courtyard for the staff and peasants who cheerily drank her health. A pretty concert brought the day to a close. Even so, the young wife had one last formality to perform; she had to be presented at Court during the days following the wedding.

Learning when to curtsey, and fitting her dress, took several days. Only then, having been presented, could Lucy Dillon, now officially Mme de Gouvernet, really begin her married life.

This almost changeless ceremonial was observed by nearly everybody. The whole Court nobility underwent it, and apart from the presentation, it was the normal procedure everywhere. Preparation for a marriage was an important business for everyone; for peasants, for the middle classes, but even more for nobles. This resulted partly from their status, and the importance of lineage in their idea of the family, but just as much too from the interests which a marriage brought into play. Once again, a wedding was less a matter of individuals than one of clans. It brought together the goods, the influence and the power of two lines. Most often it was intended as a basic element in a long term strategy of consolidation and social ascent. Matrimonial policies met differing needs, and strategies were followed accordingly. First there was what we might call the strategy of equivalence. The families being linked brought in the same capital in terms of age, worth, positions and goods. This gave the young couple the benefit of dual support and the allied families leaned upon one another, each bringing the other the same prestige potential. An example of this type of match was the marriage between the prince d'Elbeuf and Mlle de Montmorency. The two sides balanced each other in honour, in position, and in wealth. The prince d'Elbeuf was the son of Louis-Charles de Lorraine, comte de Brionne, peer and Grand Equerry of France. On his side stood Cardinal de Rohan his great-uncle, prince de Rohan and prince de Rohan-Rochefort, his uncles, the princesse de Ligne and the prince de Maison his cousins. His betrothed brought him a no less brilliant kin: besides the glorious *gens* of Montmorency, the Guines, the Broglies, the Boufflers, the Robecqs. And equality of material goods matched equality of offices and dignities. The prince d'Elbeuf received a capital sum of 55,000 l. and 60,000 l. annual income. Mlle de Montmorency was endowed with a trousseau worth 700,000 l., a capital sum of 50,000 florins, and a life annuity of 15,000 florins. In addition, the baron de Wassenaer made her a gift of a million *livres* payable on his death.[2]

In the judicial world, the Lamoignon–Feydeau marriage met the same demands of parity. Marie-Gabrielle de Lamoignon, daughter of a président in the parlement and granddaughter of Keeper of the Seals Berryer, married on 8 December 1778 Charles-Henri Feydeau de Brou, master of requests and intendant of Berry. He had family links with the Mesmes, the Boullongnes, and the Saulx-Tavanes. On the Lamoignon side, there was a similar cousinhood in the world of the parlement and government: Bernard, Castanier d'Auriac, Malesherbes. In addition to his father's succession, still undivided between himself and his sisters Mmes de Maupeou and Saulx-Tavanes, Charles-Henri had his office of master of requests. His uncle de Marville presented him with the marquisate of Dampierre, worth 360,000 l., the comté de Gien valued at 140,000 l., a house in Paris worth 100,000 l., 2,000 l. a year, and rights and credits to the value of 30,000 l. Mlle de Lamoignon received 200,000 l. in advance of her succession rights, and 200,000 l. more payable on the death of her last surviving parent.[3]

This very common type of marriage, therefore, reflected a concern to match dignities, offices and goods, and not to go beyond the relatively narrow sphere in which families reinforced similar features by linking up. Carefully chosen, such marriages promoted stability, or better still social immobility.

Some families chose a dynamic strategy, to compensate by upward movement for initial handicaps. Take the case of the maréchal de Richelieu. Despite the glory of his name, his own qualities and the great positions he held, he could not hide the fact that he was only a Vignerot, a descendant certainly of the great Cardinal, but only on the female side. This was why he wanted to add nobility to his arms by marrying a Guise. But this marvellous alliance was still not enough, and the utmost care was needed when it came to establishing their children. His daughter wished to marry the comte de Gisors, son of the maréchal de Belleisle, and the handsomest and bravest gentleman of his time. 'Thank you so much', said the maréchal, 'but I have no desire to give my daughter to the grandson of Superintendent Fouquet. I do not say that I am a member of the house of Auvergne or Créquy! But we are too besotted with the niceties of nobility to make matches with robe people.' And so Septimanie de Richelieu had to marry the greatest lord in the Netherlands, Casimir d'Egmont-Pignatelli.[4]

But what a mistake to think that robe and sword made up two separate orders! Marriages show this very well. The two bodies were so tightly bound together that nothing, except an old reflex which was completely out of date by the eighteenth century, suggested that robe and sword were two distinct worlds. One contract will be enough to show the extreme confusion that had come about between two completely intermingled nobilities.[5] Charles, duc de Clermont-Tonnerre, from an illustrious family whose nobility was among the soundest in the kingdom, married on 4 June 1741 Marie-Anne Le Tonnelier de Breteuil, from a most honourable family, but a robe one. She was the daughter of François-Victor, minister and Secretary of State for War. Among her kinsfolk were the d'Argensons, one of the oldest robe families in the kingdom, the Lefèvres de Caumartin and d'Ormesson, and Machault d'Arnouville, all enjoying the highest judicial positions. The duc de Clermont-Tonnerre counted among his kinsfolk Potier de Novions, Montmorencies, Courtivrons, Béthunes. Even better: Potier de Novion, from the same family as the ducs de Gesvres, was a simple counsellor at the parlement, and Nicolay, prime president of the chamber of accounts, was nephew to a marshal of France. So the upper robe were on good terms with the leading barons of France. At the highest level, there was only one nobility. But after all, are we not dealing with one world? If their origins differed, their age was often great in both cases, and fame through the robe was the equal of that gained by the sword. The anomaly, according to first principles, came with the integration of holders of 'soap for scum'.

In the eighteenth century there appeared a new and brasher type of alliance between plutocratic newcomers and the upper nobility. To be sure, even here it was a matter of marriage between nobles. But if the status of the couple was indeed equal, their weight was not. It was complementary. It was the alliance of two qualities – lineage on the one hand, wealth on the other. It was characteristic of this type of marriage that it did not necessarily depend on economic imperatives. To be sure, it was still common, as in the days of Mme de Sévigné, for old stock to 'manure its lands'. The attitude of the marquis de Créquy clearly shows the reluctance of certain families to make ill-matched alliances. Mlle de Froulay owed her marriage to the marquis de Créquy to the chance which had made her a rich heiress. All the Créquy lands were mortgaged to the hilt, and the marriage would not have taken place without the inheritance which suddenly came to his intended. 'M. de Créquy would have been compelled to ally with some financial family, a thing never known in his house, and which so vexed him that he could scarce but bridle at it, and not wed at all.' The Créquys belonged to that small kernel of a score of families whose origins were the most ancient in the kingdom. They had remained, as Mme de Créquy's *Memoirs* make abundantly clear, alien to the century's trends, hostile to modernity, and astonished by the changes they witnessed with bewilderment. Stock just as old – the Montmorencys, for example – behaved very differently in marriage matters.

Should we then take Mme de Sévigné's ironies too literally? Did noble families only take on daughters and sons of merchants and financiers under economic pressure? Come now! That would be to under-estimate the true position of businessmen in a society which recognised their primary importance, as well as the character of these families marked out by lifestyle, culture and refinement more as a model than as a miraculous reserve for high society, whose beacon they now were and which fell over itself to copy them. A financier's daughter with a fat dowry? A bottomless gold mine to buy out mortgages and set up magnificent quarters? Yes, of course. But also a likeable, witty wife of superior education, ready for the fashionable world and the Court. For she had been brought up for this. Even Mme de Sévigné and Saint-Simon, touchy and suspicious souls, spared no eulogies on the marriage of the maréchal de Lorges to the daughter of one Frémont, who was not yet Guardian of the Treasury but already the richest individual in France. 'Is not the maréchal de Lorges too fortunate? Dignities, great estates and a pretty wife! She has been raised as if intended one day to be a great lady.'[6]

It was a sort of predestination. The alliance of dignity and wealth was so natural that children were intended for it from their earliest years. Financiers brought up their daughters as ready-made duchesses. Such marriages, still thought of under Louis XIV as unequal, were high fashion by the eighteenth century. It was not two names, but a fortune and a name, that were being matched; that is, two equally prized and complementary qualities. For the dignity of a house was also based on wealth. A financier was not just a bag of money. The intellectuals, led by Diderot and Voltaire, had too often identified their cause with the fight against plutocracy, for him not to come out of it as something more. But a financier was also somebody who mattered in the state. The responsibilities he took on, for his greater profit, made him a servant of the king and invested him with dignity and power. His sons made their way in the law or the army. He cut a figure in town, mixed in the best society, and often kept a *salon* crowded with courtiers. Far from being a lifebelt for penniless noblemen, he was an honourable and even brilliant personage. Often his only problem was in choosing. There were hardly any great noble families who had not felt the attraction of financiers: integration between the two worlds was total, and irreversible. In the eighteenth century, only absurd provincials would talk about a misalliance when a Grimod married a Jarente daughter and the daughter of Baudard became comtesse de Puységur.

These were modern marriages which reflected well on everyone. Nobody any longer felt ashamed of these trend-setting matches which people had once tried to pass off with sharp remarks and a contemptuous attitude towards those whom show was made of wanting only for their money. Besides, did not a girl from financial circles occupy the stool of a duchess very worthily? The duchesse de Chaulnes was a Bonnier daughter, the duchesse de Choiseul was the granddaughter of Crozat, the duchesse d'Aumont the daughter of Mazade. The involvement between the smartest nobility and financiers was so deep, so inextricable, that in the end nobody any longer knew, when two families became linked, which was making the better match. Take Henriette Mazade. When on 10 September 1771 she married Louis-Alexandre d'Aumont, duc de Villequier, what did she bring to her husband? A tasty dowry of a million, agreed. But also a range of kinsfolk whose dignity yielded in nothing to his own genealogy. It was true that her father, Treasurer of the Funds of the Estates of Languedoc, was still on the threshold of nobility, having just got in through an office of King's Secretary. But who were his brothers, his brothers-in-law, and his cousins? The marquise de Foucault, the marquise de la Ferrière whose husband was a lieutenant general in the army, comte de Pons Saint-Maurice, First Gentleman to the duc d'Orléans, the vicomtesse de Rochechouart, the comtesse de Lévis, the marquis and the Marquise de Chauvelin and the farmer-general Grimod de la Reynière who himself had married Suzanne de Jarente.[7]

Most of the great financial families followed the same pattern. The Crozats were related to the whole Court (see genealogy, p. 126).

The Olliviers, merchants in Poussan at the end of the seventeenth century, in the eighteenth got into the families of Groslie-Viriville, La Tour du Pin, Vienne, Talleyrand-Périgord, Lamoignon, d'Yvetot, Vioménil. There would be no difficulty in citing dozens of others. It is hardly too much to say that without financiers, the upper nobility could not have have survived. Sénac de Meilhan was very struck by this: 'The riches of financiers became the resource of straitened families, and alliances proliferated between the most illustrious lines and opulent financiers.'

In this way marriage gave the upper nobility a grip on public funds. Already in control of the highest ranks in the army, bishoprics in the church, and Court offices, they added state finances to the sectors they already monopolised. They drew on the profits of receivers and farmers-general in the form of the dowries which regularly served the

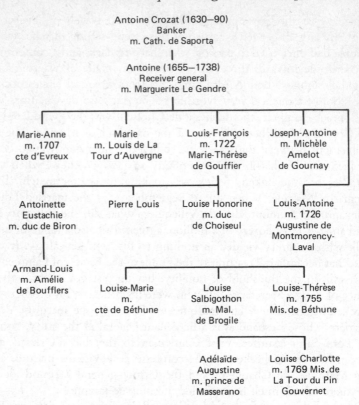

purpose of refurbishing families unable to maintain themselves without these repeated indrafts of new money. Already related to the Crozats, the Choiseuls restored themselves yet again in this way through the Pâris family. The Montmorencys, themselves related to the Crozats, also pursued dowries from the Ollivier de Sénozans and the Tavernier de Boullongnes. Their consistent policy was to swallow up financiers and add their revenues to those they enjoyed already.

Thus, what made up the higher sphere of the nobility should be understood less in terms of seniority and genealogy than in terms of power centres: Court and army, upper magistracy and higher clergy, and the royal finances. The revenues and the powers deriving from these dominant sectors of the absolutist state were, thanks to marriage alliances, entirely in the hands of a small group of families, the only ones truly bound out of self interest to the maintenance of the system.

They too would be the ones for the most part to make up that shrinking kernel which encouraged Louis XVI's desire to resist in 1789.

Attitudes were not appreciably different among the provincial nobility. The tendency towards noble endogamy was offset by the need to rebuild compromised fortunes, by the narrow range of choice and by the social importance of a middle-class elite who lorded it in the towns. Marriage between nobles, however, remained the norm which was not flouted except with extreme care. Before marrying their children into the nobility the middle classes generally took the trouble to become ennobled. D'Artaguiette bought an office of King's Secretary and only gave his daughter to Péruse d'Escars after this preliminary, which if not necessary was at least advisable to anyone who wished to make a good showing. Pierre Poivre took letters of ennoblement before Bureaux de Pusy married his daughter Julienne. In the Lyonnais, the ennobled middle class offered the best prospects, and nobles did not hesitate to make alliances with municipal officials and King's Secretaries. A typical case was that of the Mont d'Or family, descended from a crusading knight in 1166: Joseph in 1749 married the heiress to a middle-class Lyons family, Catherine Burtin, and their son in turn took Eléonore de Villars, daughter of a King's Secretary. The Norman Bailleul, a rich commoner ennobled by letters-patent, married all his daughters into the nobility. His sons-in-law were the baron de Wimpfen, the marquis de Saffray, and the comte d'Albignac. Some even had no qualms about going outside the order. The marquis de Rostaing married the daughter of a master grocer, although it is true that the latter's brother was taking his first steps into the nobility with an office of King's Secretary. In Provence, Maurice Agulhon has come across numerous examples of non-noble marriages among the Castellane-Mazaugues, or the Villeneuve-Bargemonts who had ordinary middle-class kinsfolk. The Angevin Leclerc de Juigné had also taken the plunge.[8] For the moment statistics are impossible. A high percentage doubtless still married within the nobility. But it is important that there were numerous evasions of this rule. And in fact the phenomenon only appears aberrant because our idea of old regime society is too rigid. Rich middle class and nobility were hand-in-glove in provincial towns. There was no gap between the two, and marriage reinforced their basic unity. It goes without saying that the lower one went in the scale of position and income, the more difficult marriage within the nobility became; but middle-class marriages were not accepted for all that. It is true that many commoners with genealogical luck were prepared to marry their daughters to penniless noblemen. But still, that was none too frequent, and for two complementary reasons. Petty squires were often too attached to their family trees, which were all they had; and as for urban commoners, they had higher ambitions for their children. It was in the countryside above all that the petty rural middle class and straitened gentry came together most often. Such alliances made it possible to top up inadequate incomes and sometimes saved a family from total ruin. Not always, though. Antoine Tartas de Romainville, an Angevin nobleman whose name was threatened with extinction through penury, married the daughter of a small yeoman who brought him some property; but he still could not avoid leaving his children completely without means.[9]

A serious study of the matrimonial behaviour of the nobility under the old regime would be necessary to get beyond the impressionistic picture which we have to accept today. In spite of that, for the moment we can draw some valid conclusions, at least for the higher nobility.

On the one hand, and doubtless most importantly, the nobility adopted matrimonial strategies based both on defensiveness and openness. They had built up alliances within narrow spheres in order to avoid the dispersion of offices, honours, and inheritances. But at the same time they absorbed the biggest source of profit that absolutist monarchy had created: the fiscal system, and the offices more-or-less dependent on it; banking and business in some of their official activities. The fact that they absorbed the Crozats, the Peyrencs, the Pâris, the Baudards and so many others, at one and the same time royal accountants, speculators and middle-class businessmen, at the very moment when a capitalist economy was developing alongside the taxation system, is clear evidence of their desire and need to add to their broad source of profits a dynamic sector which they had begun to invest in long before,[10] but which in the eighteenth century they came to dominate completely.

On the other hand, not being part of the social pyramid of a society of vassals since the beginnings of absolute monarchy during the sixteenth century, they were not touched by the mechanisms which underlay it, and had had to compete in the sort of society that the monarchy had organised to sap feudal power and build up its own authority. Just as they were compelled to open the second order to servants of absolutism until they blended in completely, they opened up too, with the rise of fiscal and commercial capitalism, to these new powers whose absorption both guaranteed their survival while accelerating their transformation.

This integration took place largely by way of matrimonial strategies which rounded off what the monarchy had begun. After the disappearance of a society based on vassalage, the state had created the elements of an order of clients who steadily took over from the remnants of the old nobility. Reforms and exclusions were framed to eliminate those whose uncertain loyalty could not be tightly controlled. By the creation of vast numbers of jobs it brought a mass of zealous servants into the second order, recruited from the opulent middle classes who alone could meet the financial demands of a regime that sold offices wholesale. Owing everything to the crown, and strangers by origin and recruitment to the old feudal society, they became the stoutest upholders of absolutism. In this way feudalism was undermined and the ambitions of the upper third estate satisfied.

Yet state service could not be expanded at will. As capital accumulated and culture became more democratic, the build-up of ambitions among wider groups of the population ran into the problem of numerical limits. Saturation point was reached without gratifying everybody's aspirations. Social pressure even ran up against attempts at reaction and social monopoly, attenuated fortunately by the individual loopholes made by matrimonial policies. But during the last decades of the old order the evolution of society accelerated the demand for promotion. The importance now enjoyed by money, the snobbery of intellectualism, the fashionable play of social contacts: at the moment when the juridical definition of the orders came once more under discussion, for example when the Ségur law shattered noble unity by excluding recent nobles from military privileges, all these changes therefore put in place of the society of orders a society of contacts where identities were lost amid social confusion. One way or another, nobility and middle class were moving towards amalgamation. But not all at the same rate. Whereas the nobility thought infiltration was enough, the middle classes wanted a tidal wave. Impatience on one side and reserve on the other demanded some compromise. The crown was in no position to elaborate one. So it came about against the crown. Later, the Revolution would disguise for a time the results of the alliance struck between the elites. But post-revolutionary society would reap its fruit. The notables of the Empire would be its first manifestation, with a long future ahead.

7

The nobility against the old regime

The *cahiers de doléances* – grievance lists which constitute the last will and testament of the old France – are the widest, most detailed and truest test of opinion ever made in *ancien régime* France, and we might add that we have no comparable survey for any other period in the country's history.

This picture of the French outlook is exemplary in more ways than one. It covers the whole country, from the remotest villages in the cold lands of the Auvergne and the Pyrenees, down to the fertile plains and urbanised regions. More important still, it gives us the opinion of different groups in the population; not a dubious amalgam in which undifferentiated social levels are mixed up and lose all identity, but a separate picture for each functional group under the traditional division of society into orders. Although at the level which concerns us here, that of the *bailliages*, this system has the disadvantage for the third estate of overestimating the weight of educated town dwellers as opposed to the rural population, for my purpose its advantage is clear: the nobility alone drew up their own *cahiers*. So their picture is neither warped nor filtered. It certainly did happen that the third estate and the nobility were sufficiently aware of the closeness and similarity of their demands to draw up their *cahiers* in common. In practice, this coming together would have happened more frequently if the third and the nobility had been the only ones involved. Negotiations often failed over the question of the clergy. The nobility on several occasions refused to join in with the third so as not to embarrass the clergy and give the impression that, in breaking ranks with the first order, they were joining an anti-clerical coalition. Rejection of drafting in common, both on the third and the second order's part, should not in any case be interpreted as evidence of opposition, much less hostility. The weight of tradition argued for separate *cahiers*. Most often the two orders exchanged their *cahiers*, and each borrowed what they considered relevant from the other.

There were just over 160 noble *cahiers*, Brittany having refused to draw any up as it also refused to elect deputies. They spoke for the nobility and the nobility alone. But they spoke for the whole nobility. All nobles, even the poorest, even those whose nobility was most recent, took part in the assemblies. Some *bailliages* witnessed the arrival of armigerous yokels, noblemen dressed like poor peasants, and collections had to be made to pay the costs of their stay. Those not born noble were also allowed in: any holder of an ennobling office who had spent the regulation time in it had a right to take part without discrimination. It has sometimes been thought and said that in certain *bailliages* only fief-owning nobles took part in the assemblies. In practice, they were the only ones to enjoy favourable, but purely honorific, treatment: they received an individual summons. The others were notified by public notices, and took umbrage at it. To be sure, fief-holders were over-represented. They won the privilege of sending proxies in all *bailliages* where they held fiefs. In this way large land-owners could make their voice heard in two, three, four or more assemblies. It is true that some assemblies, not wishing to boost the influence of the big landowners, refused to count proxies, but they then found their decisions quashed by the Privy Council as contraventions of the rules it had laid down.

Within the noble assemblies procedure was democratic. All decisions were taken by majority vote. It was possible for influential people to affect the discussions. But combinations were chiefly active when it came to electing deputies, when personal ambitions could readily come to the surface. For the drafting of *cahiers* commissioners were elected, generally about ten of them; they were chosen above all for their competence, and every article was subsequently discussed and approved by the whole assembly. So the *cahiers* are not the voice of a minority or an elite cut off from the body of the nobility, but rather that of the whole group. This quality accounts for many aspects of the demands, such as for example the interest shown in the poor nobility who were not excluded either from the assemblies or their decisions. By the same token, preferences expressed were not only those of the richest or most influential; all the levels which made up the nobility, with nothing in common except their membership of the second order, had their say and affected the results.

The *cahiers* which we must now analyse form much the most faithful, most reliable, and widest survey of noble opinion. We can see from them, at several levels, first how the nobility viewed old regime society, a view based on knowledge of reality but also not without illusions and wishful thinking; and then their thoughts on the organisation of government, a matter singled out for particularly lucid criticism and questioning whose radicalism was not exceeded by the bold strictures of the third estate.

The vote question

Once the doubling of the third was settled and accepted by the nobility, the third estate derived no advantage from this concession unless vote by head was allowed rather than the traditional procedure in which each order, whatever its composition and its numerical importance, enjoyed a single equal vote. This practice had obvious advantages for the nobility. First it accorded with tradition, the ancient 'constitution' of the realm, made up of three independent, hierarchically arranged orders. To give up three houses was to challenge not only this constitution, which in spite of its unwritten character was not seriously questioned – on the contrary, it was seen as the only lawful reality which successive absolute governments had drained of meaning. It was also to challenge the very structure of society as it was still fairly universally perceived by contemporaries. The house of the nobility, which liked to think it brought together all that was most remarkable in France for dignity, wealth and often talent, in this sense enjoyed a pre-eminence over the commons which seemed destined to assure it of an often decisive role in the Estates General once they met, a leadership which might seem quite proper to refuse to give up.

If the third estate had everything to gain from vote by head, the nobility risked having its wings clipped if it accepted it. By siding with the clergy or by employing its right of veto, it might outmanoevre the third estate and dominate the Estates in whatever it wanted. So it is wise to be very careful in analysing the replies which the nobility was to give to the question put to it. Their privilege might indeed seem excessive; the decision expected from them demanded a renunciation, a public-spiritedness never asked of any political power before or since, and to respond positively, which meant self-destruction, required either huge indifference, unprecedented generosity, or a sharp political awareness that could only flow from a lucid analysis of history, the social situation and the state's needs.

It was in fact a complex problem, and we must avoid reducing it to simple choices. It was not a matter of whether the privileged orders would succeed by preserving the traditional forms in stifling the voice of the third estate, or whether, under vote by head, the nobility would be absorbed, swallowed up, and prevented from making its voice heard within a now all-powerful commons. It was accepted that things would happen differently from the Estates of Blois or those of 1614. The nobility were not unaware that the third, knowing their own strength, wealth and enlightenment, would not allow themselves to be led by the nose. They were able to draw the appropriate conclusions.

The advantage won by the third in being granted representation double that of each of the privileged orders forced the latter to come clean. Either they could accept that voting should be by head, in which case the measure would take on its full significance with the deputies of the third equalling those of the two first orders in number and playing the role in the Estates-General that they were demanding and which Sieyès among others was advocating; or the privileged orders could uphold voting by order, and so show their attachment to tradition, their desire to keep the third in a minority position, and their determination to make their weight felt in the assembly's decisions, which would deprive the third of their hoped-for victory.

On the basis of the nobility's refusal, until 27 June, to join in with the commons to verify powers in common, historians of the Revolution until now, without looking closely at the matter, have depicted the nobility as systematically hostile to voting by head. Some years ago an American historian, although not part of the French revolutionary historical tradition, reached the same conclusions, working it is true not on original documents but on the notes of Beatrice Hyslop. The work of Sasha Weitmann, which concludes that the nobles were open to new ideas and that there was a close correspondence between their demands and those of the third estate, stops short at this point, even though it is the crucial one, the thermometer of noble liberalism, the true measure of their conversion to a new or renewed society, the proof of desire or unwillingness to build a Nation on modern foundations taking account of recent developments and popular aspirations. So it has been necessary to look again carefully at the *cahiers*. A quantitative analysis of this sort has the advantage of describing reality in black and white terms and of fixing its colours. Hesitations, second thoughts, and ambiguities disappear, and language is reduced to a set of pros and cons. Without therefore giving up the advantages of a quantitative analysis, it has also been necessary to give the exercise soul, to touch up the complexion of this anonymous Leviathan, in other words to personalise the quantification. The relatively small quantity of *cahiers* to look at makes this approach possible. It remains to be seen whether the novelty of the results has justified the attempt. It emerged very quickly that the simple alternatives of vote by order and vote by head were not always opted for positively one way or the other. Many *cahiers* took much more qualified positions. One *bailliage* would leave it up to its deputies to judge and choose what seemed to them the most appropriate method of voting according to their preferences, those of their order, the intentions displayed by the Estates-General, and circumstances. Others would not address the issue, showing thus their wish not to influence directly a decision which seemed to them to lie with the assembled Nation. A certain number of *cahiers*, feeling some reluctance to give up vote by order definitively, adopted a compromise solution: vote by head on all matters relating to taxation, the common interest and the constitution, and by order on everything concerning the particular interests of each order.

Only a substantial minority came out unreservedly for mandatory voting by order: 41.04%. Often this result was only reached after quite a hard struggle. At Châtillon-sur-Seine vote by order was carried by 18 votes to 13; at Blois, after a preliminary discussion, 43 votes for voting by head confronted 51 for the traditional form. Whatever the majority by which this result was carried, vote by order became absolutely mandatory for all the losers, and the deputies were to withdraw rather than accept another form of voting. Motivations, when they were mentioned, were put in disinterested terms. Villefranche de Beaujolais refused to contravene a rule that had been part of 'the constitution of the monarchy since the ordinances of 1355 and 1336 passed by the Estates-General, who alone were empowered to revoke them'. Gien ordered their deputy to vote by order so that 'one part moderates another, and the three orders form their opinions separately so that they are not carried away by any excitement, that a question may have time to be discussed by men of wisdom before being decided; intrigue in one order will then be held up by uncertainty as to another's way of thinking'. The fears entertained by some over the risk of a stormy assembly in which cunning leaders might push through ill-thought-out decisions should not be underestimated; the worries of the advocates of vote by order were not necessarily self-interested. Generally, however, it appears likely that the dominant concern was to preserve the nobility from being lost in the throng, to avoid its voice being swamped in the general drift, and to keep a say of its own, doubtless with the unspoken thought of being able to block the third estate with the help of the clergy when necessary.

A very small minority were in favour of mandatory vote by head (8.2%), but if to this percentage we add all those who, while not calling for mandatory vote by head, showed themselves amenable to it or prepared to accept it if the general wish or interest of the Nation dictated, the result is close to the former figure: 38.76%. Here class interests clearly took second place. Dôle, which did not opt for mandatory vote by head, declared that: 'Since it is for the Nation assembled in the Estates-General to pronounce on the form most advantageous to its deliberations, our deputy is left the liberty to decide whatever form the majority adopts.' They went on: 'We dare to believe that the numerical equality granted to the representatives of the third estate is a sign of the real equality in voting that ought to exist between this order and the other two combined.' Provins spoke in much the same terms: 'Let the Estates pronounce on the question of voting by head or by order according to the general good', and they advised their deputy to regard himself 'less as a nobleman than as a Frenchman, less as our particular representative than as the Nation's, and may all particular interests disappear in his eyes before the general interest'. The implication is clear: all the *bailliages* who did not dare speak out clearly expected the Estates-General to settle the question in favour of vote by head.

Finally there was a third category of *cahiers* whose stance was more ambiguous. They represent 20.14% of those examined, and they fall into two groups.

First there were those who had chosen vote by order but did not make it an inflexible principle. A *bailliage* of this sort might demand that meeting and voting by head should occur whenever there was no unanimity among the orders. This formula robbed vote by order of its obnoxiousness; it prevented the nobility from exercising a right of veto and blocking decisions it might oppose.

The second group adopted a selective formula: votes by order for certain issues, by head for others. Occasionally the common area was very limited: vote by head was reserved for anything concerning money matters and taxation. For other *bailliages* on the other hand it was very wide - taxation, matters of common interest, the constitution.

The figures again:

Requiring vote by order	41.04%
Requiring or countenancing vote by head	38.76%
Mixed voting	20.14%

In these circumstances it is no longer possible to maintain that the nobility had a firm position on voting. They were quite evenly divided between intransigents and liberals, with a moderate element whose position was often a compromise between a hard line and a progressive one.

If we take into account not the *bailliages* but deputies who were mandated, we get somewhat different results: vote by order and mixed voting diminish, and vote by head increases. Out of 245 deputies whose instructions are known (from a total of 282), 99 or 40.40% were to declare for vote by order; 27, or 11.02% for vote by head; 78 (31.83%) were instructed to accept vote by head; the instructions of 41 deputies (16.73%) called for mixed voting.

Vote by order	40.40%
Vote by head	42.85%
Mixed voting	16.73%

Because all the nobles in a *bailliage* met in its main town it is not possible to distinguish between rural and urban nobilities. The most that can be done is to distinguish between large towns, above all those with parlements, and *bailliages* with high rural populations. Out of ten seats of parlements entirely within a *bailliage*,[1] six (Paris, Rouen, Bordeaux, Dijon, Besançon, Douai) declared for vote by order; one (Aix) for mandatory vote by head, two for accepting vote by head (Metz and Toulouse), and one for mixed voting (Nancy). Can we conclude from this that the parlements were an instrument of noble reaction? It was not simply the involvement of magistrates but the decisive role played by their attachment to judicial traditions in the decisions taken. However, as the case of Aix shows, there was no unanimity in the attitudes of members of the parlements. This ambiguity is found again among those who were elected: some magistrates would sit in the assembly among the liberal nobles.

The geographical distribution of voting preferences brings out two French nobilities. One great square linking La Rochelle, Vesoul, Bourg and Tarbes marks out an area where progressive trends had made little impact; vote by order was broadly the preference there.

Cut off on the map were the south east, Dauphiné, Provence and Languedoc, where vote by head and mixed voting came out markedly ahead. North of a line from Coutances to Vesoul, vote by order was in a clear minority and preferences were divided between various shades of vote by head or mixed voting. The south west, Burgundy, Franche Comté, Normandy, Picardy and Champagne were the most traditionalist bastions of unchanging France. Dauphiné, Provence and Artois and Flanders in the north were the most consciously advanced. Around Paris, little towns like Senlis, Meaux, Provins, Melun, Dourdan, Montfort l'Amaury and Châteauneuf-en-Thimerais also made up a progressive belt around a capital more receptive to tradition.

So the deep-rooted legend that the nobility and the third estate were opposed to each other on the fundamental question of voting is no longer worth dwelling on: it shows how much history writing has been marked by ideological presuppositions. The attitudes of the nobility were very varied, and on this issue they showed themselves not to be lagging behind but on the contrary – if we take account of the consequences for the order as a decision to destroy itself – a wish for openness and the radicalisation of their desire for change. It shows how their political analysis coincided with that of the third estate, or rather that minority of the third estate which drew up the *bailliage* cahiers after cutting out popular elements and most demands that the middle classes did not put forward for themselves. There were too many links between the nobility and the elite of the third estate for a great part of the second order to cling to an isolation which might prove dangerous in the long run: to bring about the profound reforms they dreamed of, nobles needed these hardworking and purposeful commoners with aspirations so like their own, and in whom nobles might see competitors to be sure, but in no case enemies. Their criticisms of the old order were too much like those being made at the same moment by the third estate for any doubt to remain about the fundamental identity of the two orders and their solidarity against a universally derided establishment.

The old order criticised

A reading of the *cahiers* brings out evidence that would hardly be worth underlining if generations of historians had not been quite so happy to cover it up. Existing only for the greater good of the nobility, intended to gratify its desire for power, to safeguard and increase its privileges and to strengthen its dominance and inherited destiny to possess the state, the political and social order suited noble wishes, such as they were, and if nobles accepted the meeting of the Estates-General, that could not be to bring about reforms, but to consolidate their own position. This simplistic view rested on a double hypothesis: that nobles were satisfied, and that self-interest alone drove them on.

The first of these views results from a misunderstanding of the state of the nobility. Courtiers might well be satisfied with a situation that gave them all they wanted. But who were they to be confused with the nobility? Did not the latter have cause for complaint in underpaid military service, and almost total neglect? Influence? They had none. Service? Not only were they paid badly and irregularly, but even the esteem which nobles lent it was not rewarded. Higher ranks were reserved for courtiers. What about the king's favours? The nobility had never even glimpsed them. Pensions, royal bounty, prebends, all went to courtiers. Even social institutions were diverted from their purpose. Military schools set up to educate nobles of inadequate means mostly took in very different people – the rich. But surely the existing order, even if it left nobles with no governmental influence and no share of favour, at least gave them the freedom and benefit of their privileges? Indeed, nobles were at the mercy of ministerial despotism. Without mentioning the *lettres de cachet*,[2] noble status itself was not guaranteed. By the simple decision of a minister an officer might be cashiered, without discussion and without a court order. The nobility was at the mercy of unchecked authority, as defenceless and dependent as any other social group, and it would be hard to understand in these conditions how nobles could harbour or have demands different from the third estate, since like them they felt exploited and put-upon.

As to the second hypothesis, that self-interest alone drove them on, it stems more from polemics than objective analysis. In any case the issue is not well put that way. Political calculation quite as much as generosity lies behind any conversion to liberalism. Privileges as real as tax-exemption or seigneurial rights ought to have had unanimous support if the nobility was as keen to keep what it had as has been claimed. But that was not the case. And it was certainly asking a lot to expect a minority, simply under the pressure of opinion, to give up ideas of justice, the state's interests, and inherited privileges. Such a renunciation took clear-sightedness and courage, which only came as the upshot of a crisis of conscience, a genuine mental revolution. This was brought about by the thought of the Enlightenment which was widely

diffused throughout various levels of the nobility through the medium
of reading and perhaps most of all the provincial academies; through
pondering the inadequacies of the established order as a result of daily
contact with its realities; and through the shock experienced by the
'Americans', all those French officers to whom the war had revealed a
society that shone in their memory. The revelation of the American
constitutions translated by La Rochefoucauld in 1783, with their democracy, their checks and balances and their guaranteed freedoms, had
given rise to a concomitant rejection of absolutism and the abuses it
spawned. Among contemporaries of American independence a new
political ideal, a dream of a freer and more equitable society, offset
the influence of a tradition they had learned to resist together. Privileges did not weigh heavily against the ideal they brought back. They
at least were ready to give them up. But more generally, the nobility
took an independent enough line: out of concern for the state, and
because they were ready to step down, they put the interests of the
Nation before their own.

The seriousness of this awakening led the nobility to call in question
both the political and social orders. The line of historians who hold
the nobility to be the main obstacle to change is that nobles' sole concern was to retard innovation, and to preserve intact a society that
favoured them. But was that the case? The greater part of their grievances show a desire not to preserve but to change, abolish, destroy,
replace. The society and government whose merits they were supposed
to extol hardly ever found favour in their eyes. They complained across
the board of its arbitrariness, its despotism, its waste, its disorder, its
injustice. They wanted to change everything. Give men guarantees,
and the Nation its rights; put power under the control of the people's
representatives, abolish privileges that encumber the rest of the Nation.
The old order was painted in the blackest colours. Absolutism meant
ministerial despotism, financial anarchy, favouritism, a badly run kingdom; it meant men's freedoms flouted, and their money wasted.
Irresponsibility and nepotism everywhere, favour where merit should
rule. Never has a political system and a society been so dissected and
condemned.

Despotism as a system of government was condemned for its inefficiency and its immorality. How did the nobility picture the despotism they were denouncing? The king? He made very little appearance
in their grievance lists. This was because the person of the king figured
little in the nobility's analysis of the situation. The king was himself

the plaything of a system that kept him prisoner. This system was ministerial despotism: abuse of power by ministers in their departments; the irresponsibility of ministers appointed by favour, toppled by intrigue, often incompetent yet blocking the way to merit for fear that by giving it play they would raise up their own replacements and introduce competence and talent to great offices. They ruled according to their caprices, swayed by influence and the interest that had raised them, heedless of justice or continuity, undoing today what their predecessors had done yesterday, guided by arbitrariness, hampering the course of justice by *lettres de cachet* and evocation of cases from the normal courts, wily at serving their friends and finding out loop-holes. The *cahiers* named names, and denounced miscarriages of justice. Colonel de Moreton, cashiered without due process of law, became a symbol of ministerial arbitrariness. His name crops up in a dozen *cahiers* and others mention his case without naming him. The intendants were not spared either: settling cases in the secrecy of their offices, taxing at will, running their provinces heedless of the aspirations, resources or the interests of the inhabitants, they personified a ruinous centralising spirit which spread the depredations of ministerial despotism throughout the kingdom. Nor was the Court spared; it deceived the king, milked the treasury with an ever-open hand, siphoned off royal bounty, monopolised jobs, high rank in the army, and governorships.

Despotism, favouritism, intrigue, irresponsibility, waste – these were the governmental vices that the nobility sought to reform.

Looked at rather more closely the discontents become more specific, and the wish for reform more marked. Criticism of the government was methodically organised around three fundamental complaints: ministerial and bureaucratic arbitrariness, restrictions on individual liberty, and bad management of public services. And the call for change centred on new values: democratisation of government, individualism, and rationalisation of the state.

Reaction against the arbitrary power of ministers was general. Not depending on the king, they were in fact dependent on nobody but themselves, were answerable to nobody, and governed autocratically. They had to be watched, kept out of mischief, forced to explain their conduct publicly, take blame for their mistakes and be punished for their evasions and prevarications. Over 85 % of the *cahiers* called for the Nation to have the right to judge them. Under the new constitution they would be answerable before the assembled Estates-General.

Against the intendants, the living image in the provinces of ministerial despotism, the verdict was even more severe. Their administration was condemned for its abuses and its inefficiency. When not calling for their pure and simple abolition (22%), the *cahiers* wanted their authority replaced by that of provincial estates or freely elected uniform assemblies (80%) which would take over all or part of their powers. Wherever it was found arbitrary power was unequivocally condemned. 82% of the *cahiers* demanded the abolition of the commissions and evocations[3] which removed cases from ordinary justice, 69% wanted abolition of *lettres de cachet*, 44% the limitation of imprisonment without a court appearance to a maximum of 24 hours. The condemnation of bureaucratic absolutism brooked no appeal. The body of the kingdom's nobility called with all its desires for liberalisation and democratisation of the state, guaranteed and judged by permanent or periodic sittings of the Estates-General.

Condemnation of the old order's restrictions on individual liberty in all its forms was universal, and was symbolised by the call for the destruction of the Bastille and other state prisons. The nobility demanded the blanket suppression of *lettres de cachet*, and freedom to settle and move about inside and outside the kingdom. Guarantees were insisted on. Sixty per cent of the *cahiers* demanded that liberty should be declared 'inviolable and sacred' for all citizens without exception. For these nobles who are said to have been defenders of the old order and traditional values, was there any danger greater than freedom of thought and of the press? Yet almost the whole of the nobility insisted on it, regarding it as the most enviable part of individual liberty. Censorship was condemned; everyone should have the right to think and to publish whatever they wanted on their own responsibility.

The organisation and workings of public services came in for systematic criticism from the second order. They were criticised both for their abuses and their weaknesses. Financial organisation was a favourite target. First it was accused of working without control. The treasury was prey to greedy courtiers who combined together to surprise the king's good faith or dissuade him from resisting. Hence the call for the abolition of bearer drafts (*acquits de comptant*). These were orders to pay sent to the royal treasury without indication of the nature or purpose of the payment. The payee did not have to give a receipt, and the chamber of accounts could not investigate them. In these conditions no proper accounting was possible, and the king could spend part of his budget as he liked without anybody knowing how. The state's budget was also burdened by a mass of *gages*, salaries and emoluments attached to quite useless offices, jobs and places which weighed down the expenses side while benefiting nobody since no real duties were entailed in these sinecures. The nobility called for their abolition, adding at the same time that of anomalous pensions. This was no minor reform: pensions might run to some 10% of the Nation's budget, so that to cut down on them was not a modest economy. The nobility were not fooled by poor management of the fiscal system and its unsuitedness to a far-reaching exchange economy. The waste which followed from the independence of the receivers-general, the irrationality of a system with a pointless proliferation of heads of receipt and expense which discouraged all attempts to set up national accounting, were emphatically denounced. If only 10% of the *cahiers* called for the abolition of the receivers-general, over 41% demanded that the administration of direct taxes should be in the hands of provincial assemblies or estates who would pay any monies not spent locally directly into a national fund. A desire for efficiency and economy came together here with aspirations to decentralisation. As to indirect taxes, they were deemed crushing, unjust, not to say in-human, in every case contrary to the interests of the people and the economy. They came under the fiercest attack of all: tolls and stamp-duties to be abolished; the salt monopoly to be abolished or at least moderated (51.5%); internal customs duties to be abolished (64.17%). So the fiscal system of the old order was entirely rejected: the nobility's abandonment of their fiscal privileges (89%) took away the last stone in a hated edifice.

Did the judicial system find any more favour in noble eyes? The civil and criminal codes, deemed archaic, no longer suited to the progress of manners, and often inhuman, were the object of general disapproval. A total recasting was called for, under a commission of specialists convened to draft them anew. The most detailed *cahiers* set out a plan for the new legislation. They stipulated safeguards for accused persons: trial by jury, right to a counsel, reasoned verdicts, the abolition of torture and ignominious interrogation, criminal prosecution in public, restriction of the death penalty, improvement of prisons. They also went into judicial processes, calling for them to be simplified and speeded up; and they severely criticised the recruitment of judges: if 4.98% of the *cahiers* were in favour of keeping venality of office, 31.4% called for its abolition. Nearly 10% demanded that judicial office should only be achieved through open competition or election, but others called for a long probationary training: magistrates should have had several years' experience at the bar, or before going to a sovereign court they should have served in a lower one. A minority (5.22%) even called for justice to be dispensed without fees.

On the army, criticism dwelt essentially on two points: the unsuitability of its discipline to the character of the Nation and the dignity of its citizens; and the scandal of the proliferation of useless ranks designed to gratify the ambitions and greed of people well connected at Court. We shall come back to the radicalism of the protest against inequality of rewards between different classes of the nobility and the exclusion of the third estate.

The organisation of the economy came in for no less rough treatment. There were protests against checks on the freedom of trade and circulation of goods, against abuse of monopolies which damaged industry, against the misdeeds of guilds, mysteries and corporations, the diversity of weights and measures, all impediments holding back the development of free enterprise and the rise of a market economy. The nobility wanted rid of them all.

And so it was the whole political, social and economic organisation of the old order that the nobility was calling into question, no holds barred. Far from being upholders of the past, they looked much more like iconoclasts. This innovating attitude was the result of a coming together of variables which all pushed in the same direction. The Enlightenment and the exchanges born of its diffusion, the American example and that of England, increasing discussion of power questions in clubs and academies, at least from the time of the Entresol, and the rise of individualism linked to the recognition of merit, all these pointed the same way. The nobility no longer reacted to problems with the reflexes of an entrenched, inward looking, aloof group, but in the same way as all elites affected by the movement of the Enlightenment. The gap between the nobility and the elite of the third estate had been very largely bridged. Everywhere, in societies, salons, academies, masonic lodges, nobles and middle classes had embarked on a common approach and had elaborated the model of the new society that the desires of both were now calling for. They knew that it would not come into being in a fratricidal struggle, but would be their common achievement. They had common interests, common ideals, and they knew it. A great part of the nobility sought like the middle class to shatter the oppressive framework of the bureaucratic state. On this point the nobility was some way ahead. Ever since they had tried to break Louis XIV's absolutism they had clung on, despite the defeat of *polysynodie*, to their nostalgia for a society freed from tyrannical oppression. Nobles and middle classes knew that they would only break the chain by putting in place of the society of orders and privileges, or of conflicting interests which the state used to build up its authority by playing one off against another, a society of individuals with the same rights and the same duties, subordinate to the common interest.

8

A plan for society

All that experience and human intelligence had thought up, discovered and elaborated over three centuries may be found in the *cahiers*. The various abuses of the old monarchy are there set out, and remedies proposed; all forms of freedom are called for, even press freedom; improvements of all sorts requested for industry, manufactures, trade, roads, the army, taxation, state finances, schools, physical education, etc.[1]

Even today we cannot fail to get this impression that the *cahiers* at one and the same time pushed back and fixed the limits of political liberation, when the most tolerant regimes are still far from bringing about all the aspirations that 1789 let loose. Complete freedom of the press and *habeas corpus* are still, two centuries after the meeting of the Estates-General, unmet demands. It is, then, well worthwhile to dwell for a moment on these *cahiers* which set out, for France and further afield, until now and perhaps still for tomorrow, a social ideal based on the dignity of mankind and respect for the individual, a society in which the state would not be some monstrous and intolerant Leviathan grinding down the citizen the better to enslave him in the name of a dubious efficiency, but a harmonious compromise between necessary authority and reasonable freedoms. How could we not reflect a moment on this plan for society which met some resistance almost everywhere even before its promise came to fulfilment? Were men unsuited to tolerance and freedom? Would France only be the land of the free because she had been better able than others to dream of it? In 1789, at least, Alice – I mean France – went through the looking glass. The dream became a reality.

A word about procedures: they are not without value in understanding the great events impending. And to be sure, events there would be – glorious, bloody, immortal. But the greatest of all was surely this faceless celebration, even before the Estates-General met, when the whole of France saw the chance to change its destiny, met together in enthusiasm and excitement, to suggest a fraternal society and throw down to future generations a challenge which they have not yet entirely taken up.

A faceless coming together it may have been, but everyone joined it with great spirit and fervour. The general regulation of 24 January 1789 and the particular regulations of March and April laid down the ground rules for the meetings of the *bailliage* assemblies which would draw up grievance lists and elect deputies to the Estates-General. For nobles, the form of summons did not respect equality. Some were summoned individually by *bailliage* lieutenants – fief holders; others were informed by public posting of letters of summons. The rich got priority. They held fiefs in several *bailliages* at once; they had the right to be represented in each by proxies, as did wives in joint possession and minors who were heirs to fiefs. Though unequal, therefore, suffrage was almost universal for the nobility. Paris enjoyed special regulations. Every noble who could prove residence in the capital was allowed into his district assembly. Paris was divided into 20 departments, so it had 20 primary assemblies which had to elect representatives in the ratio of one to ten. But the assemblies thought this reduction too severe, and they elected one representative for every five nobles. There were in all 208 for 1,000 electors. In Lorraine-Barrois the map of the *bailliages* was so dense that to grant a deputy to every one of them would have produced an imbalance in the national representation. So here a special regulation was needed which grouped them, and deputies were chosen by a process of re-election. The same procedure was applied to Provence.[2]

Despite the enthusiasm aroused by the meetings, there is no doubt that some did not turn up. But not in any great numbers. If we compare the number of nobles, as we have calculated them, with the numbers present at the assemblies, we note that they largely tally. Besides, there was something else. The king's orders were explicit, and absence could be noted against those not obeying; failure to appear on the electoral lists might later be interpreted as proof of lack of nobility. In any case the interest of being able to take part could not have left the vast majority of the nobility indifferent. Nevertheless some noblemen spurned their order and preferred to go to the third estate assemblies. On the other hand some individuals of uncertain standing were able to slip into the ranks of the nobility. Foreign lords with holdings in France were also allowed into the assemblies, sometimes not without fierce resistance. For instance at Gex it took a clear order from the king to get the Protestant nobility of Geneva admitted to the assembly. In this way the whole nobility, petty or great, rich or poor, old or recent, took part in drawing up the *cahiers*. Despite everything, a certain imbalance emerged in favour of wealth. Was it not, in the absolutist state, the great rising quality?

The makeup of the assemblies varied according to each *bailliage*, and their nobilities had features which differed everywhere. How many individual biographies or *bailliage* prosopographies could we not use to throw the fullest light on the diversity of the French nobility? The myth that it was a unitary body has been cut from Harlequin's cloak. We do not have enough information. Occasional pointers nevertheless allow us, for lack of anything better, to draw up professional profiles. At Nîmes, out of 162 electors, 71 gave no profession: from the rich landowner with country houses, fiefs, high and low justice, to the petty gentleman on his tiny patch, this category of 'unemployed' (*oisif* – which included some who did cultivate the land, even if somebody else's), covers much vagueness. Of the rest, 87 were soldiers, 4 were magistrates. At Nancy, seat of a sovereign court, out of 209 participants, 42 were magistrates, 25 soldiers, 5 advocates, 5 teachers, 1 financier. In Paris outside the walls, there was extreme diversity: from a total of 323 electors, soldiers came first at 108, magistrates 48. Then come councillors of state, masters of requests, financiers, king's secretaries, aldermen, a financial administrator, a surgeon, a member of the Academy of Sciences and a mathematician.

Some 130 surviving *cahiers*, setting out noble grievances with often prolix rhetoric: several thousand pages presenting delicate problems in reading and exploitation. A quantitative approach was essential. Was a computer necessary? In the end it was possible to quantify by hand. A debatable decision, yet one which had a considerable advantage in putting information together: there was no reduction to a prefabricated framework and so it was possible not to overlook any shades of meaning, reservations, or uncertainties. Did that make up for insurmountable weaknesses in handling the material? No doubt. Handling the cards on which each grievance was recorded proved difficult. At first sight it seemed essential to record everything, without exception, distinction or degree of importance. Local grievances could be quite as important as national ones. In particular, recording everything allowed me to trace a differential geography of levels of awareness, to pick out the *bailliages* able to rise to abstract concepts, to go beyond local demands to national aspirations. Two categories were eliminated: strictly local grievances which never appear in more than one or two *cahiers*. One *bailliage*, for example, might call for the strengthening of proofs of nobility for admission to the convent for young noble ladies in their town; no other grievance voiced a similar wish on the national scale. On the other hand, when a *bailliage* requested the establishment of a second convent reserved for noble daughters, I took account of this demand because it fits in with the very general desire to increase outlets for the nobility. For one category of grievances matters could be compressed. Supposing a *bailliage* called for the suppression of the *aides* (excise taxes) and then demanded in a whole series of complaints the abolition of each one of these taxes by name, I only counted this as a single grievance. The advantages of the policy are obvious. First the total number of grievances is brought down to 5,000, which makes them easier to handle. Above all, it avoids inflating certain groups of grievances disproportionately, and putting too much weight on categories in which the *cahiers* were only too willing to hold forth at length (taxation), to the detriment of other series where whole strings of points were less easy to put together (government). To leave out strictly local grievances was certainly a regrettable loss. But for my purpose it matters little.[3]

The *cahiers* of 1789 presented the nobility, like the other orders of the realm, with an occasion for freely denouncing the abuses of the old order. But their originality, in comparison for example with those of 1614, lay in going far beyond criticism. They called for reforms, but above all, they went on naturally from denouncing flaws to thinking politically, and elaborated and put forward a veritable plan for society. It was a new state and a new society that was outlined and built up, sometimes very strikingly, throughout the long litany of their demands.

Sorting grievances into great thematic masses clearly shows the politicisation of the nobility and its desire, new and paradoxical in the context of the society of the absolutist state, to see set up an individualist and liberal society. The three newest themes – demand for power, individual freedom and equality between citizens – alone make up 50% of the items. It was essential to rearrange them. Without misrepresenting the dense wordiness of the documentation, the grievances can be broken down under six general rubrics.

Under the first rubric, more than half the grievances, 67 out of 133, called for a constitution or charter of the Nation's rights. 50% of the *cahiers* asked for one to be drawn up, and for it to become the law of the land. The demand for a constitutional monarchy was just as marked

	Grievances	%
Rights of the Nation and the King	133	2.68
Individual rights	907	18.31
Privileged orders:		
nobility	527	10.64
clergy	298	6.01
Equality between third and nobility	327	6.60
Political demands	1,298	26.20
Institutional	1,463	29.53

in the other *bailliages*, even though not so clearly put. Despite a few stereotyped forms of words expressing gratitude to Louis XVI as 'restorer of liberties', the king had a negligible place in noble preoccupations: in all they only devoted 0.6% of their grievances to him personally. Four *cahiers* called for formal recognition of his inviolability, and 28 (or less than 21%) were for vesting full executive power in him. This imbalance between the Nation and the king was made even more obvious by the demand for guarantees for the freedom of the citizen.

This in fact was a major demand: individual liberty. 907 grievances, 18.31% of the whole. The nobility were more interested in precise guarantees than statements of principle. Only three *cahiers* called for a declaration of rights. But 81, or 60.44% demanded recognition of individual liberty. Guarantees against governmental arbitrariness focussed on exceptional courts, evocation of cases to the Privy Council, extraordinary judicial commissions, and special tribunals, all of which the *cahiers* very widely wanted abolished, and *lettres de cachet*, imprisonment without due process and release on bail. The nobility were unanimous (88.05%) in calling for recognition of freedom of thought and of the press.

Grievances concerning the interests of the second order reached a high number, 10.64%. But they did not all spring from self-interest. Some called for the ending of favours enjoyed by certain privileged categories such as the Court nobility, while others wanted the nobility to be opened to talent or merit. Six per cent of grievances concerned the clergy: but only 2.05% showed a desire to keep it as an order; the rest, on the contrary, were against it.

Recognition of equality between the third estate and the nobility was demanded in 6.60% of grievances on varying but important points from equality of taxation to equal access to public office.

Political demands made up the most important heading: 26.20%. They put forward three basic demands: legislative power, control over the executive, and decentralisation.

Under the heading 'Institutions' I have brought together the other grievances relating to all the great public services. First comes justice (8.68%) then finances and taxation (8.29%), trade, industry and agriculture (5.37%), the army (3.53%) health and public education (2.54%).

The tabulations show first the total number of grievances for each type of demand, in the second column the percentage of *cahiers* where a given grievance is put forward, and finally the percentage of the 4953 grievances contained in the 134 *cahiers* under analysis (about 30 have not been recovered).

	Grievances	%	%
I. RIGHTS OF THE NATION AND THE KING			
Constitution or Charter of the Nation's Rights	67	49.99	
King to be sacred and inviolable	4	2.98	
King to be sole executive	28	20.89	
Salic law to be kept	22	16.41	
Catholicism to be dominant religion	12	8.95	
Total	133		2·68
II. INDIVIDUAL RIGHTS			
Declaration of rights	3	2.23	
Individual freedom to be inviolable and sacred	81	60.44	
None to be tried except by natural judges	92	68.65	
No imprisonment without court appearance for more than 24 hours	59	44.02	
Abolition of evocations and extraordinary commissions	110	82.08	
Abolition of exceptional courts	61	45.52	
Abolition of Waters and Forests courts only	14	10.44	
Abolition of *lettres de cachet*	92	68.65	
Release on bail (except for major criminal cases)	24	17.9	
Abolition of prerogative courts (*tribunaux d'attribution*) (Royal councils, court of requests, provost's courts, special courts)	6	4.47	
Bastille and other state prisons to be destroyed	15	11.19	
No interference with private mails	67	50	
Freedom of settlement and movement	8	5.97	
Freedom of thought and the press	118	88.05	

	Grievances	%	%
Abolition of all personal servitude	7	5.22	
Deputies to be inviolable	40	29.85	
Rights for minorities	29	21.64	
Army not to threaten citizens' freedom	6	4.47	
Property to be inviolable	64	47.76	
Due process for comte de Moreton	11	8.20	
Total	907		18.31

III. PRIVILEGED ORDERS

I. NOBILITY

(a) Grievances aimed at preserving noble rights

	Grievances	%	%
Honorific prerogatives to be preserved	53	39.55	
Non-nobles not to carry arms	26	19.40	
Usurpations of nobility to be traced	9	6.71	
A heralds' court to verify nobility	11	8.20	
Ordinance of 1781 on entry to regiments to be confirmed	4	2.98	
Ordinance of 1781 to be revoked, possession of transmissible nobility to suffice for entry	21	15.67	
Seignorial courts to be retained and improved	23	17.16	
Only one order of nobility to be recognised	12	8.95	
Saint-Cyr and the Military School to be reserved for poor nobility	15	11.19	
Seignurial rights to be retained	24	17.16	
Separate noble tax-rolls to preserve distinctions	5	3.73	
Protest against doubling third estate	3	2.23	
No equality of taxation	3	2.23	
Exemption for lands cultivated by own hands (*vol du chapon*) to be retained	4	2.98	
Financial sacrifices to be accepted only for the moment	3	2.23	
Noble monopoly of commissioned ranks to be retained	9	6.71	
Nobles to have preference	2	1.49	
Vote by order	55	41.04	
Total	282		5.69

(b) Corporative demands

	Grievances	%	%
Nobles to be allowed to engage in trade and other non-servile professions	32	23.88	
Criminal record not to affect families	12	8.95	
Abolition of heredity in office	30	22.38	
Favours and upper ranks not to be reserved for courtiers	5	3.75	

	Grievances	%	%
Venal nobility to be abolished; nobility to be the reward for service	60	44.77	
Useless ennobling offices to be abolished	12	8.95	
Noble chapters to be established	13	9.70	
Visible distinctions for nobles	3	2.23	
Thought to be given to circumstances of poor nobility	16	11.94	
Protection for poor nobility or compensation for sacrifices it makes	11	8.20	
Total	194		3.91

(c) *Liberal demands*

Virtue, courage and professional merit to be ennobled	32	23.88	
Officers of *bailliage* and *présidial* courts to be ennobled in 2nd or 3rd generation	3	2.23	
Seigneurial rights to be abolished or bought out	11	8.20	
Labour service, or dues in kind, or common obligations (*banalités*) to be bought out	7	5.22	
Privileged access to appeal courts (*committimus*) to be abolished	53	39.55	
Total	106		2.14
General Total	527		10.64

2. CLERGY

(a) *Hostile demands*

Clergy to pay off its debt	5	3.73	
Income of prelates to be reduced	4	2.98	
Pluralism to be forbidden	39	29.10	
Vestry fees to be abolished	14	10.44	
Concordat to be renounced	7	5.22	
Bishops and incumbents to reside	53	39.55	
Commendatory abbacies to be reduced or abolished	7	5.22	
Monasteries to be reduced or reformed	4	2.98	
Mendicant and useless or non-teaching orders to be abolished	17	12.68	
Vows under 25 to be abolished	11	8.20	
Order of the clergy to be abolished	4	2.98	
Diversion of revenues during vacancy (*économats*) to be abolished	4	2.98	
Tithe	20	14.92	
All religious festivals to be on Sunday	7	5.22	
Total	196		3.95

	Grievances	%	%
(b) *Demands favouring the Clergy*			
Benefices and stalls to be set aside for retired parish priests and curates	6	4.47	
Circumstances of parish priests and curates to be improved	17	12.68	
Stipends payable to vicars from impropriated tithes (*portions congrues*) to be increased	34	25.31	
Investigate retirement for priests	3	2.23	
Debts incurred by the clergy on the state's behalf to be absorbed into the debts of the nation	4	2.98	
Debts payable to the Court of Rome to be abolished, and bishops to be allowed to grant dispensations	38	28.35	
Total	102		2.05
General Total	298		6.00

IV. DEMANDS FOR EQUALITY BETWEEN THIRD ESTATE AND NOBILITY

	Grievances	%	%
Equality of access to all public offices	6	4.47	
Repeal of the law closing entry into military posts to the third estate	4	2.98	
Officers risen from the ranks to be allowed to reach all ranks and distinctions	6	4.47	
Formalities humiliating for the third estate to be abolished	7	5.22	
Penalties to be the same for all orders	12	8.95	
Relief (*franc-fief*) to be abolished	23	17.16	
Equal liability to taxation	116	88.54	
Specific demand for all to be subject to the same taxes in the same form and with the same name	21	15.67	
Privileged access to appeal courts (*committimus*) to be abolished	53	39.55	
Vote by head plus mixed voting	79	58.90	
Total	327		6.60

V. POLITICAL DEMANDS

I. NATIONAL LEVEL

	Grievances	%	%
Legislative power	94	70.14	
Estates-General (permanent or periodic)	134	100	
Consent to taxation	121	90.29	
Ministers to be answerable	114	85.07	
Control of executive: Accounts to be submitted	67	50.00	

	Grievances	%	%
Taxes to be abolished and recreated until provision made for their replacement	23	17.16	
Annual publication of expenses	65	48.50	
Expenditure of each department to be fixed	80	59.70	
No taxes to be granted before the adoption of constitutional laws	52	38.80	
Taxes to be granted only until next session of Estates-General	91	67.91	
Legitimate debt to be consolidated	87	64.92	
Improper pensions to be abolished and an annual list to be published	90	67.16	
Total	1040		20.99

2. LOCAL LEVEL

	Grievances	%	%
Provincial estates to be set up everywhere	109	81.34	
Intendants to be abolished	47	35.07	
Provincial estates to be empowered to levy and assess taxes	55	41.04	
Parlements (to be the Nation's guarantors for the enforcement of laws, 40; to verify superintending and administrative laws, 7)	47	35.07	
Total	258		5.20
General Total	1298		26.20

VI. INSTITUTIONS

1. JUSTICE

	Grievances	%
Offices: to remain venal	4	2.98
venality to be abolished	42	31.34
Civil and criminal codes to be reformed	105	78.35
Trial by jury	6	4.47
Defending counsel to be created	32	23.88
Simpler and swifter procedures	28	20.89
All useless levels of jurisdiction to be abolished	7	5.22
Justice to be free	7	5.22
Fees to judges (*épices*) to be abolished	6	4.47
Magistrates to be irremovable	38	28.35
Courts to give reasons for verdicts	9	6.71
Torture and convicts' interrogation-stool (*sellette*) to be abolished	12	8.95
Confiscation of goods as a penalty to be abolished	6	4.47
Courts to be brought closer to those under them	23	17.16
More parlements to be set up	18	13.43
Legal costs to be cut	21	15.67

	Grievances	%	%
Criminal prosecution to be in public	13	9.70	
Restriction of death penalty	13	9.70	
Justices of the peace to be set up	4	2.98	
Magistrates to have previous experience at the bar	12	8.95	
Judicial office to be elective or open to competition	13	9.70	
Prisons to be improved	8	5.97	
Law to be less severe for unmarried mothers	3	2.23	
Total	430		8.68

2. ARMY

	Grievances	%	%
Military life to be given fixed laws	42	31.34	
Soldier's position to be improved or pay raised	11	8.20	
Humiliating punishment to be abolished	52	38.80	
Troops to be employed for road-building and public works	12	8.95	
Governors and their lieutenants to be abolished	18	13.43	
Military bases with commands attached to be reduced	6	4.47	
Number of general officers to be reduced	9	6.71	
Militia to be replaced	5	3.73	
Mounted police (*maréchaussée*) to be increased	20	14.92	
Total	175		3.53

3. FINANCES

	Grievances	%	%
Lotteries to be abolished	24	17.91	
Bearer-credits (*acquits de comptant*) to be abolished	7	5.22	
Apanages of royal princes to be abolished, suppressed or modified	19	14.17	
Useless offices, jobs and places to be abolished	35	26.11	
Total	85		1.71

4. TAXATION

(a) *Administration*

	Grievances	%
General tax farms to be abolished	3	2.23
Receivers-general to be abolished	13	9.70
Auctioneers and valuers to be abolished	33	24.62

(b) *Indirect taxes*

	Grievances	%
Abolition of excise duties (*aides*)	36	26.86
Abolition of stamp duties (*droits de marque*)	11	8.20
Abolition of stamped paper duties (*contrôle*)	7	5.22
Constant, clear and moderate rates for stamped paper duties	60	44.77

	Grievances	%	%
1% tax on office values (*centième denier*) to be abolished	14	10.44	
Salt monopoly (*gabelle*) to be moderated	11	8.20	
Salt monopoly to be abolished	58	43.28	
Customs barriers to be transferred to frontiers	86	64.17	
Customs barriers not to be transferred to frontiers	3	2.23	
Investors, capitalists, industrialists and merchants to be taxed	58	43.28	
Indirect taxes, above all on luxury goods, to be preferred	6	4.47	
Private tolls (*péages*) to be abolished	12	8.95	
Total	411		8.29
(c) *Trade, industry, agriculture*			
Absolute freedom of trade and traffic in grain and goods	26	19.40	
Monopolies harmful to industry to be abolished	55	41.04	
Guilds, mysteries and corporations to be abolished	18	13.43	
Uniformity of weights and measures	27	20.14	
Dispensations, state letters and safe-conducts to be abolished	50	37.31	
Loans at interest to be allowed	37	27.61	
Arts, trade, manufacturers and agriculture to be encouraged	12	8.95	
Division and conversion to use of heaths and commons	9	6.71	
Improvement of agriculture	3	2.23	
Commercial treaty with England to be reviewed	3	2.23	
Rigorous laws against bankrupts	16	11.94	
Various	10	7.46	
Total	266		5.37
(d) *Health and Public Education*			
Beggary to be rooted out	40	29.85	
Hospitals and institutions for foundlings to be increased	8	5.97	
Surgeons and experienced midwives to be established everywhere	23	17.16	
National education to be reformed and improved, and schools to be set up for all classes in society	55	41.04	
Various	76	1.53	
Total	202		4.07

What a host of new and explosive proposals! Laid piously at the feet of the throne, would they have had any fate other than to be buried in ministerial files? But they were sent to deputies, often with express mandates, and safeguards to forestall any attempt by the king or his ministers to prevent the new constitution from working. And what a revolution this constitution was to be! Nothing less than the death certificate of the absolutist state. The old regime monarchy, absolute in the sense of unchecked despite the dreams of the parlements, and arbitrary in the sense of lacking safeguards for the subject, was to be supplanted by a monarchy that was constitutional and liberal. Administrative monarchy, ruling France through commissioners, controlling municipalities, was to yield to a decentralised state and provincial autonomy. The society of orders, where each estate, and inside each estate each corporate body, was locked into its own set of privileges, duties and rights, was to give way to an individualist society where each citizen, subject to the same laws, enjoyed the same rights.

The constitution, as outlined by the nobility's *cahiers*, was to be based on the principle, introduced to France by Montesquieu and England, of the separation of powers. The king – whose sacred and inviolable quality, incidentally, was rarely stipulated, perhaps because this was self-evident – was invested with executive power. Twenty-one per cent of the *cahiers* were for explicitly allowing him this prerogative, but even with the others there is no doubt that this power was not to be shared, once checks and balances had been thoughtfully devised to prevent any abuse in its exercise. The totality of legislative power was to belong to the Nation alone, represented in the freely elected Estates-General. Over 70% of the *cahiers* made this demand unequivocally. The assembly, whether permanent or periodically but regularly convoked, found itself assigned a triple function: it was to enjoy legislative power in all its plenitude and nothing would have the force of law without its approval; it was to consent to taxation – any levy raised without its consent would be illegal and those who authorised its collection would be subject to prosecution; it was to control the executive – all ministers would be answerable to it and subject to its judicial powers. It would have oversight of the public finances: ministers and officials would have to lay their accounts before it; and it would fix the expenditure of each department, confirm pensions and publish a list of them each year.

The *cahiers* were careful, suspicious even. They took infinite precautions to avoid any attempt by government to bring reform plans to nothing or to preserve ways of recovering control later. Almost 40 % of the *cahiers* were against voting any funds before the constitution was adopted. To be sure of the future, and aware that the tables might be turned, the great majority (68 %) were against granting taxes beyond the fixed date when the Estates-General reconvened. Should they not be called on time in a legal way, then all taxes would lapse and those who ordered their collection would be arraigned. Powers constrained, guaranteed independence for the legislative, control of the executive by the Nation, but that was not all. The constitution must safeguard the fundamental liberties of each individual. The society dreamed of by nobles in 1789 was a liberal one, in which the strongest and most extensive guarantees would be given to citizens against any temptation on the part of those in power to behave arbitrarily, to stifle opinion, or to interfere with national representation: freedom of the individual, of movement, of thought, of the press, inviolability of deputies, of property, of minorities (Protestant and Jewish), and guaranteed public employment. Nobody was to be judged except by his natural judges, all special courts to be forbidden, *lettres de cachet* to be abolished. Demands made for the protection of citizens, such as no imprisonment without charge for more than 24 hours, release on bail, and openness of prosecution have still not entirely been met in the late twentieth century.

With constitutional monarchy, liberal monarchy, the nobility deliberately turned their backs on the absolutist state. What they were proposing very closely matched the model being put forward at the same moment in the *cahiers* of the third estate. But absolute monarchy also meant centralisation, discretionary powers for commissioners and their abuses, local liberties flouted. And so the nobility called for the blanket abolition of the intendants who carried the arbitrariness of government out into the provinces, and the setting up throughout the kingdom of freely-elected provincial estates in which the three orders would be equally represented. What would they do? Their functions would be varied and extensive. Assessment and levy of taxes, deployment of monies necessary to the province, payment of the rest into the treasury, authorisation and supervision of public works. So each province would freely administer itself, live on its own resources, manage its own budget and works, beyond the reach of government constraint, the caprice of ministers, and the abuses of intendants. It was, then, a new state that the nobility was proposing, constitutional, liberal, decentralised, in a word the antithesis of the absolutist state. But it was also a new society.

The society of orders, already long compromised, and by the monarchy itself, still lingered on. Fully aware of this basic fact, the nobility showed itself ready to speed up the evolution. Over 60 % of the *cahiers*, as we have seen, accepted the uniting of the orders in a single assembly where only individuals would count, and where corporate bodies would no longer have powers or real existence. The privileges which gave the order its cohesion, cut it off from the rest of the Nation, removed it from common obligations, and in a word made it a body apart and a brilliant exception to the status of citizenship: all this the second order agreed to give up. The wish to put an individualistic society in place of a corporative one was expressed in the demand for equality: without distinctions of order, personal status, or birth, equality of all before the law and abolition of juridical privileges (almost 40 % of the *cahiers* called for the abolition of the right of *committimus*), equality of penalties, for even a degrading death meant hierarchy among convicts; equality of taxation (over 88 %), a sign of low birth in a society of orders but a symbol of citizenship in a society responsible for its own destiny. The majority of *cahiers* showed themselves very haughty over honorific privileges. Even so a radical fringe was ready to push the frontier of equality further out: access for all, without distinction of birth or status, to public office and military ranks, abolition of distinctions and formalities humiliating for the third estate. That was the outer limit of noble liberalism. The third estate had wished for nothing further. Not yet.

In place of a society of inherited superiority, privileges and distinctions, the nobility put forward a society of free citizens, equal in law, subject to the same duties, a society in which, under the government of a controlled monarchy, the individual was subject only to a law that was uniform, clear, rid of all imprecision and all arbitrariness, weighing equally, under cover of an authority freely accepted, for and by all without exception.

Such a reformation of state and society would have remained incomplete if the electors had not gone into further detail about institutions. And so, anxious to leave no grey areas, the *cahiers* set out in great detail the reforms to be introduced in the army, the law, finance, trade and industry, health and public education, the struggle against beggary, and relief for the poor and foundlings.

In the law, three great reforms. A recasting of the civil and criminal codes whose drafting should be entrusted to a commission of experts and be inspired by humanitarian and liberal principles; trial by jury to be established, allow accused persons the benefit of a counsel, that is a competent defender, abolish torture and the convict's stool, practices worthy of barbarism, limitations on the death penalty. The courts – after abolition of all those shown to be useless – would be brought closer to those subject to them, and the number of supreme courts of appeal increased. All courts would be obliged to give reasons for their judgments, and criminal proceedings would become public. As to magistrates, they should be tenured in order to guarantee judicial independence, but venality of office was to be abolished, and appointments made by competition or election. With better administration, the judiciary would henceforth be certain of its independence in the face of government and would offer all guarantees to those coming into contact with it. A well-regulated, equitable judicial system, safe from the executive and inspired by the humanitarian principles so widely diffused by the Enlightenment, was an indispensable complement to the freedom of the citizen, and it seemed so necessary that the nobility devoted almost 9 % of its demands to the subject.

It was impossible not to be concerned, at the moment when taxation was being subjected to consent, with the administration of the finances and the most burning question of all, the management of public funds. Financial control by the Estates-General was as much a means of bringing pressure to bear, in fact of blackmailing the executive, as a condition of sound management. With a concern for rationality which despite timid attempts the monarchy had never been able to impose on its administration, the *cahiers* also called for the abandonment of practices leading to disorder such as the use of bearer-credits, excessive pensions, useless offices, and, with even more vigour, the abolition of tax officials (provincial estates would henceforth appoint their own receivers), excises, tolls, and the much-execrated salt monopoly.

Military men found much to deplore in endless changes of regulations, favouritism and the arbitrary decisions of ministers. The nobility, which often thought of the army as its own preserve (25.% of the *cahiers* asked that the second order's exclusive right to provide officers should be upheld) wished to modify both its constitution and its spirit. On two points the army of Louis XVI provoked discontent and bitterness among nobles: the monopoly of upper ranks in the hands of the Court nobility, and the code of discipline which was thought humiliating and degrading to the honour of an enlightened and generous Nation. Breaking here again with the dogma of prescriptive rights, privileges of birth and innate dignities, the nobility demanded that senior ranks should only in future be awarded for merit and that officers risen themselves from the ranks (whose condescending title of 'officers of fortune' should be replaced by 'officers of merit') should be able to aspire to any rank and dignity. As to discipline, an imitation of the Prussian model had recently been introduced in France, and many officers thought it incompatible with the character of the Nation: corporal punishment, beating with the flat of the sword, were all the more resented in that ever since the chevalier d'Arc an ideological trend had tended to idealise the soldier as a hero in a cult of spartan honour and devotion to the fatherland. The *cahiers* which had absorbed most from the social lessons of the Enlightenment for their part took up a demand of the third estate, and it must be said it took some courage to do so. It was not completely without justification that the nobility could claim to reserve to itself a monopoly of ranking military posts, although in practice this never actually came about. Most of the other professions, which often brought the middle classes a fortune, were in principle closed to nobles, if not by law at least by prejudice.

The third estate in its requests should not overlook the fact that all the doors of fortune are open to them, that all proper means of enrichment are theirs, whereas ecclesiastical laws forbid these same means to the clergy, and prejudices not yet gone do not allow the nobility to take them up: indeed for a great number of its members there is only the career of arms, an honourable profession, no doubt, but ruinous for most of those who embrace it. Trade is a prolific mine that all classes are not yet allowed to exploit.

Admittedly the career of arms sometimes brought renown, but rarely wealth. Nobles serving in the armies, declared the *cahier* of Béziers, were ordinarily one of the poorest classes in the kingdom. And yet the nobility were attached to this profession by 'patriotic' ideology as much as by their own interests. Some however were prepared to open it up to commoners. They did so in the name of a principle which had profoundly imbued the noble outlook over half a century: merit. The concept of nobility had in fact changed. Alongside the honour attached to heredity, merit was accepted as another criterion of definition. The nobles of Langres were so convinced of it that they subscribed unreservedly to this maxim provided by the *cahier* of the three orders: 'The idea of nobility brings to mind either a precious heritage passed on in the blood, or a glorious reward for works useful to the homeland; it is a decoration received from ancestors or obtained by services.' The *cahier* of Châteauneuf-en-Thimerais drew the logical conclusion from this mental revolution: 'Let all citizens be eligible for all ecclesiastical, civil and military employments, which ought to be the prize and reward of virtue and merit and not the preserve of a privileged class; lack of birth should no longer be an obstacle; talents, conduct and courage should be the most honorable of passports.' It is true that all the nobility were not so explicit. Twenty-five per cent, as we have seen, wished to reserve commissioned rank to nobles alone; and scarcely 8% formally demanded access for all to all posts. The others, who declared no view, had at least given up their comfortable certainties and left the boldest to speak in their name.

The same uncertain attitude came out in the handling of important questions raising the issue of other noble privileges. Seigneurial rights were the object of violent attacks and the nobility could not be unaware that these rights were under challenge. Yet only 30% of the *cahiers* mention them: 17% to call for their continuance, 13% for their abolition. So the nobility was divided on this point and most expected the Estates-General themselves to settle the question.

Did the nobility at least uphold the pretensions of their brother order, the clergy? The solidarity which could have existed between the privileged orders had no effect at any time. Nobles themselves raised the issue of the existence of orders and privileges. The clergy, above all the upper clergy and regulars, were very roughly handled by noble *cahiers*. Some even went so far as to demand purely and simply the abolition of the order. Most of them attacked the leaders of the church, the bishops and benefice-holders: their income should be reduced, they should be compelled to reside – these were the commonest demands. On the other hand the nobility, witnessing every day the wretchedness of many vicars and curates, showed themselves concerned to improve the lot of these pastors who were often the outcasts and pariahs of christian society: their stipends should be raised (generally to a level of 1,000 l. or 1,200 l.), they should be allowed decent retirement and have benefices and stalls set aside for them. Concerned to clean up the clergy and raise its moral level, the *cahiers* wished to forbid vows under 25, reform the monasteries, abolish mendicant, useless and non-teaching orders.

The nobility also showed themselves very sensitive to the problems of health and public education: 2.54% of their grievances were devoted to national education (41% of the *cahiers* called for schooling for all classes of society), the poor and foundlings, to the spreading of surgeons and experienced midwives throughout the countryside, and to the rooting out of the unqualified and impostors.

Can we still be surprised at the interest shown by the nobility in trade and industry? They had entered the realms of capitalist exchange long before, some of them with the dynamism we have seen, and almost all of them through the system of lending and borrowing. Their desire to enter still more directly into economic life was forcefully expressed in demands for the removal of all bars to free initiative. In practice the nobility had long been bound up with capitalism, and particularly fiscal capitalism, but they wanted more: recognition of their right to become involved in productive activities had been granted by the monarchy long before; it was the third estate which held out against it, and the *cahiers* tried to force their hand. And that was why, with little concern to uphold the corporative system, the nobility called for the abolition of guilds and corporations and all privileged monopolies.

So then, what about the nobility making common cause with an order of things in which the Nation could no longer recognise itself? Bitterly defending outdated structures to hold on to their privileges and reinforce their positions in a state which identified itself with them? Or were they not rather building up, in full communion with the third estate, a war machine designed to bring down absolutism and put in its place a constitutional and liberal state whose very existence would be intended to safeguard the citizen against all arbitrariness and guarantee the right to happiness to all? Breaking with centuries of heredity which reserved the privilege of wellbeing to a minority, was not the nobility demanding the generalisation of happiness? All the *bailliages* might have placed at the head of their *cahiers* this demand from the nobility of Blois: 'The goal of any social institution is to make those who live under its laws as happy as possible. Happiness ought not to be confined to a small number, it belongs to all.'

Do the state and society dreamed of by nobles on this eve of revolution show a singularity which places the nobles in a parallel cultural world, not reactionary (because it was obviously forward-looking) but at one remove from the national culture? Or on the contrary did they embrace the most common aspirations in order to bind themselves unreservedly into the new society which was then emerging? Comparison with the *cahiers* of the third estate – of the middle classes, in fact – gives the answer; a positive one. The offshore island of the nobility had been joined up to the mainland. In an excellent unpublished thesis an American historian, Sasha Weitman, has analysed the content of the *cahiers* of the three orders[4] so we are in a position to compare results.

The call for liberty, so great among the nobility, is there in the third estate *cahiers* quite as clearly, though slightly less emphatically. The following tabulation amply demonstrates the similarity between the two orders:

	Third	Nobility
Freedom of the press	74%	88.05%
Abolition of judicial evocations	40	82.08
Abolition of *lettres de cachet*	74	68.65
Mandatory defending counsel	35	23.88

So the nobility was slightly ahead of the third, more preoccupied with safeguarding total freedom of expression, more sensitive to the pressures that the authorities could bring to bear on free information. On the other hand they were less keen to seek guarantees against judicial abuses. In giving up their privileges, the nobility showed themselves very forward, sometimes more so than the third estate itself, even where the latter had nothing to lose and everything to gain:

	Third	Nobility
Equal taxation	86%	88.54%
Abolition of *committimus*	54	39.55
Abolition of seigneurial dues	64	13.74

The nobility only fell clearly behind on seigneurial dues, but we have already seen that theirs was a passive attitude, with most of the *cahiers* not taking a view and a small percentage demanding that they be explicitly confirmed.

In fact, if a methodical comparison were fully made, the *cahiers* of the two orders would almost entirely correspond. The only divergence would appear where opposing interests clashed: the third, for example, and for obvious reasons, was much more inclined than the nobility to call for the abandonment of discriminatory practices in the recruitment of public officials. But in essentials – the construction of a liberal and constitutional state, an egalitarian and individualistic society, and decentralised government – there was a perfect identity between the two orders. The rivalry which some, like Sieyès, tried to whip up in 1789 to set against each other the elites of the third, speaking through the general *cahiers* of the third estate, and the nobility, was already a political ploy to bring out rival candidates for power.

The middle class and the nobility look, in their lists of grievances, like allies determined to bring down a discredited order and put in its place a new one about which in a very broad measure they had common ideas. If they became divided, that could only be over the means of making the transition and who would bring it about; not on the principles.

Conclusion

At this special moment in history, when a Nation discovered and revealed itself; in the year of '89 when, having passed through the fair times of the European Enlightenment, absolutism was collapsing in France in the innocent fires of the first rays of liberty; on this eve of Revolution big with a future in which all the durable regimes to come, even republican ones, aimed at and succeeded in restoring the political old regime by incessantly increasing the scope of the state's dominion, an impersonal power in the hands of professional wielders of power; at this charmed moment when everything seemed possible but common sense suggested the wisdom of limiting change; here let us stop for the moment to take stock.

Nobody in France wanted any more of the absolutist state. The nobility it had created, favoured and pampered, but not satisfied, opened divorce proceedings against it on the basis of an exhaustive range of complaints, resentments and . . . finding a new partnership. With the Nation, discovered miraculously after long reflection begun under the rod of a champion of reason of state, that ambivalent standard of all despotisms; with the third estate from which they sprang, and whose conflicts and ambitions they tirelessly re-enacted within their own frontiers; with liberty, that hope of peoples who had lived through the fanaticism of their rulers; with the State of their dreams: unburdensome, heedful of the desires of its people, working for them and not for itself, purged of its eternal, frenzied concern for passive obedience, no longer master and tyrant but servant and dependant.

Nobody in France wanted any more of society as the old order had conceived it. No? What about the nobility who benefited from inequality, who enjoyed privileges both honorific and real, and a superiority recognised, however resentfully, by public opinion? Would they give up all this? Come now! Let us not push paradox to absurd lengths – which means not calling received ideas into question. The *cahiers*? Opportunism. So they crossed the Rubicon? Only to fight a bitter rearguard action. Or is all this an illusion?

Perhaps quite simply because of the way the problem has been put. Surely all hope of understanding the French crisis is vitiated by bringing every attempt at explanation back to a single proposition. By introducing the class struggle into a society of orders, all perspectives have been warped. The orders themselves were only a transparent envelope enclosing a multiplicy of bodies in constant conflict; from one order to another bodies were united by community of interests, but cut off one from another by legal frontiers. Rivalry between third estate and nobility was largely theoretical and counterfeit. Rivalry between nobility and nobility is more accurate, as had long been the case. In a word, this was the general pattern and the second order was its hero; it was enough henceforth to harmonise the melody, for the theme had been found. It was in fact within the nobility that the debate took shape, it was there that the wager of Enlightenment emerged: birth against merit. It was within the second order that the third estate played its cards, and won. It was those who had secured ennoblement who brought the cause of merit to triumph; they who had demanded the abolition of discriminatory practices which set birth apart in a privileged position. Their cause blended with that of the elite of the third estate. In this way the nobility was a special laboratory, a school in which the middle class learned the elements of egalitarian revolution. Equality of elites. For those who had been ennobled (as more or less all nobles had, according to varying requirements)[1] and for the middle class too, what was at stake was the widening of privilege to embrace merit or its equivalents – money and culture. A real convergence of interests, even when concealed by specific rivalries, could not fail to mobilise the two orders against the only beneficiaries of narrow privilege: the Amphitryons of the Court, confused and rightly condemned with the state which they symbolised.

The 'first Revolution' united nobles and commoners against the absolutist state and against restrictive privilege. Because this was an Enlightenment revolution and the upshot of the debate between birth and merit. It was a revolution of elites, a revolution for equality at the top. Beyond, the Enlightenment was largely left behind.

Afterword to the English edition

The French edition of *La noblesse au XVIIIe siècle* ended there. That decision seemed justified by the unity I wished to give to an argument which the *cahiers* of 1789 seemed to round off. To go further would have been to write another book, take another course, and broach new research on the nobility in the Revolution. So the book in a sense stopped short, leaving the reader still hungry and, given what was known of the attitude of the majority of the nobility since the meeting of the Estates-General, took a line which seemed to give the lie to all later developments. So it seems useful, for the English-language reader, to add some explanations which I hope will resolve this apparent contradiction.

The nobility is more or less roundly associated in France with ideas of counter-revolution, emigration and plots. It is no part of my intention, to be sure, to deny the reality of the reaction, or even to attempt to play it down. But what needs to be explained is both the reason for a turnabout which might be found surprising, and the breadth of a conversion that nothing seemed to presage. Since the nobility throughout the eighteenth century had shown itself hostile to absolutism, and expressed in its *cahiers* a liberalism and a wish to see the regime transform itself into a constitutional monarchy tightly controlled by a national assembly, it can only come as a surprise to see it flying to the help of this same absolutism and fanatically opposing all the decrees of the Constituent Assembly. This unexpected turnabout presents a problem, and to come to terms with it is not enough to turn to psychological explanations; for there might appear to be a gap between the attitudes taken by the representatives of the second order and the intentions expressed by their constituents. Nor is it proved that the move towards a line of resistance was as general as we might think from the stubbornness of the deputies to the Estates-General alone. Even they were not all of one mind, and a group among them committed themselves openly to the Revolution without hesitation or regret.

168

But the majority wanted nothing to do with it. They had hoped that the Revolution would assure them of a leading position: they saw with horror that they would have to share both responsibilities and advantages. With an inconsistency which shows how deluded they had been, they now came to the aid of stricken absolutism for fear of being carried away along with it. Called to plunge, and be diluted in the ocean of middle-class elites, and by so doing give up a specific identity, the nobility divided. Some saw in the new order the end of a long road and the price to be paid for reconquered freedoms; others the death certificate of a long and prestigious history. The latter, doubtless the most numerous (but should we not distinguish between the nobility of the country and its imperfectly representative deputies?) persuaded themselves that their existence was bound to the survival of a regime whose grave they had madly helped to dig. This radical turnabout arose spontaneously from the fear of annihilation: suddenly the nobility was nothing and the exaltation of the Nation had only left it with a very unequally shared capital: glory, which for the faceless and undistinguished mass of nobles without a history, meant emptiness and anonymity. Doubtless it was not by chance that, alongside and to the left of Mirabeau, the aristocratic deserter and revolutionary, there stood several of the greatest names in France – d'Aiguillon, La Rochefoucauld, La Fayette, Lameth ... glory, wealth and prestige, whereas on the right those who longed for former days took for their leader the half-matured product of 'soap for scum' – Cazalès. The historic nobility lost nothing by an equality which could not efface its fame; but for King's Secretaries on the other hand it brought bankruptcy. Admittedly the frontier was not always so clearly marked; there were petty nobles who embraced the Revolution, and great lords (often linked with the Court, and prisoners of its favours) who resisted it. But it is true that the list of the first nobles to side with the third estate lays out the story of the second order before our eyes, in a brilliant array of ancient armorial bearings. Their privilege protected them because it was rooted in history and could not be eclipsed. The others merely owed their apartness to inequality: it was to be extinguished with the regime which guaranteed it.

The nobility was demanding first place in the redistribution of powers; and when the third estate refused to let itself be deprived of its hopes, nobles preferred to give up all their dallying with reform rather than fit themselves into the uniform mould of the reconciled elites. But we must be careful: fusion between the elites did not fall

entirely short. It partly came about within the Constituent Assembly
and doubtless even more in local and departmental administration
where nobles and commoners co-operated, in the same work of transforming affairs, to establish new constitutions and reorganise the kingdom. The most realistic nobles agreed to sharing, sometimes even
enthusiastically, but we must await the results of patient research to
assess the scale of an acceptance which work under way on 'notability'
under the Revolution allows us to glimpse: from it we can follow the
careers of many nobles who accepted the Revolution and offices in
communes, districts and departments, and were often enthusiastic
members of the first revolutionary clubs.[1]

Nevertheless, in the Constituent Assembly the majority of the nobility became entrenched in haughty rejection of any concessions. Only
one deputy in five or six broke of his own accord with the temptation
of sterile isolation. The majority's obstinacy poses a problem, for it
entailed the abandonment of all the principles hitherto upheld and a
total realignment behind the absolutism they had fought so much
against. Throughout the session they backed the king and his authority,
whereas their *cahiers* had uniformly demanded legislative power and
control of the executive for the assembly. So, then? Were they fore-
swearing their convictions, or had the *cahiers* gone far beyond what they
wanted? Had they only been expressing the thought of a noble intelligentsia who had contrived to impose their wishes on a deluded or
intimidated majority? Only careful study of the procedures and biographies of those who drew them up will give us a decisive answer.

In any case the blending of elites discernible in the course of the
century ran into a double agony: fear of losing an agreeable collective
identity, and, perhaps even more deeply felt, fear of seeing equality
established within the group, no longer according to traditional criteria
of organic deference, but through selection according to distinctions
which the century had slowly elaborated and which the nobility had
more or less knowingly and willingly embraced: personal distinction,
merit, talent. What they had accepted in small doses, and even benefited from, revolted them when it threatened to swamp them. But
then the signs which, over the eighteenth century, had seemed to point
to a coming-together of elites, appeared as a mere snare, and events
had shown their true nature: illusions or false appearances. Such a
conclusion would deliberately overlook the psychological factors –
which operate naturally in contradictions – in individual and collective
behaviour. That at the last minute the nobility should hesitate to

take a decisive step and not give up differences it was proud of; that it should have been afraid to see its identity vanish and then take refuge once more in an image of the past that it had itself helped to obscure: none of this should surprise us. It is in times of crisis that there often occurs this phenomenon of identification with an archaic model, rejected when things are going well, but turned to fanatically when danger becomes immediate or provocation intolerable. It might be said that such a psychological explanation is not enough to comprehend complex reality. And indeed it is only used here as a heuristic hypothesis. All it does is to underline the importance of the human problem arising in '89: the nobility was ill-prepared for coping with it because only its elites had followed and often led the cultural evolution of the age; these progressive leaders had no doubt asked too much of the group and overestimated its strength; certainly they were surprised by its ability to resist. For, and it is a fact we must come back to again and again, a not-inconsiderable fraction of the nobility backed the Revolution, kept up the struggle against absolutism, co-operated with the third estate, and took the lead in resisting the king in the Constituent Assembly. There even emerged, on the left in the Assembly, a 'triumvirate' which brought together, in common opposition to Mirabeau's middle way, Lameth, Duport and Barnave; in other words, a courtier, a magistrate and a commoner, bringing in their wake the most forward 'Jacobin' nobles. We have yet to assess the numbers of those who everywhere backed the Revolution, contributed to its successes, and were willing to sit on directories and run communes. We also need to get clear what part was played by opportunism, and what by conviction. But we can be sure right away that the whole nobility did not turn against the Revolution. Some of them, still to be counted, helped alongside the third estate to make up the new political elites of the constitutional revolution. So they did not all betray the ideas expressed throughout the century, and the new institutions were established with their co-operation. Even so the issue is not yet settled. What is certain is that the nobility split – showing once again its disunited character and the frequency of the rifts running through a group gathered together under a common name but divided by everything. The eighteenth century had often brought out inner rivalries; '89 provided a break. Some, perhaps most, turned to tradition, inertia's alibi; others took on the legacy of the Enlightenment; some, like Condorcet or Kersaint, took it to its ultimate conclusion, whilst others – Le Pelletier, Châteauneuf, not forgetting Orléans – went far beyond.

And yet we still have not done with the contradiction between the intentions set forth in the *cahiers*, and the attitude taken by the majority of deputies. The instructions of the electors had only given explicit orders to join with the third estate to a very small number of representatives; but a slender majority had clearly expressed the wish that the method of voting chosen should not lead to confrontation and that there should be no obstinate resistance which was deemed bad for the interests of the state and harmony within the Assembly. If the deputies had shown the same conciliatory spirit as their constituents, the balance of strength in the chamber of the nobility would have been reversed. But, as a result of frequent tumults in assemblies easily carried away by turbulent characters (and in the chamber of the nobility all the good orators and most active members, such as Cazalès, La Quenille and d'Antraigues, were on the most extreme right); as a result too of the seductive ploys of the extremist Court faction (Artois and Polignac), able by attentions or flatteries to win over a number of dazzled provincials – and also on account of the very imperfect representative quality of the deputies (who belonged almost entirely to the military caste and had been elected less for their opinions than the prestige of their uniform) – many delegates interpreted their instructions as they saw fit, and took advantage of the indecision in their *cahiers* to reject all compromise. Some even went so far as to flout the explicit intentions of their constituents. When instructions were not mandatory they were generally interpreted by deputies in the least liberal sense. Even deputies from the same *bailliage* could be found divided: thus, according to the wishes of those who instructed them, the two elected for Haute-Marche were to accept the decision of the Estates-General; yet one of them joined the third estate after the royal proclamation enjoining this on 27 June, whereas the other protested against the same declaration. But betrayal was most blatant at Nîmes. The *cahier* of this seneschalcy – one of the most liberal in the kingdom – specifically ordered its deputies to join with the third estate and only to vote by head; yet they refused to join up, and protested against the abolition of privileges and against all the decrees of the Constituent Assembly.

The nobility, then, had often elected the least appropriate representatives for bringing about the change that some of them wanted and others were resigned to accepting. We ought not to confuse the ordinary nobleman who sought compromise and often profound reforms, and the deputy imprisoned by longing for the past, or prey to the Court's sometimes frenzied quest for confrontation with the third estate. We might think, without too much speculation about what we do not know, that part of the nobility recognised themselves in the work of the Constituent Assembly and disapproved of the sterile opposition of the majority of their representatives. If the blending of elites only came about very partially within the Assembly, we might suspect that in the country at large matters went very differently, and the constitution of 1791 was to stiffen individual inclinations still further. So the century's efforts had not been entirely lost; the imperial regime, still some years off, was to put an end to the war between the nobility and the elite of the third estate, reconcile them completely at last, and thus finally settle a conflict arbitrarily sustained by fanatics long beyond its natural span, despite the efforts of those, too often forgotten, who had long seen it as nothing more than an outmoded squabble.

Notes

Abbreviations

AD   *Archives départementales*
AN   *Archives nationales*

Notes to Introduction

1 A system under which only those of distinguished lineage might be presented to the king [Tr.].
2 *Obligations de l'état religieux.*
3 Ségur, *Mémoires.*
4 See his letters to Burke, notably that of 6 December 1790, published by H. V. F. Somerset in *Annales historiques de la Révolution Française* (1951), pp. 360–73.
5 *Mémoires* (Pléiade edn.), vol. 5, pp. 611–12.
6 *Ibid.* p. 610.
7 The 1781 law was aimed less at the middle class than at the recently ennobled. In practice four degrees of nobility were required, or lineage of about a century, in order to achieve a commission without rising from the ranks. On this subject see the work of D. Bien in the bibliography.

Notes to Chapter 1

1 See Saint-Simon's description of the annulment of Louis XIV's will and codicil.
2 Fénelon, *Plans de gouvernement concertés avec le duc de Chevreuse pour être proposés au duc de Bourgogne* (November 1711).
3 *Principes fondamentaux d'un sage gouvernement.* A supplement to his examination of conscience on the duties of kingship.
4 Boulainvilliers, *Essai sur la noblesse française.*
5 See F. Furet, and M. Ozouf, 'Mably et Boulainvilliers: deux légitimations historiques de la société française au XVIIIᵉ siècle', *Annales, E.S.C.* (1979).
6 *Mes Pensées,* 'des dignités'.

7 Mably, *Observations sur l'histoire de France*: 'So long as fiefs were not hereditary, distinctions granted to lords were merely personal. Their nobility was
not passed on in the blood, and left their children in the common class of
citizens until they swore the oath of fealty between the prince's hands. In
a word, there were two different classes of citizens, but all families were of
the same order. Everything changed when fiefs became hereditary; new
lords of a new sort thought themselves superior to others, and the idea of
nobility we have today began to take shape.'

8 By de La Roque, *Traité de la Noblesse*, 1678.

9 D'Argenson, *Mémoires*.

10 *Voyage en Orient*, quoted by L. Pingaud, *Un agent secret sous la Révolution et
l'Empire* (1893).

11 *Mémoire sur les Etats Généraux* (1788) D'Antraigues' ferocity towards courtiers was not entirely disinterested. He had applied for the honours of the
Court and had been rejected on grounds of insufficient proofs of eligibility.
He was descended from an ennobled financier under Henry IV. His bitterness reinforced and perhaps exceeded his convictions.

12 *Mémoire sur les Etats Généraux.*

Notes to Chapter 2

1 Derogatory term for offices bought in order to ennoble the buyer [Tr.].

2 *Les magistrats du Parlement de Paris au XVIIIe siècle* (Paris, 1960).

3 'L'aristocratie parlementaire française à la fin de l'Ancien Régime', *Revue
historique* (1952), pp. 1–14.

4 C. Carrière, 'Le recrutement de la cour des comptes d'Aix-en-Provence',
81e Congrès des sociétés savantes (1956).

5 M. Gresset, *Le monde judiciare à Besançon (1674–1789)*.

6 This was also the average length for a career. See for example Gresset on
Besançon.

7 A.N. V².

8 D. Labarre de Raillicourt, *La noblesse militaire* (1962).

9 According to F. Bluche and P. Durye, *L'anoblissement par les charges avant
1789*, the following municipal offices ennobled in the eighteenth century:

Angers:	Mayor, (1st degree) (4 years), deputy mayor, 1st degree (for short periods only).
Angoulême:	Mayor, 1st degree (variable tenure, 3–20 years), deputy mayor, 1st degree (for short periods only).
Bourges:	Mayor, 1st degree (variable tenure, 4–20 years).
Lyons:	Provost of Merchants [mayor], 1st degree (annual, to 1764); 4 *échevins*, 1st degree (annual to 1764, then bi-ennial).
Nantes:	Mayor, 1st degree (2 years).

Paris:	Provost of Merchants, 1st degree (annual, no commoner in the eighteenth century), 4 *échevins*, 1st degree (2 years), King's procurator, clerk, town receiver, 1st degree (20 years).
Poitiers:	Mayor, 1st degree (variable, 4–20 years), deputy mayor, 1st degree (20 years).
Toulouse:	12 then (from 1732) 8 *capitouls*, 1st degree (1 year to 1778, 2 from 1778–83, 4 after 1783).
Perpignan:	Noble citizens or honoured burgesses, 1st degree.

10 See on this subject M. Cubells, 'A propos des usurpations de noblesse en Provence sous l'Ancien Régime', *Provence historique* (1970).

11 For Paris, the letters are in the archives of the court of accounts, A.N. series P. For Brittany, J. Meyer, *La noblesse bretonne au XVIIIe siècle*; for Burgundy, Jules d'Arbaumont, *Les anoblis de Bourgogne* (1867).

12 These grounds are set out in Dauvergne's contribution to *Mélanges présentés à Marcel Reinhard* (1972).

13 A.N. P 5557, 5488, 5591, 5592, 5269, 5417, 5392, 5765, 5763, 5105, 5298, 5444, 5134.

14 Involved in this study are Christine Favre, Françoise Bluche, Guy Chaussinand-Nogaret, François Furet and Jean-Louis Vergnaud. My thanks to François Furet, Director of the Historical Research Centre, for allowing me to use this study here.

15 A.N. series P.

16 La Roque, *Traité de la Noblesse* (1768).

17 Boulainvilliers, *Essai sur la noblesse de France* (1732).

18 *Observations sur le préjugé de la noblesse héréditaire* (1789), p. 29.

Notes to Chapter 3

1 It is worth noting that today the old French nobility, whose entry standards are very pertinently set, does not recognise certificates as proofs of nobility.

2 The right to take any case in which one was involved automatically before a sovereign court.

3 On the problem of money in the army, see E. G. Léonard, *L'armée et ses problèmes au XVIIIe siècle* (Paris, 1958).

4 Only the Knights of Malta and members of some chapters (like Remiremont for example which the Bourbons could not enter because the Medicis were there) in France had to provide proofs by quarterings in both the male and female lines.

5 M. Grau, *De la noblesse maternelle, particulièrement en Champagne* (1898); A. de Mauroy, *Un dernier mot sur la noblesse maternelle en Champagne* (1913).

6 The authenticity of the letter of 9 January 1774 from Louis XV to the duc d'Aumont has sometimes been challenged (De Broc, *Essai historique sur la noblesse de race*). Even if it is apocryphal its message is confirmed in other

ways. The comte de Puisaye thus wrote to the king: 'The honour of being presented to your majesty and of access to your carriages is a particular favour which you can grant or refuse as you wish'. A.N. M 608.

7 H. Carré, *La noblesse de France et l'opinion publique au XVIIIᵉ siècle.*

8 *Cahier* of the third estate of Nemours.

9 A. D. Hérault, C 5172.

10 Quoted by Taine, *Les origines de la France contemporaine*, vol. 1, p. 28.

11 A. D. Aveyron, C 1615.

12 Louis-Philippe, *Mémoires* (1973).

13 Capitation of Aurillac, published by M. Leymarie, 'Redevances seigneuriales en Haute-Auvergne', *Annales historiques de la Révolution française* (1968), p. 378.

14 Capitation of the election of Laon, published by de Sars in *Mémoires de la Fédération des Sociétés Savantes de l'Aisne* (1957).

15 R. Forster, *The House of Saulx-Tavanes. Versailles and Burgundy, 1700–1830* (1971).

16 *Etat des pensions sur le Trésor royal* (5 vols., 1789).

17 This was merely the salary. Gifts and various advantages attached to these offices raised their yield considerably.

18 A.N. O¹ 714. Court offices.

19 *Mémoires de Mme. Campan.*

20 A.N. O¹ 748. Royal Household.

21 A.N. T 471–2.

22 *Rapport du comité des pensions à l'Assemblée Nationale* (1790).

23 A.N. M 643. Governors and income from their posts, 1750.

24 A.N. T 348/2.

25 Y. Durand, *Les fermiers-généraux au XVIIIᵉ siècle* (1971), p. 108: the marquise de Cramayel drew 16,500 l. in 1780 in interest on money invested with Alliot de Mussey.

26 See below, Ch. 5.

27 A.N. B III 135, *Journal historique . . . de la commission nommée par les colons résidant à Paris depuis le 15 juillet 1788 . . . rédigée par le marquis de Gouy d'Arcy commissaire rapporteur.*

28 Pre-revolutionary money was reckoned in *livres*, *sols* and *deniers*, exactly like British pounds, shillings and pence.

29 A.N. T 153, 150, "Tableau du revenu du comte et de la comtesse de Choiseul-Gouffier', 1777.

30 A.N. T* 557, 11.

31 A.N. T* 491/3.

32 A.N. T* 24/4.

33 A.N. T* 201/90.

34 A. D. Seine D4B6/104 and 86.

35 A.N. AF 4 1076, lists of the twelve most highly assessed payers of the land tax in each department, drawn up around 1803–5.

36 C. Girault, 'La noblesse sarthoise' *La Province du Maine* (1954–5).

37 A.N. AF 4 1076.

38 *Etat des pensions sur le Trésor royal* (1789).

39 Jacqueline Préjean, 'Une famille noble dans la deuxième moitié du XVIIIe siècle' (typewritten *thèse de troisième cycle*, University of Paris I).

40 A.D. Gard 1E 989.

41 A.D. Hérault 1F 459.

42 *Ibid.* L 1513.

43 A. Young, *Travels in France during the years 1787, 1788 and 1789* (ed. C. Maxwell, Cambridge, 1929), p. 166.

44 *Ibid.*

45 On this subject see J. Meyer, 'Un problème mal posé: la noblesse pauvre. L'exemple breton, XVIIIe siècle', *Revue d'Histoire moderne et contemporaine* (1971), pp. 161–88.

46 There are many examples of this type of noble in the files of the Tribunal of the Marshals of France, A.N. AB XIX.

47 A.N. BA 85. Minutes of the assembly of the nobility of Villefranche.

48 *Travels through France and Italy* (1766), letter IV.

49 J. Fournée, *Etudes sur la noblesse rurale du Cotentin et du bocage normand* (1954).

50 Leymarie, 'Redevances seigneuriales', cited above, n. 13, pp. 299ff.

51 H. du Mas, 'Cadets de province au XVIIIe siècle', *Mémoires de la Société d'Agriculture d'Angers* (1902), p. 21.

52 A. Clergeac, 'Une famille de gentilshommes campagnards: les Chabannes', *Revue de Gascogne* (1903), p. 97.

53 Abbé Bernier, *Essai sur le tiers état rural en Basse Normandie au XVIIIe siècle* (1891), pp. 157–8.

54 L. Tuetey, *Les officiers sous l'Ancien Régime* (1908), p. 26.

55 A.N. AB XIX.

Notes to Chapter 4

1 *Polysynodie* was an experiment in government under which each department was put under the supervision of a council of great noblemen. It was abandoned in 1718 after only three years of operation. [Tr.]

2 *Mémoires* (Pléiade edn.), vol. 1, p. 125.

3 Tilly, *Mémoires* (Mercure de France edn.), p. 314.

4 For example, comtesse de Chatelaillon paid for the following lessons for her daughter:

> 72 l. to M. Huart for three months' dancing lessons.
> 96 l. to M. Leprince for four months' singing lessons.
> 72 l. for three months' harp lessons.
> 72 l. for three months' clavichord lessons (A.N. T 390/2).

5 Marquise de La Tour du Pin, *Mémoires d'une femme de 50 ans*.

6 Mme. de Genlis, *Mémoires*.

7 On the education of girls, see A. de Luppé, *Les jeunes filles de l'aristocratie et la bourgeoisie à la fin du XVIIIᵉ siècle* (1924); F. Rousseau, *Histoire de l'abbaye de Pentemont*; L. Parey, *La princesse de Ligne*.

8 G. Dupont-Ferrier, *Du collège de Clermont au Lycée Louis-le-Grand* (1921).

9 H. L. Bouquet, *L'ancien collège d'Harcourt* (1921).

10 At Beaumont-en-Auge, Tiron, Pont-le-Voy, Sorrèze, Rabais (Benedictines) La Flèche (Brothers of the Christian Doctrine), Vendôme, Tournon, Effiat (Oratorians), Auxerre (Congregation of Saint-Maur), Brienne (Minims), Pont-à-Mousson (Canons regular of Saint-Sauveur).

11 J. Fabre de Massaguel, *La vie quotidienne à l'école de Sorrèze* (Académie des Sciences de Haute Garonne, 1972).

12 C. de Montzey, *Institutions d'éducation militaire* (1866).

13 A.N. T 390–2.

14 C. de Carné, *Les pages des écuries de Roi* (1900).

15 Tilly, *Mémoires*, Ch. 1.

16 Mme de Créquy relates in her memoirs that it was the fashion to starve children. No soup, no meat, no fruit, jam or pastry. The Béthune sons broke into their grandmother's kitchen at dead of night. The most quick-witted of them attacked the cat's food. While at Mme. de Créquy's, the prince de Montbarey's sons were discovered with lips red from eating sealing-wax.

17 Lauzun, *Mémoires*.

18 M. Dumoulin, 'Les académies parisiennes d'équitation', *Bulletin de la société des vieux papiers* (1922); O. Raguenet de Saint-Albin, 'Livre des pensionnaires et externes de l'académie d'équitation d'Angers', *Revue d'Anjou* (1914).

19 Préjean, 'Une famille noble dans la seconde moitié du XVIIIᵉ siècle'.

20 Du Mas, 'Cadets de province au XVIIIᵉ siècle'.

21 G. Valous, 'Une existence de célibataire à la veille de la Révolution', *Le Correspondant* (1926).

22 E. Perrin, 'Les oisivetés d'un gentilhomme forézien, Claude Harenc de la Condamine', *Amitiés foréziennes* (1921).

23 G. Blondeau, 'Journal du chevalier de Belchamp', *Annuaire de la société d'histoire de Lorraine* (1930).

24 See, for example, Bluche, *Magistrats du Parlement de Paris*, pp. 244–7 for the education given to future magistrates.

25 This and other examples come from D. Roche, *Le siècle des lumières en province. Académies et académiciens provinciaux, 1680–1789* (1978).

26 Meyer, *Noblesse bretonne au XVIIIᵉ siècle*, vol. 2, pp. 1162–1177.

27 *Ibid*.

28 Bluche, *Magistrats du Parlement*, pp. 290–6.

29 A.D. Hérault Q 474.

30 A.N. T 471/1. Boisgelin's library.

31 'Le livre français à la fin de l'Ancien Régime', *Annales E.S.C.* (1973), pp. 735–44.
32 Roche, *Siècle des lumières*.
33 *Mémoires*, p. 105.
34 *Béatrix*.
35 *gentilshommes: gens-tue-hommes* or *gens-pille-hommes*.
36 H. Carré, 'Querelles entre gentilshommes campagnards du Poitou au XVIIIᵉ siècle', *Revue du XVIIIᵉ siècle* (1914).
37 A.N. X2. Gilbert de Beaucouvert was condemned in 1760 to be beheaded for murder. The marquis de Bellay, 31, was condemned by the Châtelet for violent behaviour. Convicted of murder in 1770, François de Gallier, 39, was reprieved for a payment of 10 l. for prayers and the same sum in alms. Clément de Gaulles de Gouvron, 50, was convicted of murder at Rheims. In 1755 de Boisvilliers de la Roberdière was condemned to be beheaded for the same reason as Romorantin. Chassin de Chabret was reprieved after condemnation for murder. Mars de Fontelure, convicted of fratricide at Riom, was condemned to have his hand and head cut off on 15 April 1785. Charles Thébault de La Touche was condemned to lose his life in 1784 for murder and robbery.
38 A.N. AB XIX 1404.
39 A.N. X2, inventory.
40 A.N. X2b 1087.
41 A.N. X2A 849.
42 P. Guiral, 'Un noble provençal contemporain de Sade: le marquis d'Antonelle', in *Marquis de Sade* (1968).
43 *Justine, ou les malheurs de la vertu* (1791).

Notes to Chapter 5

1 *Développement et défense du système de la noblesse commerçante* (1757).
2 A.D. Hérault C2720.
3 A.N. F 12 p. 49.
4 A.N. F12 101 p. 321.
5 G. Richard, 'La noblesse de France et les sociétés par actions à la fin de l'Ancien Régime', *Revue d'Histoire économique et sociale* (1962).
6 A.N. T 471¹.
7 A.N. T 551/1.
8 A.N. T 291.
9 A.N. Minutier central, XIV, 479.
10 *Ibid.*, XVI ,857.
11 *Ibid.*, XIV, 478.
12 *Ibid.*
13 *Ibid.*, CVIII, 683.
14 *L'armement nantais dans la deuxième moitié du XVIIIᵉ siècle* (1969), pp. 91–3.

15 A.N. 94 A Q.

16 G. Chaussinand-Nogaret, 'Une entreprise française en Espagne au XVIIIe siècle', *Revue d'histoire moderne et contemporaine* (1973).

17 A.N. Minutier central, XCV, 372.

18 A.N. Colonies C 14 (46–7), T 514 (14), T 200 (1); minutier central, XXX, 483.

19 D. Ozanam, *Claude Baudard de Saint-James* (Paris, 1969). See too A.N. T 461 (1).

20 A.N. F 12, pp. 375, 384, 459, 481, 563, 593, 739; 107, p. 80.

21 A.N. F12 106, p. 781.

22 *Ibid.*, p. 1339.

23 *Ibid.*, 107, p. 205.

24 *Ibid.*

25 *Ibid.*, p. 412.

26 *Ibid.*, pp. 614, 756, 854.

27 A. Cochin, *La manufacture des glaces de Saint-Gobain* (1865).

28 A.N. Minutier central XXX, 483; F 12 1339.

29 On the mechanisation of cotton production, see C. Ballot, *L'introduction du machinisme dans l'industrie française* (1923).

30 Charles-Louis marquis Ducrest, brother of Mme de Genlis, published an *Essay on Hydraulic Machines* in 1777.

31 Ballot, *Introduction du machinisme*, pp. 394–5.

32 On this see Jacques Payen, *Capital et machine à vapeur au XVIIIe siècle* (1969), pp. 137ff.

33 A.N. Minutier central XXX 459.

34 *Ibid.*, XXX 469.

35 See E. A. Wrigley, 'Modernisation et révolution industrielle en Angleterre', *Annales E.S.C.* (1973).

36 A.N. T 522/2; F 12 1301–4; see too Rouff, *Les mines de charbon* (1922).

37 B. Gille, *Les origines de la grande industrie métallurgique en France* (1947).

38 'Les nobles métallurgistes dans le département de l'Eure de 1789 à 1815', *Actes du 87e congrès des sociétés savantes* (1963).

39 A very incomplete list of grantees of mining concessions includes the following names: marquis de Pons (La Frugere, Auvèrgne), comte de Rangouse (Aurillac), duc de Chaulnes (Brittany), marquis de Rastignac (Périgord), prince de Bauffremont (Franche-Comté), marquis de Traisnel (Hainault), duc de Guines (Artois), marquis d'Ornemans (Lorraine), marquis de Mondragon (Saint-Chamond), marquis de Foudras (Lyonnais), marquis de Bermond (Le Bousquet d'Orb), baron de Ferroul (Laurens and Fougillon, Languedoc), baron de Comère (Neffies, Languedoc), princesse de Saint-Pons (Agillanet, Languedoc), comte de Vezins (Roucoulet, Montauban), marquis de Basleroy (Littry, Normandy), duc d'Aumont (Boulonnais), comte de Praslin (Cheffreville, Normandy), comte de Chatenay (Lagny), baron de Montejean (Montejean, Anjou), comte de Lévis (Foulon,

Roussillon), Guyton de Morveau, advocate-general at the parlement of Dijon, who like Jars had experimented with coke smelting (Châlon-sur-Saône) and whose mine at Saint-Brin supplied a glassworks, duc de Clermont-Tonnerre (La Reville, Autun) who also owned a glassworks at Epinac, comte de Buffon, Guyton de Morveau, the chevalier de Richard and Tolosan (Vassy) (A.N. T 238 and 522/2). A similar survey could be made for lead and silver mining. The grants in Couserans and Comminges belonged entirely to the marquis de Vellepinte and the comte de Betous de Gestas. In this region the forges were entirely in the hands of the nobility: Mme de Polignac (Oust), comte d'Ercée (Alos and Aulus), comte de Sabran (Massat), de Montgrenier (Arbas) (A.N. H 69 and T 522/2°). More important still were the acquisitions made by the duc de Béthune-Charost at Roche-La-Molière and by the marquis de Solages at Carmaux, where he set up glassworks, not to mention the comte de Buffon and his forges at Montbard.

40 A.N. X2^b 1431.
41 A. de Saint-Léger, *Les mines d'Anzin et d'Aniche* (1938).
42 A.N. T 1146. 1, 2, 3.
43 A.N. F 14 7890(7).
44 A.N. Minutier central, XXXIII, 638.
45 *Ibid.*, XIV, 492.
46 *Ibid.*, XXVI, 619, 631, 643, 647, 651, 654.
47 Chaussinand-Nogaret, 'Une entreprise française en Espagne'.
48 A.N. AP 2, dossier 2.
49 On the Wendels, see R. Sédillot, *La maison de Wendel de 1704 à nos jours*, (1958).
50 G. Richard, 'De la sidérurgie à la métallurgie de transformation. L'entreprise de Dietrich de Niederbronn de 1685 à 1939', *Actes du 88e congrès national des sociétés savantes* (1964).
51 *Houille* means coal, so 'coal merchant' [tr.].
52 On Le Creusot, see Ballot, *L'introduction du machinisme*; Sédillot, *Maison de Wendel*; Ozanam, *Baudard de Saint-James*; and G. Chaussinand-Nogaret, *Gens de Finance au XVIIIe siècle* (1972).
53 For a rapid survey, see Chaussinand-Nogaret, *Gens de finance*. Three works offer a closer acquaintance with the world of the financiers: H. Lüthy, *La Banque protestante en France* (2 vols., second edition, 1972); G. Chaussinand-Nogaret, *Financiers de Languedoc* (1970); Durand, *Les fermiers-généraux au XVIIIe siècle*.
54 Sénac de Meilhan, *Le gouvernement, les mœurs et les conditions en France avant la Révolution* (1862 ed.).
55 See Chaussinand-Nogaret, *Gens de finance au XVIIIe siècle*.

Notes to Chapter 6

1 Marquise de la Tour du Pin, *Mémoires d'une femme de 50 ans.*
2 A.N. Y 61 f. 343$^{\text{vo.}}$ and ff.
3 A.N. Y 62 f. 196 and ff.
4 Marquise de Créquy, *Mémoires.*
5 A.N. Y 61 f. 359$^{\text{vo.}}$ and ff.
6 Letter to Mme. de Grignan, 8 April 1676.
7 A.N. Y 61 f. 413$^{\text{vo.}}$ and ff.
8 M. Agulhon, *La vie sociale en Provence intérieure au lendemain de la Révolution* (1970).
9 Du Mas, 'Cadets de province au XVIIIe siècle', pp. 121–5.
10 See D. Dessert, 'Finances et société au XVIIe siècle', *Annales E.S.C.* (1974).

Notes to Chapter 7

1 We cannot count Grenoble, for example, because its *cahier* was drawn up by the Estates of Dauphiné.
2 Sealed orders signed by the king and not subject to judicial review [tr.].
3 Removal of cases by royal order from the ordinary courts to the Privy Council.

Notes to Chapter 8

1 Chateaubriand, *Mémoires d'outre-tombe*, Bk. 5, Ch. 11.
2 The assembly of each *bailliage* chose representatives who met together at Nancy, Mirecourt, Sarreguemines and Bar-le-Duc. In Provence only Aix, Marseilles and Arles sent their own deputies directly. Castellane, Draguignan and Grasse met at Draguignan; Digne, Forcalquier, Sisteron and Barcelonette met at Forcalquier; Brignoles, Hyères and Toulon at Toulon.
3 François Furet and Denis Richet have long been engaged upon a quantitative analysis of the *cahiers* as a project of the *École pratique des hautes études.* They have established an analytical framework which I have used here, with modifications for the needs of my subject. Sasha Weitman, in a very fine thesis, has analysed the general *cahiers* of the three orders; nevertheless I thought it useful to go over the *cahiers* of the nobility myself for my own purposes.
4 Weitman, 'Bureaucracy, democracy and the French Revolution' (1968).

Notes to Conclusion

1 Proof of about a century's nobility was required for the army and about three centuries for the Court.

Notes to Afterword

1 See *Grands notables du premier Empire*, a series which the *Centre national de la recherche scientifique* began to publish in 1978.

Bibliography

Sources mentioned in footnotes are not referred to again here. For the *cahiers* I have preferred to use the originals in series BA and B III of the Archives Nationales rather than the published versions in the *Archives parlementaires*.

This bibliography only includes works I have consulted. On the nobility it may be complemented by the excellent one to be found in Jean Meyer's thesis *La Noblesse bretonne au XVIIIe siècle* (1966).

Titles of the most often cited learned journals are abbreviated as follows:

Annales–Annales E.S.C.
A.H.R.F.–Annales historiques de la Révolution française.
R.H.M.C.–Revue d'histoire moderne et contemporaine.

Adam, A., *Le mouvement philosophique dans la première moitié du XVIIIe siècle*, 1967.
Agulhon, M., *La vie sociale en Provence intérieure au lendemain de la Révolution*, 1970.
Alès de Corbet, *Origine de la noblesse française*, 1766.
Allonville, comte d', *Mémoires secrets*, 1835.
Althusser, L., *Montesquieu, la politique et l'histoire*, 1959.
Antraigues, comte d', *Mémoire sur les Etats Généraux*, 1788.
Arc, A. de Sainte-Foy chevalier d', *La noblesse militaire ou le Patriote français*, 1756.
Argenson, marquis d', *Considérations sur le gouvernement de la France*, 1764.
Mémoires, 1858.
Ariès, P., *Histoire des populations françaises et leurs attitudes devant la vie*, 2nd ed., 1971.
Aron, R., 'Social structure and the ruling class', *British Journal of Sociology*, 1950.
'Classe sociale, classe politique, classe dirigeante', *Archives européennes de sociologie*, 1960.
Babeau, A., *La vie militaire sous l'Ancien Régime*, 1889–90.
Les établissements d'instruction à Paris en 1789, 1889.
Ballot, C., *L'introduction du machinisme et l'industrie française (1780–1815)*, 1923.
Barber, E., *The Bourgeoisie in Eighteenth-Century France*, 1955.

Barthélemy, E. de, *La noblesse de France avant et depuis 1789*, 1858.
  Les ducs et les duchés français avant et depuis 1789, 1867.
Baudrillart, H., *Gentilshommes ruraux*, 1894.
Beaune, H., *Voltaire au collège*, 1867.
Behrens, B., 'Nobles, privileges and taxes in France at the end of the Ancien
  Régime', *Economic History Review*, 1962–3.
Benoit, A., *L'école des cadets-gentilshommes du Roi de Pologne à Lunéville*, 1867.
Bergasse, *Observations sur le préjugé de noblesse*, 1789.
Bertin, E., *Les mariages dans l'ancienne société française*, 1879.
Bien, D. D., 'La réaction aristocratique avant 1789', *Annales*, 1974.
Bloch, M., *Les Rois thaumaturges*, new edn., 1961.
Bluche, F., *Les magistrats du Parlement de Paris au XVIIIᵉ siècle*, 1961.
  L'origine des magistrats du Parlement de Paris, 1956.
  Les honneurs de la cour, 1957.
Bluche, F. and Durye, P., *L'anoblissement par les charges avant 1789*, 1962.
Bluche, F., *La vie quotidienne de la noblesse française au XVIIIᵉ siècle*, 1973.
  'L'origine sociale du personnel ministériel français au XVIIIᵉ siècle', *Bulletin
  de la Société d'histoire moderne*, 1957.
Bois, P., *Paysans de l'Ouest*, 1960.
Boiteau, P., *L'état de la France en 1789*, 1861.
Bosher, J., *French Finances. From Business to Bureaucracy*, 1970.
Bottomore, T. B., *Elites and society*, 1964.
Bouillé, Marquis de, *Mémoires*, 1821.
Boulainvilliers, *Essai sur la noblesse de France*, 1732.
Bouquet, H. L., *L'ancien collège d'Harcourt*, 1891.
Bourrachot, L., 'L'administration des biens d'une baronnie quercynoise', *Bull.
  Soc. Etudes litt. du Lot*, 1934.
Bouton, A. and Lepage, M., *Histoire de la franc-maçonnerie dans la Mayenne*, 1951.
Bouvier (J.) and Germain-Martin, *Finances et financiers d'Ancien Régime*, 1955.
Bouyala d'Arnaud, A., 'Un gentilhomme provençal au XVIIIᵉ siècle: le
  marquis d'Eguilles', *Provincia*, 1960.
Braudel, F. and Labrousse, E., *Histoire économique et sociale de la France*, vol. II, 1970.
Brelot, C., *La noblesse en Franche-Comté de 1789 à 1808*, 1972.
Broc, Vicomte de, *Essai historique sur la noblesse de race*, 1877.
  La France sous l'Ancien Régime: les usages et les mœurs, 1899.
Buat, Comte du, *Eléments de la politique*, 1773.
Burguière, A., 'A Reims: diffusion des Lumières et cahiers des Etats Généraux',
  Annales, 1967.
Campan, Madame, *Mémoires*.
Carcassonne, E., *Montesquieu et le problème de la constitution française au XVIIIᵉ
  siècle*, 1927.
Carné, G. de, *L'école des pages*, 1886.
Carré, H., *La noblesse de France et l'opinion publique au XVIIIᵉ siècle*, 1920.
Cassirer, E., *The philosophy of the Enlightenment*, 1951.

Carrière, C., 'Le recrutement de la cour des comptes d'Aix', *81ᵉ Congrès des Sociétés savantes*, Caen, 1956.

Chabaud, A., 'Essai sur les classes bourgeoises dirigeantes à Marseille en 1789', in *Assemblée générale de la commission centrale des comités départementaux*, 1939, vol. I.

Champion, E., 'La conversion de la noblesse en 1789', *Révolution Française*, 1893.

Charmeil, J. P., *Les trésoriers de France à l'époque de la Fronde*, 1964.

Chartier, R., 'Un recrutement scolaire aux XVIIIᵉ siècle: l'école royale du génie de Mézières', *R.H.M.C.* 1973.

Chassant, A., *Nobles et vilains. Recherche sur la noblesse et les usurpations nobiliaires*, 1857.

Chateaubriand, R. de, *Mémoires d'Outre-tombe*, 1964.

Chaunu, P., *La civilisation de l'Europe des Lumières*, 1971.

Chaussinand-Nogaret, G., 'Aux origines de la Révolution: noblesse et bourgeoisie', *Annales*, 1975.
    Gens de finance au XVIIIᵉ siècle, 1972.
    Les financiers de Languedoc, 1970.
    Une histoire des élites, 1975.
    'Les Jacobites au XVIIIᵉ siècle', *Annales*, 1973.
    'Une entreprise française en Espagne', *R.H.M.C.*, 1973.
    'Capitalisme et structure sociale', *Annales*, 1970.

Chevalier, J., *Le Creusot*, 1946.

Chevalier, L., *La situation économique de la noblesse dans le Lyonnais*, 1941.

Chevallier, P., *Les ducs sous l'Acacia*, 1964.
    La première profanation du Temple maçonnique, 1968.
    Histoire de la Franc-maçonnerie française, 1974.

Choiseul, Duc de, *Mémoires*, 1907.

Clergeac, A., 'Une famille de gentilshommes campagnards aux XVIIᵉ et XVIIIᵉ siècles', *Revue de Gascogne*, 1903.

Cobban, A., *The Social Interpretation of the French Revolution*, 1964.

Cochin, A., *La manufacture des glaces de Saint-Gobain*, 1865.

Collas, A., *Un cadet de Bretagne: Châteaubriand*, 1949.

Colombet, A., *Les parlementaires bourguignons à la fin du XVIIIᵉ siècle*, 1937.

Condorcet, *Œuvres*, 1847–9.

Constant, J. M., 'L'enquête de noblesse de 1667 et les seigneurs de Beauce', *R.H.M.C.* 1974.

Coyer, Abbé, *La noblesse commerçante*, 1756. *Supplément à la noblesse commerçante*, 1757.

Créquy, Marquise de, *Souvenirs*.

Cubells, M., 'A propos des usurpations de noblesse en Provence sous l'Ancien Régime', *Provence historique*, 1970.

Dainville, F. de., 'Collèges et fréquentation scolaire au XVIIIᵉ siècle', *Population*, 1955–7.

Debien, G., 'Défrichement et reprises des fermes en Poitou à la fin du XVIIIᵉ siècle', *A.H.R.F.* 1968.

Decouffé, A., 'L'aristocratie française devant l'opinion publique à la veille de la Révolution', *Etudes d'histoire économique et sociale du XVIIIᵉ siècle*, 1966.

Devyver, A., *Le sang épuré*, 1974.

Doyle, W., 'Le prix des charges anoblissantes à Bordeaux au XVIIIᵉ siècle', *Annales du Midi* (1968).

    The Parlement of Bordeaux and the End of the Old Regime 1771-1790, 1974.

Duby, G., *Guerriers et paysans*, 1973.

    Hommes et structures du Moyen Age, 1973.

Dugas, L., 'Une éducation d'autrefois: enfance et jeunesse de Châteaubriand', *Revue Bleue*, 1929.

Duméril, M., *La légende politique de Charlemagne et son influence au moment de la Révolution*, 1878.

Dumoulin, M., 'Les académies parisiennes d'équitation.' *Bulletin de la société des vieux papiers* (1922).

Dupont-Ferrier, G., *Du collège de Clermont au lycée Louis-le-Grand*, 1921-5.

Dupront, A., 'Cahiers de doléances et mentalités collectives', *Actes du 89ᵉ Congrès des Sociétés savantes*, 1964.

    'Formes de la culture de masses: de la doléance politique au pèlerinage panique', in *Niveaux de culture et groupes sociaux*, 1967.

Durand, Y., *Les Fermiers Généraux au XVIIIᵉ siècle*, 1971.

Egret, J., *La pré-révolution française*, 1962.

    Le Parlement de Dauphiné et les affaires publiques dans la deuxième moitié du XVIIIᵉ siècle, 1942.

    Louis XV et l'opposition parlementaire, 1970.

    'L'aristocratie parlementaire française à la fin de l'Ancien Régime', *Revue Historique*, 1952.

Elias, N., *The Court Society*, 1983.

Etat nominatif des pensions du Trésor royal, 5 vol., 1789, B.N. Lf81, 3.

Faure, E., *La disgrâce de Turgot*, 1961.

Fénelon, *Plans de gouvernement concertés avec le duc de Chevreuse pour être proposés au duc de Bourgogne* (novembre 1711).

    Principes fondamentaux d'un sage gouvernement. Supplément à l'examen de conscience sur les devoirs de la royauté.

Ferrières, marquis de, *Mémoires*.

Fleury, vicomte, *Le prince de Lambesc*, 1928.

Fontenay, H. de, *Napoléon, Joseph et Lucien Bonaparte au collège d'Autun*, 1869.

Ford, F. L., *Robe and Sword*, 1953.

Forster, R., 'The provincial noble: a reappraisal', *American Historical Review*, 1963.

    The House of Saulx-Tavanes, 1971.

    The Nobility of Toulouse in the Eighteenth Century, 1960.

Fournée, J., *Etude sur la noblesse rurale du Cotentin et du bocage normand*, Istina, 1954.

Franklin, A., *Ecoles et collèges à Paris au XVIIIe siècle*, 1897.

Frijhoff, W. and Julia, D., *Ecole et société dans la France d'Ancien Régime*, 1975.

Furet, F., 'Le catéchisme révolutionnaire', *Annales*, 1971.

Furet, F. and Daumard, A., *Structures et relations sociales à Paris au XVIIIe siècle*, 1961.

Furet, F. and Richet, D., *The French Revolution*, 1970.

Gallier, A. de, *La vie de province au XVIIIe siècle*, 1877.
Le marquis d'Aubais, 1870.

Garden, M., 'Niveaux de fortune à Dijon', *Cahiers d'histoire*, 1964.

Genlis, Madame de, *Mémoires*.

Geoffroy, S., *Répertoire des procès-verbaux des preuves de noblesse des gentilshommes admis aux écoles militaires de 1751 à 1792*, 1899.

Girault, C., 'La noblesse sarthoise', *Province du Maine*, 1954–5.

Godechot, J., *France and the Atlantic Revolution of the Eighteenth Century: 1770–1800*, 1965.

Goncourt, E. et J. de, *La Femme au XVIIIe siècle*, 1862.

Goodwin, A., 'The social structure and economic and political attitude of the French nobility in the XVIIIth century', *Congrès international des sciences historiques*, Vienna, 1965.

Goodwin, A. (ed.), *The European Nobility in the Eighteenth Century*, 1953.

Goubert, P., *L'Ancien Régime*, 1973.

Grau, M., *De la noblesse maternelle, particulièrement en Champagne*, 1898.

Gresset, M., *Le monde judiciaire à Besançon (1674–1789)*, 1975.

Gruder, V. R., *The Royal Provincial Intendants: a Governing Elite in Eighteenth Century France*, 1968.

Guillory, *Le marquis de Turbilly, agronome angevin au XVIIIe siècle*, 1862.

Hartung, F. and Mousnier, R., 'Quelques problèmes concernant la monarchie absolue', *X^e congrès international des sciences historiques*, Rome, 1965.

Hazard, P., *The European mind 1680–1715*, 1953.

Hecht, J., 'Un problème de population active au XVIIIe siècle: la querelle de la noblesse commerçante', *Population*, 1964.

Hennet, L., 'L'école militaire de Paris', *Journal des sciences militaires*, 1886.

Hyslop, B. H., *L'apanage de Philippe-Egalité*, 1965.

Jalenques, L., 'La noblesse de la province d'Auvergne au XVIIIe siècle', *Bulletin d'Auvergne*, 1911.

Kolabinska, M., *La circulation des élites en France. Etude historique depuis la fin du XIe siècle jusqu'à la Révolution*, 1912.

Labatut, J.-P., *Les ducs et pairs en France au XVIIe siècle*, 1972.

La franc-maçonnerie et la Révolution française, A.H.R.F., 1969.

Laroque, L. de and Barthélemy, E. de, *Catalogue des gentilshommes . . .* 1860 et sq.

La Roque, G. A. de, *Traité de la noblesse*, 1678.

Lassaigne, J. D., *Les assemblées de la noblesse de France aux XVIIe et XVIIIe siècles*, 1962.

La Tour du Pin, Madame de, *Mémoires d'une femme de cinquante ans*.

Lauzun, duc de, *Mémoires*, 1928.

Le Bihan, A., *Francs-maçons parisiens du Grand Orient de France*, 1966.
  Loges et chapitres de la Grande Loge et du Grand Orient de France, 1967.

Ledoux, E., 'La profession de foi scientifique du marquis de Rostaing', *Mémoires de l'Académie de Besançon*, 1930.

Lefebvre, G., 'Les classes en 1789 et leurs vœux', *Annales d'histoire économique et sociale*, 1930.
  Les paysans du Nord pendant la Révolution française, 1924.
  La Révolution française, 1963.
  Etudes orléanaises, 1962.

Léon, P., *Economies et sociétés pré-industrielles*, 1970.
  La naissance de la grande industrie en Dauphiné, 1954.

Léonard, E. G., *L'armée et ses problèmes au XVIIIe siècle*, 1958.

Le Roy Ladurie, E., 'Pour un modèle de l'économie rurale française au XVIIIe siècle', *Mélanges de l'Ecole française de Rome*, 1973.
  Les paysans de Languedoc, 1966, rééd., 1974.
  'Révoltes et contestations rurales en France de 1675 à 1788', *Annales*, 1974.

Levron, J., *Daily life at Versailles in the seventeenth and eighteenth centuries*, 1968.

Lévy, C. F., *Capitalistes et pouvoir au siècle des Lumières*, 1969.

Leymarie, M., 'Rentes seigneuriales et produit des seigneuries de l'élection de Tulle', *A.H.R.F.*, 1970.

Lezay-Marnesia, marquis de, *Plan de lecture pour une jeune femme*, 1784.

Ligou, D., 'La franc-maçonnerie française au XVIIIe siècle: position des problèmes et état des questions', *Information historique*, 1964.

Louandre, C., *La noblesse française sous l'ancienne monarchie*, 1880.

Luppé, A. de, *Les jeunes filles de l'aristocratie et de la bourgeoisie à la fin du XVIIIe siècle*, 1924.

Lüthy, H., *La banque protestante en France*, new edn., 1970.

Mably, *Observations sur l'histoire de France*, 1765.

Mas, H. du, 'Cadets de province au XVIIIe siècle', *Société d'Agriculture d'Angers*, 1902.

Marion, M., *Dictionnaire des institutions de la France aux XVIIe et XVIIIe siècles*, 1923, 2nd edn. 1968.

Marmontel, *Mémoires*, 1818.

Marsay, vicomte de, *De l'âge des privilèges au temps des vanités*.

Marx, R., *La Révolution et les classes sociales en Basse-Alsace*, 1974.

Massé, R., *Varennes et ses maîtres*, 1956.

Mauroy, A. de, *Un dernier mot sur la noblesse maternelle de Champagne*, 1913.

Mauzi, R., *L'idée de bonheur dans la littérature et la pensée française au XVIIIe siècle*, 1960.

Menestrier, Père, *Les diverses espèces de noblesse et les manières d'en dresser les preuves*, 1685.

Méthivier, H., *L'Ancien Régime*, 1961.

La fin de l'Ancien Régime, 1970.

Meyer, J., *La noblesse bretonne au XVIIIe siècle*, 1966.

'Un problème mal posé: la noblesse pauvre', *R.H.M.C.*, 1971.

L'armement nantais dans la deuxième moitié du XVIIIe siècle, 1969.

Noblesses et pouvoirs dans l'Europe d'Ancien Régime, 1974.

Moisson de Brécourt, *Essai sur l'éducation de la noblesse*, 1747.

Monin, H., *L'état de Paris en 1789*, 1889.

Montbarey, prince de, *Mémoires*.

Montesquieu, *Œuvres complètes*, 1964.

Montzey de, *Institutions d'éducation militaire jusqu'en 1789*, 1866-7.

Morazé, C., *Les bourgeois conquérants*, 1948.

Mornet, D., *Les origines intellectuelles de la Révolution française*, 1933.

Mougel, F. C., 'La fortune des princes de Bourbon-Conti à la veille de la Révolution', *R.H.M.C.*, 1971.

Mousnier, R., *La vénalité des offices sous Henri IV et Louis XIII*, 1945.

'Monarchie contre aristocratie au XVIIe siècle', *XVIIe Siècle*, 1956.

Muteau, C., *Les collèges de province jusqu'en 1789*, 1882.

Oberkirch, baronne d', *Mémoires*, 1970.

Ordres et classes. Communications réunies par D. Roche, 1973.

Ozanam, D., *Claude Baudard de Saint-James*, 1969.

Pareto, V., *Œuvres complètes*.

Payen, J., *Capital et machine à vapeur au XVIIIe siècle*, 1969.

Perrin, E., 'Mœurs et usages d'autrefois: les oisivetés d'un gentilhomme forézien', *Amitiés foréziennes*, 1921-2.

Poitrineau, A., *La vie rurale en Basse-Auvergne au XVIIIe siècle*, 1965.

Poncelet, abbé, *Principes généraux pour servir à l'éducation des enfants, particulièrement de la noblesse française*, 1763.

Préjean, J., '*Une famille noble dans la deuxième moitié du XVIIIe siècle: le baron et la baronne de Schömberg*', (Unpublished thesis).

Puy de Clinchamps, P. du, *La noblesse*, 1959.

Ribbe, C. de, *Les familles et la société en France avant la Révolution*, 1879.

Ribier, A. de, 'Les anoblissements et les confirmations de noblesse en Auvergne', *Bulletin historique Auvergne*, 1922 et sq.

Richard, G., *Noblesse d'affaires au XVIIIe siècle*, 1975.

Richelieu, duc de, *Mémoires*, 1871.

Richet, D., 'Elite et despotisme', *Annales*, 1969.

La France moderne. L'esprit des institutions, 1973.

Robin, R., *La société française en 1789: Semur-en-Auxois*, 1970.

Roche, D., 'Recherches sur la noblesse parisienne au milieu du XVIIIe siècle: la noblesse du Marais', *Actes du 86e congrès national des sociétés savantes*, 1962.

'Milieux académiques provinciaux et société des lumières', in *Livre et société dans la France du XVIIIe siècle*, 1965.

Le siècle des lumières en province, 1978.

Rochemonteix, C. de, *Un collège de Jésuites aux XVIIe et XVIIIe siècles: La Flèche*, 1889.

Rothkrug, L., *Opposition to Louis XIV. The Political and Social Origins of the French Enlightenment*, 1965.

Roton, A. de, *Les arrêts du Grand Conseil portant dispense du marc d'or de noblesse*, 1951.

Rouff, *Les mines de charbon*, 1922.

Ravitch, N., 'The social origins of French and English bishops in the XVIIIth century', *Historical Journal*, 1965.

Reinhard, M., 'Elite et noblesse dans la seconde moitié du XVIIIe siècle', *R.H.M.C.*, 1956.

Reiset, comte de, *Modes et usages au temps de Marie-Antoinette*, 1885.

Grandes dames et aventurières, 1905.

Saint-Albin, O., 'Livre des pensionnaires de l'académie d'équitation d'Angers', *Revue Anjou*, 1914.

Sainte-Beuve, *Causeries du lundi*, vols. XII and XIV, 1857.

Saint-Germain, J., *Samuel Bernard. Le banquier des Rois*, 1960.

Saint-Jacob, P. de, *Les paysans de la Bourgogne du Nord au dernier siècle de l'Ancien Régime*, 1960.

Saint-Léger, A. de, *Les mines d'Anzin et d'Aniche*, 1935.

Saint-Priest, *Mémoires*, 1929.

Sars, M., 'La situation financière de la noblesse du Laonnais à la veille de la Révolution', *Mémoires de la fédération des sociétés savantes de l'Aisne*, 1957–8.

Sédillot, R., *La maison de Wendel de 1704 à nos jours*, 1958.

Sée, H., 'La doctrine politique des Parlements au XVIIIe siècle', *Revue d'histoire du droit*, 1924.

Ségur, comte de, *Mémoires*, 1827.

Sénac de Meilhan, *Le gouvernement, les mœurs et les conditions en France avant la Révolution*, 1862.

Sentou, J., *Fortunes et groupes sociaux à Toulouse sous la Révolution*, 1969.

Sereville, E. de and Saint-Simon, F. de, *Dictionnaire de la noblesse*, 1975.

Sieyès, *Qu'est-ce que le tiers état?* (éd. R. Zapperi), 1970.

Six, G., 'Fallait il quatre quartiers de noblesse pour être officier à la fin de l'Ancien Régime?', *R.H.M.C.*, 1929.

Soboul, A., *Précis d'histoire de la Révolution française*, 1962.

La civilisation et la Révolution française, I. *La crise de l'Ancien Régime*, 1970.

Stael de Launay, Madame de, *Mémoires*, 1829.

Taine, H., *Les origines de la France contemporaine*, 1876.

Talleyrand, *Mémoires*.

Taylor, G. V., 'Noncapitalist wealth and the origins of the French Revolution', *American Historical Review*, 1967.

'Types of capitalism in eighteenth-century France', *English Historical Review*, 1964.

Thibaut, L., *Le mécanicien anobli. Pierre Joseph Laurent*, Thesis, Université de Lille, III.

Tilly, comte de, *Mémoires*, 1965.

Tocqueville, A. de, *The Ancien Régime and the Révolution* (ed. H. Brogan, 1971).

Tourzel, duchesse de, *Mémoires*, 1969.

Tréca, G., *Les doctrines et les réformes de droit public en réaction contre l'absolutisme de Louis XIV dans l'entourage du duc de Bourgogne*, 1909.

Trudon des Ormes, A., 'L'état civil des citoyens nobles de Paris en 1789', *Mémoires de la société de l'histoire de Paris et de l'Ile de France*, 1899.

Tuetey, *Les officiers sous l'Ancien Régime*, 1908.

Vaissières, P. de, *Gentilshommes campagnards de l'ancienne France*, 1903.

Valous, G., 'Une existence de célibataire à la veille de la Révolution', *Le Correspondant*, 1926.

Vivie, O. de, *Un cadet en 1792: Charles de Cornier*, 1886.

Vogué, marquis de, *Le duc de Bourgogne et le duc de Beauvilliers, lettres (1700–1708)*, 1900.

Vovelle, M., *Piété baroque et déchristianisation: attitudes provençales devant la mort*, 1971.

The fall of the French Monarchy, 1787–92, 1983.

'Sade, seigneur de village', in *Le marquis de Sade*, 1968.

Warren, R. de, *Les pairs de France sous l'Ancien Régime*, 1958.

Weitmann, S., 'Bureaucracy, democracy and the French Revolution', unpublished *PhD of the Washington University*, 1968.

Weulersse, G., *La physiocratie à la fin du règne de Louis XV*, 1959.

Les physiocrates sous les ministères de Turgot et de Necker, 1950.

Young, A., *Travels in France during the years 1787, 1788 and 1789* (ed. C. Maxwell), 1929.

Supplementary bibliography

Bien, D. D., 'The secrétaires du roi: absolutism, corps and privilege under the Ancien Regime', in E. Hinrichs, E. Schmitt and R. Vierhaus (eds), *Vom Ancien Regime zur Französischen Revolution*, 1978.
'The army in the French Enlightenment', *Past and Present*, 85 (1979).
Cobban, A., *Aspects of the French Revolution*, 1968.
Doyle, W., 'The parlements of France and the breakdown of the Old Regime, 1770–1788', *French Historical Studies*, VI (1970).
'Was there an Aristocratic Reaction in pre-revolutionary France?', *Past and Present*, 57 (1972).
Origins of the French Revolution, 1980.
'The price of offices in eighteenth century France', *Historical Journal*, 27, (1984).
'Dupaty (1746–1788). A career in the late Enlightenment', *Studies on Voltaire and the Eighteenth Century* (1984).
Ellis, G., 'The "Marxist Interpretation" of the French Revolution', *English Historical Review*, 93 (1978).
Forster, R. 'The survival of the nobility during the French Revolution', *Past and Present*, 37 (1967).
Merchants, Landlords, Magistrates. The Depont family in eighteenth century France, 1980.
'The French Revolution and the "new" elite, 1800–1850', in J. Pelenski (ed.), *The American and European Revolutions, 1776–1848*, 1980.
Goodwin, A., 'The social origins and privileged status of the French eighteenth century nobility', *Bulletin of the John Rylands Library*, XLVII (1964–5).
Grassby, R. B., 'Social status and commercial enterprise under Louis XIV', *Economic History Review* 2nd series xiii (1960–1).
Greenlaw, R. W., 'The French nobility on the eve of the Revolution. A study of its aims and attitudes, 1787–9' (Unpublished Ph.D thesis, Princeton, 1952).
Higonnet, P., *Class, Ideology, and the Rights of Nobles during the French Revolution*, 1981.
Johnson, D. (ed.), *French Society and the Revolution*, 1976.

Lucas, C., 'Nobles, bourgeois, and the origins of the French Revolution', *Past and Present*, 60 (1973).

Meyer, J., 'La noblesse française au XVIII⁰ siècle: aperçu des problèmes', *Acta Poloniae Historica* xxxv i (1977).

Runciman, W. G. 'Unnecessary revolution: the case of France', *Archives of European Sociology*, xxiv (1983).

Scott, S. F., *The Response of the Royal Army to the French Revolution*, 1978.

Shapiro, G. and Dawson, P., 'Social mobility and political radicalism: the case of the French Revolution of 1789', in W. O. Aydelotte, A. G. Bogue and R. W. Fogel (eds), *The Dimensions of quantitative research in History*, 1972.

Stone, B., 'Robe against Sword: the Parlement of Paris and the French aristocracy, 1774–1789', *French Historical Studies*, ix (1975).

Taylor, G. V. 'Revolutionary and non-revolutionary content in the *cahiers* of 1789: an interim report', *French Historical Studies*, vii (1972).

Index